INVISIBLE POETS

INVISIBLE POETS

Afro-Americans
of the Nineteenth Century

JOAN R. SHERMAN

University of Illinois Press

URBANA   CHICAGO   LONDON

Publication of this work was supported in part
by a grant from the Andrew W. Mellon Foundation.

To
Bernie,
Laurie, Jon, and Dan

———

PREFACE

Anthologies of Afro-American literature typically imply that black poetry began with Phillis Wheatley (1753–84), disappeared for over one hundred years, and only reemerged with Paul Laurence Dunbar (1872–1906). Actually, however, at least 130 black men and women published poetry in America during the nineteenth century. I have chosen twenty-six of these individuals for intensive study, hoping to construct for the first time certain significant profiles of their life experiences and to appraise the qualities and import of their poetry.

My introduction explains the need for such a study and brings the twenty-six poets together by way of a demographic survey, a chronological overview of their poetry in its historical-cultural setting, and a consideration of criteria for assessing their work. Each of these poets is then presented individually with a documented biography and critical analysis of all his known poetry. Bibliographies of the poets' works are followed by a bibliographical essay which details materials available for research in black literature, especially for the nineteenth century, and suggests procedures followed and problems encountered in this study.

The seven appendices record other poets I located but did not treat comprehensively for various reasons. Thirty-six individuals in Appendix A published significant quantities of poetry and prose in the last century, and they deserve further detailed attention. Appendix B lists sixty-eight occasional poets who produced less (from one to several poems) before 1900. Little or nothing is known about them, except for a handful who made their mark in other areas of Afro-American life. Appendix C enumerates nine anonymous black poets with titles and locations of their poems, and Ada, who published twelve poems in the *Liberator* from 1831 to 1837. Many poets often erroneously identified as nineteenth-century Afro-Americans are found in Appendices D and E: Appendix D lists twenty-six poets who published between 1900 and 1916 but did not, to my knowledge, appear in print before the turn of the century; Appendix E describes thirteen individuals frequently cited as black Americans who in fact were white, of doubtful racial stock, or foreign born. Appendix F discusses the Creole poets of Louisiana who wrote in French and published the first anthology of black poetry in America, *Les Cenelles* (1845). Finally, Appendix G offers bibliographies for the eighteenth-century black poets Phillis Wheatley and Jupiter Hammon.

Although he is undoubtedly a major nineteenth-century figure, Dunbar is excluded from this study because his life and works have been amply documented during the past seventy years. Dunbar's four novels, four volumes of stories, and *Complete Poems* (New York, 1913) are readily available. Dozens of periodical articles from 1896 to date offer reviews of his publications, interviews with him, his obituaries, reminiscences of him, and periodic reevaluations of his poetry. Moreover, Dunbar is represented in most black literary histories and collective biographies (and many white ones). Among full-length Dunbar studies are: Lida Keck Wiggins, *The Life and Works of P. L. Dunbar* (Naperville, Ill., 1907; rpt. Kraus, 1971); Benjamin Brawley, *Paul Laurence Dunbar, Poet of His People* (Chapel Hill, 1936; rpt. Kennikat, 1967); Victor Lawson, *Dunbar Critically Examined* (Washington, D.C., 1941); Virginia Cunningham, *Paul Laurence Dunbar and His Song* (New York, 1947); Mary Hundley, *The Dunbar Story, 1870–1955* (New York, 1965); Tom Scott, *Dunbar: A Critical Exposition of the Poems* (New York, 1966); and Addison Gayle, Jr., *Oak and Ivy: A Biography of Paul Laurence Dunbar* (Garden City, 1971). Dunbar manuscript materials are in the Schomburg Collection of the New York Public Library and the Ohio Historical Society Archives.

To gather reliable biographical and bibliographical data for the poets, I corresponded with persons and organizations throughout the United States. Their generous responses are acknowledged in the notes to each poet's chapter which they made possible. I wish to thank Ernest Kaiser and the staff of the Schomburg Collection for courteous and ample cooperation; also Mrs. Dorothy B. Porter, Joseph H. Reason, and the staff of the Howard University Moorland and Spingarn Collections, and Donald A. Sinclair of Rutgers University Library for their kind assistance. My thanks are due the Rutgers University Research Council, which provided a grant for publication expenses. I am more grateful than words can say to Walter E. Bezanson, Tilden G. Edelstein, and Ronald Gottesman, who encouraged, guided, and edited my work for two years. For a bounteous gift of cheerful endurance and loving support, my husband, Bernard I. Sherman, and my children, Laura, Jonathan, and Daniel, have my deepest appreciation.

Some of the material in this volume has appeared in my articles in *Negro History Bulletin, College Language Association Journal, Journal of Negro History, Virginia Magazine of History and Biography,* and *Tennessee Studies in Literature.*

CONTENTS

Key to Abbreviations and Symbols

DAB	*Dictionary of American Biography,* ed. Allen Johnson and Dumas Malone (New York: Scribner's, 1928–37)
JNH	*Journal of Negro History*
Loggins	Vernon Loggins, *The Negro Author: His Development in America to 1900* (1931; rpt. Port Washington, N.Y.: Kennikat, 1964)
NHB	*Negro History Bulletin*
Redding	J. Saunders Redding, *To Make a Poet Black* (Chapel Hill: University of North Carolina Press, 1939)
Simmons	William J. Simmons, *Men of Mark: Eminent, Progressive and Rising* (1887; rpt. New York: Arno, 1968)
VN	*Voice of the Negro*
WWCR	*Who's Who of the Colored Race,* ed. Frank L. Mather (Chicago, 1915)

SYMBOLS

✿	Most valuable sources
#	Volume not examined

INTRODUCTION

Afro-Americans of the nineteenth century are the invisible poets of our national literature. Long before Ralph Ellison's hero discovered his invisibility, the black poets were, and have remained, "as transparent as air" to white America and to a majority of their own race.[1] During the century between Phillis Wheatley and Paul Laurence Dunbar, over 130 black men and women published some ninety volumes and pamphlets of poetry plus hundreds of poems in black periodicals. But their achievements, impressive both in quantity and quality, remain unacknowledged.

None of the early poets is mentioned in American literature bibliographies and literary histories compiled by Evans, Foley, Fullerton, Roorbach, Sabin, Johnson, Blanck, Spiller, and others; bibliographies of black literature offer scanty and inaccurate references to their work. The poets are invisible in white magazines and poetry anthologies of their time and ours, and they fare little better in black literature collections. Since black poetry anthologies typically skip from Wheatley to Dunbar or, occasionally, include the same few in-between poets and the same few poems, and since the poets' books and pamphlets are out of print and their uncollected verse languishes in scattered, inaccessible periodicals, it is estimated that only 10 percent of nineteenth-century Afro-American poetry is currently available.

Not only are these black voices unheard, but the poets' very existence is also unacknowledged. Excluded from virtually all standard biographical dictionaries, collective biographies, and state literary histories, they infrequently appear in similar compilations by and about Afro-Americans, most of which were published between 1860 and 1935 and are now rare books. Moreover, the data in such collections, as well as in black literary histories and anthologies,

1. Ralph Ellison, *Invisible Man* (New York, 1952), p. 434.

are uniformly incomplete and unreliable. Derived from prefaces and introductions to the poets' works or from contemporary sketches in black periodicals, such biographies necessarily present only the most favorable facts plus apocryphal and erroneous material which has been perpetuated by all later writers. Criticism of black poetry is extremely scarce for all early writers and nonexistent for most. In no case has a critic dealt with a poet's complete works, and with rare exceptions evaluations are heavily biased. On one hand, racial chauvinism, sentimentality, or moral indignation warps critical judgment to exalt the poetry out of all proportion to its merit; on the other hand, out of ignorance, defensiveness, or racial prejudice, critics contemn the entire body of pre-Dunbar verse.

To render these Afro-Americans and their poetry visible, to strip myth and misinformation from their lives and offer the most accurate biographies and bibliographies obtainable after a century of neglect, and to assess all their poetry objectively, I chose twenty-six representative poets for intensive study and some three dozen others for brief attention. All of them published before 1900, some continued to write into the twentieth century, and their literary output varies considerably. Among the sixty-one poets for whom data was collected, many also published full-length histories, biographies, plays, or short story collections; one, Frances Harper, published the first novel by a black woman in America (1892). Three poets did translations from French or German; three wrote autobiographies; ten published, edited, and wrote for their own periodicals; almost all published essays on such topics as race, religion, politics and economics, metaphysics, literature, temperance, astronomy, and current events.

Only a handful of the poets wrote dialect verse, the charming but superficial poetry that gave Dunbar visibility and his title, Poet Laureate of the Negro Race. Rather, their work, ranging from militant, race-proud jeremiads to sentimental nature and love lyrics, faithfully conforms to nineteenth-century poetic standards. At the same time, however, the poetry is an invaluable record of over one hundred years of *black* experience as felt and articulated by some of the most sensitive and talented of the race.

The lives of these men and women are as heterogeneous as their poetry and even more extraordinary. No group of writers in any place or time has struggled to surmount lowly birth, poverty, lack of education, and life-long discrimination to produce a body of literature. For two hundred years "a peculiar disposition" of American eyes has conferred invisibility on the black poets and their achievements or has distorted what was seen. A new pair of glasses is offered here as a partial and preliminary corrective toward total realistic appraisal of the black artists' contribution to American literature.

The Poets: A Demographic Review

The twenty-six representative poets, born between 1796 and 1883, were exceptionally long-lived for their century, with an average age at death of sixty-five. It seems noteworthy, too, that those born before 1825 lived an average of ten years longer than those born after 1862. Of the twenty-four whose birthplaces could be established, eleven were Southerners and thirteen Northerners.[2] The racial stock of twenty poets was ascertained from contemporary descriptions (perhaps unreliable) and photographs or drawings of them. Two, George Horton and Elymas Rogers, were of "pure" African blood; seven others were predominantly African, five were mulattoes, and six were of predominantly Caucasian ancestry. Almost equally represented in each of these racial groups are Northerners and Southerners and those born before or after the Civil War.

The early lives, educations, and occupations of the poets vary widely. Five were born slaves and remained in bondage until Emancipation. Slavery was brief or nominal for Daniel W. Davis and Timothy T. Fortune; but Albery Whitman lived in slavery for twelve years, Islay Walden for sixteen, and Horton for sixty-six years. These five slave-born poets have nothing further in common —rather, they are a microcosm of the twenty-six poets in terms of their education and later achievements. Horton taught himself to read and write. Whitman had only a year of formal schooling, and Fortune three years. Davis graduated from high school and a seminary; Walden earned a B.A. degree from Howard University and a seminary diploma. Similarly, among the free-born poets, Noah Cannon, a circuit-riding preacher from Delaware and precise contemporary of Horton, was entirely self-taught. Five poets—James Whitfield, Harper, James Bell, John Menard, and Aaron Thompson —acquired less than a high school education. Another six poets—

2. Six poets who were from the border states (Maryland, Delaware, Kentucky, and Tennessee), slave-holding states below the free-soil border, have been included as Southerners.

Joshua Simpson, Joseph Cotter, George Rowe, James Campbell, Charlotte Forten, and Charles Clem—completed the equivalent of high school and, in some cases, additional "adult" education or religious training. Four free-born poets earned B.A. degrees at colleges or seminaries—Charles Reason, Elymas Rogers, James McGirt, and Eloise Thompson—and three went beyond the first college degree: H. Cordelia Ray earned an M.A. in pedagogy; George Vashon, the first black graduate of Oberlin College, read law and passed the New York bar examination; and George McClellan earned an A.B. and M.A. from Fisk and a B.D. from Hartford Seminary. Thus almost two-thirds of the poets in this study had only a high school education or less, and one-third had college degrees.

As might be expected, with vocational choices of Afro-Americans severely limited, a majority of the poets were teachers and ministers. Several of them combined these two vocations, and some teachers and two ministers were newspaper editors as well. Despite such overlapping, however, of the twenty-six poets eight were primarily educators, and six were clergymen representing four denominations: African Methodist Episcopal, Baptist, Congregationalist, and Presbyterian. Of all the poets, only Harper earned a living from publication and lecture-reading of her poetry. Others held jobs as a plasterer, manufacturer, barber, manual laborer, and printer; some were civil service clerks, minor municipal officials, or journalists. Although a few individuals remained in their birthplaces throughout their lives, most of the poets left home in their late teens and traveled widely for schooling or employment. For example, McClellan, a teacher and minister from Tennessee, spent his life in Kentucky, Mississippi, Alabama, New England, and California. Bell, a plasterer and lecturer born in Ohio, worked the cities North and South and spent several years in Canada and California; Whitfield, a native of New Hampshire, barbered his way from New York to Idaho to Central America and California.

Many of the poets, in addition to pursuing their vocations, avocations, and poetry-writing, worked actively with black literary and educational societies, state boards of religious denominations, lodges and welfare agencies, and national groups like the YMCA, WCTU, and NAACP. Many were in the vanguard of antislavery and civil rights organizations as officers and lecturers. Although only Whitfield affiliated with the American Colonization Society, two others, Rogers and Menard, supported emigration; but several poets vigorously opposed it, and the majority of them sought equality and justice within American society.

Like white poets of the century, many of the blacks knew one another and also maintained close ties with other Afro-American men of letters. Cotter and McClellan were colleagues in the Louisville, Kentucky, schools, as were Reason and Ray in New York City. James Bell and Whitfield and the editor Philip A. Bell were friends in San Francisco. McGirt and James Corrothers met as students at Bennett College; Vashon was a friend of the historian William C. Nell and of J. Sella Martin, a poet, activist, and editor of *New Era*. Cotter, Corrothers, Davis, and James Campbell corresponded with Dunbar (and Fortune drank with him), while John E. Bruce, the New York journalist, was an intimate of Fortune and knew Davis, Corrothers, Ray, Harper, and many more. William Wells Brown, litterateur of his day, shared a lecture platform with Harper, Boston hospitality with Forten, and at least a nodding acquaintance with every black writer of note. As poets themselves and editors of major literary magazines, A.M.E. Bishops Daniel Payne and Benjamin Tanner knew and published many of the black poets.

Outside literary circles, several poets traveled among outstanding black and white activists of the century. Bell worked with John Brown; Harper campaigned with the leading suffragettes, women's rights and WCTU workers; Reason attended the African Free School with Alexander Crummell, J. McCune Smith, and Henry H. Garnet, and he and Vashon, who had taught John M. Langston in high school, labored for black rights alongside Frederick Douglass and his followers. Fortune worked and skirmished with the great black trio, Douglass, Washington, and Du Bois, as well as with President Theodore Roosevelt. And Forten enjoyed the friendship of the stellar New England abolitionists, from Garrison to her idol, the poet Whittier. This partial list of friendships adds evidence to historians' documentation of a widespread Afro-American literary and political community which flourished throughout the century. However, only about half the poets in this study belonged to this community. Isolation of the others from one another and from contemporary race leaders is not accounted for by chronological, sectional, educational, or occupational variables. Rather, the men and women engaged in nationwide political and welfare work naturally acquired the largest circle of famous friends. Among the apolitical figures, only the later poets knew one another, either by chance or through their mutual acquaintance with Dunbar or a journalist like Bruce.

The Poetry

J. Saunders Redding, the dean of Afro-American literary critics, offers the proposition

> that American Negro literature, so called, is American literature in fact, and that American Negro literature cannot be lopped off from the main body of American literary expression without doing grave harm to both as complementary instruments of historical and social diagnosis and as the joint and articulated corpus of American experience.[3]

Black poetry of the nineteenth century strongly supports and illustrates this proposition, for it is American in subject, versification, and attitudes. Throughout the century black poetry, like the main body of white poetry, reflects and responds to the changing political, social, and cultural scene, to the events, ideologies, and leaders, black and white, that constitute American history. Naturally, black writing most vividly mirrors the changing fortunes of the black race, but these fortunes were in turn wholly a product of the American environment.

In the entire body of black verse published between 1829 and 1900 there is scarcely a trace of those qualities commonly assigned to the Negro folk temperament (or an African heritage) such as peasant irony, sensuousness, tropic nonchalance, primitive rhythms, or emotional raciness. There is much evidence, however, of other qualities lumped under the Negro folk rubric which in fact are common to black *and* white nineteenth-century poetry: sentimentality, imagination, childlike innocence, musicality, and colloquialism. Moreover, a majority of the black poets share with their white contemporaries a variety of poetic and personal values: unambiguous thought and refined sentiments; elevated language; Christian piety and morality; and an affectionate nostalgia for a simple, homely, rural life. Black poetry also exhibits the commonly deemed defects of American verse of the last century: didacticism and rhetorical shrillness, intellectual and emotional banality, diffuseness, and fondness for abstract and archaic diction and mythological-literary allusions. In addition, instead of African or Afro-

3. J. Saunders Redding, "Negro Writing in America," *The New Leader,* 43 (May 16, 1960), 8.

American song patterns, black poets employ every traditional verse form: the ode, sonnet, ballad, Spenserian stanza, ottava rima, heroic couplet, terza rima, rhymed triplet, quatrain, blank and free verse, and all standard combinations of meter and rhyme. Finally, the poets almost universally accept the century's dictum that poetry's province is to convey truth, to teach, uplift, and reform, and secondarily to give pleasure.

Despite such close and consistent adherence to American literary standards, the corpus of early black verse also supports Alain Locke's composite theory, which views Negro cultural products as distinctive hybrids resulting from interpenetration of American national and black racial traits.[4] However, these racial traits in Afro-American verse are not, as Locke suggests, the unique properties of the spirituals and folklore; rather, they are literary extensions of black life-modes which may be called "soul" and "style." Johnnetta B. Cole, writing on "Culture: Negro, Black and Nigger," finds soul and style the "essence of blackness" and the consistent themes in black American life. Soul consists of three notions: a particular brand of long-suffering weariness, deep emotion, and an aggressive sense of racial group identity. The four "life styles in nigger culture" Cole calls the street style (the hustling, stylized talking urban mode), the militant style (a fervid, urgent striving to relieve oppression), the upward-bound style (a climbing toward middle-class security and integration), and the down-home style (cherishing of traditional, rural, and Southern ways). "Blackness is best expressed," she writes, "when style combines with soul."[5]

Since a people's literature is a distillation of their lives, these sociological constructs become touchstones for identifying the essence of blackness in Afro-American poetry and for illuminating the poetry's relation to its sociohistorical context.[6] Analysis of nineteenth-century black poetry shows that as the verse (and prose

---

4. Alain Locke, "The Negro's Contribution to American Culture," *Journal of Negro Education*, 8 (July, 1939), 521–29.

5. Johnnetta B. Cole, "Culture: Negro, Black and Nigger," *The Black Scholar*, 1 (June, 1970), 40–44. The "street style" does not appear in nineteenth-century black poetry.

6. J. Saunders Redding identifies three patterns, each with a "contra-mythology" of its own into which all black writing falls, as the "race pattern," which depicts blacks as "the apotheosis of the anti-social"; the "opuscule pattern," which gives them the stature of classic, daring heroes and heroines; and the "folk pattern," which portrays them as simple, childlike creatures ("Negro Writing in America," pp. 9–10). For simplicity, I will use Cole's analogous sociological terminology to describe both the black lifestyles and the literature.

literature) shifts during the century from militant race protest, to justification of the race as "white" Americans, to romanticization of folkways and plantation experience, a diminution of blackness occurs, for the poetry loses soul. These shifts in literary posture perfectly parallel the simultaneous whitewashing of the race, its movement from a militant to an upward-bound and down-home life style in response to societal pressures.

The most distinctively black poetry appears before the Civil War. This militant verse, written by Reason, Alfred Campbell, Simpson, Whitfield, Harper, Vashon, and Rogers, is the best protest poetry of the century in terms of emotional and intellectual intensity, craftsmanship, and racial propaganda value. And it has soul: the cry of "How long, oh Lord"; the festering despair and fury of a dream deferred; lightning blasts of righteous indignation or bitter mockery; and always a proud, all-encompassing concern for the race above the individual. The militant poetry belongs to an era dominated by protest organizations, abolitionist literature, and eloquent orators. From pulpits and podiums, in petitions and calls, at meetings of the Free Negro Convention movement and a multitude of black and interracial antislavery societies, Afro-Americans clamored for freedom and equality: Douglass, Garnet, Ruggles, Crummell, Remond, Still, Nell, Ward, Forten, Payne, Ray, Cuffe, Smith, Purvis, and dozens more. David Walker's *Appeal* (1829) shocked the nation and reverberated in Afro-American periodicals for the next thirty-five years. As early as 1827 *Freedom's Journal* had sounded the liberation cry, followed by Russwurm's *Rights of All* (1829), Ray's *Colored American* (1837), Ruggles's *Mirror of Liberty* (1838), Whipper's *National Reformer* (1838), Delany's *Mystery* (1843), Douglass's *North Star*, his *Paper* and *Monthly* (1847–63). White newspapers, better known and more widely circulated, joined in protest: Lundy and Garrison's *Genius of Universal Emancipation* (1829); Garrison's *Liberator* (1831) and *Emancipator* (1833), journal of the American Anti-Slavery Society; and Child's *National Anti-Slavery Standard* (1841).

Antebellum black writers, concentrating on abolitionist and civil rights polemic, also produced a few literary works. Delany's *The Condition, Elevation, Emigration and Destiny of the Colored People of the United States* (1852) and Nell's *Colored Patriots of the American Revolution* (1855) were inspiring biographical histories. Brown's *Clotel, or the President's Daughter* (1853) and *The Escape* (1858), the first novel and play by a black man, exposed the evils of slavery. Another novel, Frank Webb's *The Garies and Their Friends* (1857), was followed by Harper's tale, "The Two Offers" (1859), and the third antebellum novel, Delany's *Blake, or the Huts of America* (1859). To provide additional outlets for Afro-American fiction and poetry as well as protest writings, blacks founded dozens of periodicals before the War, notably the *AME Church Magazine* (1841–47), Payne's *Repository of Religion and Literature and of Science and Art* (1858–63), and Hamilton's *Anglo-African Magazine* (1859–60).

By far the most popular and influential black writing were thousands of slave narratives, at least forty of them full-length accounts, written in the 1830's–1850's by fugitives or from their dictation. These vivid chronicles of life in slavery and dramatic harrowing escapes fueled abolitionist fervor up North and fearful antagonisms in the South. Many ex-slaves became celebrities of the lecture circuit and the press when their memoirs appeared, exacerbating tensions. While slave narratives give psychological and sociological perspectives on the bondsmen and the peculiar institution, black poetry of the same period reveals the thoughts and feelings of *free* Afro-Americans. Significantly, the only antebellum poetry which clings to the oral folkloristic and melodramatic traditions of the slave narratives is Simpson's antislavery song-poems, written for fugitives on the Underground Railroad. These songs satirize hypocritical white preachers and naive masters, reveal the superstitions, amusements, pious emotionalism, and shrewd trickery of the slaves in tones both self-mocking and proud. Like the narratives, Simpson's work stresses the slaves' continual ardent desire for and attempts to attain freedom, not in a future kingdom but in Canada or the North. Themes and folk qualities of the slave narratives appear to a much lesser degree in the Bible stories of Cannon (1833) and in a few earthy, humorous pieces by the slave poet Horton (1845).

Poetry by the other six antebellum writers is entirely humorless and divorced from both folklore and commonplace rural pursuits. The free blacks' verse is uniformly serious, pragmatic, moralistic, historically oriented, and intellectual even when most passionate. Reason writes stirring appeals for black enfranchisement and universal liberty (1841, 1846). Alfred Campbell, an avid Garrisonian, attacks the Church, Constitution, Fugitive Slave Law, and Southern hypocrites (1850's). Whitfield, the angriest and most pessimistic of the poets, bitterly decries national injustice and his own failure

(1853). The brilliant Vashon draws parallels between the abortive Haitian insurrection and his own chaotic era (1853), and he defends black men's rights as Americans to President Lincoln (1862). Harper, with less rancor than sorrowful melodrama, summons a vengeful God and callous mankind to witness the anguish and heroism of slave mothers, abused black women, and fugitives (1854, 1857). Finally, Rogers in two long satires appeals to law and conscience to condemn the Fugitive Slave Law, the Missouri Compromise, and the Kansas-Nebraska Act (1854, 1855). These militant poets (and several after them) also write martial or sentimental tributes to saviors of the race: Lincoln, Douglass, and Garrison hold first place in their hearts, followed by John Brown, Harriet Beecher Stowe, Charles Sumner, Robert Gould Shaw, and General Grant among the white heroes, and Daniel Payne, Cuba's Maceo, Crispus Attucks, Toussaint L'Ouverture, and Frances Harper among the blacks.

The villains of the century for all black poets are the white establishment in general and, after the Civil War, Andrew Johnson in particular. Bell, the most steadfast champion of race progress from 1862 to 1900, contributes an anti-Johnson satire of scathing effectiveness, while his lengthy odes trace the black man's history and contributions to America in peace and war. Bell commemorates all emancipations and mourns all setbacks to worldwide liberty. Although he remains proudly race conscious, he is a transitional figure whose work signals the gradual loss of distinctive blackness in poetry from Reconstruction to the end of the century, for Bell drowns the militancy and soul of antebellum writers in floods of pretentious, defensive oratory.

The years from 1866 to 1877 which saw hopes for racial equality raised and shattered were unfruitful for black poetry and black culture generally. Poets like Whitfield, Vashon, and Simpson continue to respond to the march of events with odes and songs in honor of Emancipation, the three constitutional amendments, and the Civil Rights Acts, as poets after them will do. Ray contributes an Emancipation ode, read at the unveiling of the Freedmen's Monument in Washington (1876). Harper finds inspiration in the biblical account of Israel's redemption for her full-length saga of the life and death of Moses (1869), and in 1872 she writes witty sketches of the freedmen whose colloquialisms and folksy details herald a new kind of race poetry which culminates in the dialect verse of the last two decades of the century.

Two additional approaches to race which reflect the upward-bound life style of blacks in the postwar era appear for the first time in black poetry of Reconstruction. One is avoidance, the abandonment of racial issues as a subject—either altogether as in Whitman's first poem, a "whites only" love story (1873), or by only minor acknowledgment of race (in a dedication or tribute) as in the volumes of the ex-slave Walden (1873, 1877). A second approach, also initiated by Whitman and characteristic of his work until 1900, is glorification of the race. In 1877 Whitman portrays "America's *coming* colored man" as one endowed with suprahuman physical, mental, and moral powers.

The decade of Reconstruction sounded the death knell of impassioned, militant protest and the birth of the down-home and upward-bound postures. From 1877 onward, and especially after 1890, Afro-Americans' status grew worse in North and South. Legislatures, courts, and public opinion supported systematic disfranchisement of blacks and stripped them of civil and hard-won social gains through Jim Crow laws, invalidation of the 1875 Civil Rights Act, segregation of public schools, and mob terrorism. Black inferiority was "proved" on sociological, psychological, and physiological authority, and black manhood was mocked by stage and literary portrayals of minstrel and plantation characters. Under such pressures Afro-American writers could have only one goal: to justify the race to white society.

To this end, first of all, they recounted the black man's sacrifices, strengths, and virtues in dozens of books like Flipper's *The Colored Cadet at West Point* (1878), Williams's *History of the Negro Race in America* (1883), Simmons's *Men of Mark: Eminent, Progressive and Rising* (1887), Wilson's *The Black Phalanx* (1890), Penn's *The Afro-American Press and Its Editors* (1891), Langston's *From the Virginia Plantation to the National Capitol* (1894), and the zenith of upward-bound literature, Washington's *Up from Slavery* (1900). Such works identified the race with America's work ethic and middle-class values—they "proved" blacks were white. In addition, they made the black author publishable as militant propaganda would not and gave him the opportunity to offer his race encouraging prototypes of success in a hostile world.

After a hiatus of fifteen years, dozens of black periodicals flourished nationwide in 1880–1900, all designed as showcases for black writers and as guides to race elevation. The three most successful (and enduring) magazines were church sponsored: the *AME*

Church Review (1884), *AME Zion Quarterly Review* (1890), and
National Baptist Magazine (1894) committed their pages to the
mental, moral, and religious uplift of the race and to exhibiting
black literary talent. Many other periodicals, mostly local and short
lived, began publication in these decades. They included educa-
tional periodicals issued by state teachers' associations throughout
the South and popular magazines for women and children which
dedicated themselves to the goal expressed in the subtitle of
Howard's American Magazine (1895): "Devoted to the Educa-
tional, Religious, Industrial, Social, and Political Progress of the
Colored Race."

With the same goal, from 1880 black poets magnify Afro-Amer-
ican accomplishments. They avoid race protest in favor of inspira-
tional, purely descriptive, and sentimental verse on orthodox white
subjects: nature, love, religion, poetic art, patriotism, death, home,
and mother. Poets like Ray, Eloise Thompson, McClellan, and For-
tune show a decided bias for neoclassical decorum, heightened po-
etic diction, and technical virtuosity, all far removed from the
direct, impassioned remonstrances of antebellum poets. Post-Recon-
struction poets also shift allegiance from a wrathful Jehovah and
retaliation through fire and sword to a gentle Jesus with his promise
of justice in the next world. The poetry is integrationist, at times
explicitly, more often through conscious adherence to such white
themes, techniques, and ethical attitudes. Rarely, as in the work of
McClellan, does a black poet's anguished awareness of his double
role—as an American and a Negro—disturb his verse and distin-
guish it from prevailing upward-bound varieties.

In their drive for total Americanization, no black poets after
1877 denounce a President or an oppressive law by name, although
some swipe weakly at the establishment, plead for civil rights, and
continue to publicize race achievements. In Menard's 1879 volume
over half the verses are about love, and his few race poems, though
indignant in tone, are optimistic. Whitman pursues elevation of the
race's image by exalting the Seminole Indians and Maroons, whose
struggles for freedom had ended forty years previously. Some stan-
zas in his *Rape of Florida* (1884) and poems through the 1890's
urge Afro-Americans to become "fearless manly" men and to de-
fend their natural rights to citizenship, but in general Whitman
sings beautifully of love, nature, and immortality. McGirt (1899)
intersperses didactic and sentimental verses with martial tributes
to black and Cuban heroes of the Spanish-American War, while

in a few verses he ridicules black color and class prejudice and appeals for freedmen's rights. Rowe offers one volume of uplifting and consolatory sermons in verse (1887) and another, *Our Heroes* (1890), which celebrates fifteen black luminaries. A contemporary review of *Our Heroes* conveys the intent of all such upward-bound literature:

> The glow he has cast over the originals . . . throws out all prejudice formed on preconceived poetical models. We see the goodness and nobility in every one of them . . . true manhood and womanhood in those he writes of . . . and we, impressed by what we see through him, do reverence with him. We learn to look beyond the worldly envelope of a man to the integrity of his conscience. Here should begin our race pride, which, as the author wisely says, is necessary to the growth, progress, and prosperity of any people. It should especially be placed in the hands of the young.[7]

The Afro-Americans' search for acceptance and self-improvement, both in image and materially, drew several poets into the orbit of Booker T. Washington. In the work of Cotter, Clem, Davis, and the later Harper, the Tuskegean's upward-bound ideology reaches didactic perfection. Clem (1900) counsels self-reliance, prudence, pluck, and piety; Cotter's turn-of-the-century verse sanctifies self-help, money-getting, patient accommodation, and industrial education; Davis urges work and prayer as keys to racial progress. As in every decade since 1850, Harper's work remains the prototype of black poetry. As early as 1871 she forgave the oppressor and combined her appeals for civil rights with a confident vision of racial brotherhood. During the last two decades of the century she leads the poets in uplifting verse, directed not only at raising black moral, educational, and economic status, but also at reforming the national evils of alcoholism and the double standard of sex. Several other poets of this period warn against King Alcohol, but Harper and Alfred Campbell, both militant abolitionists in the 1850's, raise the loudest cries for temperance and women's rights.

The years of repression after Reconstruction clearly redirected Afro-American energies away from militancy to defensive modes. First, the upward-bound life style took literary form as celebrations of race achievements, exhortations to match or surpass white standards, and conscious imitations of the majority's cultural products. Second, the down-home life style found expression in dialect poetry of the 1890's which mythologized the Southern past, obscured pres-

7. "Have You Seen Our Heroes?" *AMECR,* 7 (October, 1890), back page, quoted from *Plain Speaker,* Orangeburg, S.C.

ent ills, and avoided the future. Black dialect poets reinforced
stereotypes popularized in the antebellum novels of Kennedy,
Simms, and Cooke and in minstrel shows that flourished from the
1850's well beyond the emergence of Russell, Harris, and Page in
the 1880's. James Weldon Johnson vividly describes their favorite
"Negro":

> a simple, indolent, docile, improvident peasant; a singing, dancing,
> laughing, weeping child; picturesque beside his log cabin and in the
> snowy fields of cotton; naively charming with his banjo and his songs
> in the moonlight and along the lazy Southern rivers; a faithful, ever-
> smiling and genuflecting old servitor to the white folks of quality; a
> pathetic and pitiable figure.[8]

Black writers supported the minstrel tradition for many reasons:
to be safe, to escape from oppressive realities (these included all
forms of discrimination and the special socioeconomic hardships
generated by extensive urbanization of Southern blacks), to earn
money and recognition, to assuage guilt, to nourish what was often
a genuine affection for bygone simple rural joys. In addition, some
black poets channeled their sincere concern for race progress into
dialect poetry to make the black man acceptable to white America.
That is, to paint the race as servile lackeys or happy-go-lucky chil-
dren was to render it harmless, thereby countermanding the image
of demonic, menacing savages that would take vicious forms in the
novels of Thomas Dixon. To mock the black man's superstitions,
exaggerate his proverbial talent for song and dance, his gastronomic
gluttony, his love of finery, and his head-scratching impotence was
to render him a delightful object of laughter and pity without either
the intelligence or will to threaten Anglo-Saxon supremacy. Still an-
other objective of dialect verse, clearly delineated in the work of
Davis, was to show Afro-Americans their foibles and follies of
slavery days which continued to impede race progress.

With the many reasons for the black poets' minstrelsy in mind,
dialect poetry cannot be dismissed as solely a demeaning, inade-
quate sociohistorical record of antebellum black life, for it was never
intended to be factually sound. Rather, it may be appreciated for
reflecting the desires and attitudes of many black artists struggling
to survive in American society at the turn of the century and be-
yond. None of the twenty-six poets in this study wrote in dialect
before 1877—Harper's sketches of 1872 caught the rhythms of

8. James Weldon Johnson, "The Dilemma of the Negro Author," *American
Mercury*, 15 (1928), 478.

Southern black speech but did not try to reproduce the diction; but James Campbell (1887, 1895), Davis (1895, 1897), McGirt (1899), and a little later Clem and Cotter celebrated "the Negroes of the old regime" (Campbell's dedication), while Whitman and Fortune disdained dialect but favored plantation stereotypes such as the fateful octoroon. Besides its cultural significance, the dialect poetry of Campbell and Davis, particularly the former, has aesthetic merit. Its passages of lyrical beauty, its rollicking satire, foot-tapping or haunting melodies, and down-home details of church-going, fine eating, trickery, and big-wheeling are indeed charming. This verse often recalls the folk and slave narrative traditions. But twenty or thirty years after Emancipation, the seamy and brutal, demoralizing and killing aspects of slavery recorded by the fugitives were buried by popular demand, and the black poets trod the golden footsteps of their laureate, Dunbar, to offer an eager public roses without thorns. With W. D. Howells's introduction to Dunbar's *Lyrics of Lowly Life* (1896), dialect verse became respectable, fashionable, and profitable for black poets. In the first two decades of the twentieth century dialect pieces by Dunbar, Corrothers, J. Mord Allen, John Holloway, Ray Dandridge, and many others found honored niches in white periodicals which for two hundred years had wholly ignored the writings of Afro-Americans.

Criteria for Evaluation

Nineteenth-century Americans admired poetry for its moral, social, and sentimental strength expressed in easily comprehensible language and conventional forms. Popular poetry was true to the beauties or the pathetic realities of life and responsive to national causes. The work we esteem today—of Poe, Melville, Whitman, Dickinson—for its verbal complexities, ambiguity, irony, symbolical richness, and originality of thought and design was ignored or ridiculed by the large poetry-reading public (and critics) of its time. Rather, they worshiped Bryant, Whittier, Holmes, Longfellow, Riley, and hundreds of minor poets who instructed, inspired, and amused them.

Black poetry of the last century had scarcely any audience and no critical theorists. Rare notices of it in black periodicals praised the poets for demonstrating the abilities of the race and the poetry for promulgating true Christian and American values. In the twentieth century, when early black poetry was noticed at all, the same

pragmatic standards were applied, combined at times with a bio-
graphical-historical approach that marveled at the very existence
of verse by early Afro-Americans. When black critics, applying the
aesthetic norms of the New Criticism, finally glanced at the poems
as poems, they found them valueless; the work could not justify its
autonomy, severed from its creators and their intentions, its his-
torical milieu, and its propagandistic effects.

Modern black critics have reached no consensus on critical stand-
ards for black writing. As Darwin Turner explained in 1970:

> Despite 50 years of criticism of Afro-American literature, criteria for
> that criticism have not been established. Consequently, some readers
> judge literature by Afro-Americans according to its moral value, a
> few for its aesthetic value, most by its social value, and too many
> according to their response to the personalities of Black authors.[9]

Until very recently, Turner observes, black literature was evaluated
solely "according to the criteria established and approved for white
American writers," whether the prevailing criteria were moral, so-
cial, aesthetic, or personality values. Many new black critics, how-
ever, demand that Afro-American writing be judged "according to
an aesthetic grounded in Afro-American culture" which stresses the
styles and traditions of the black experience and the degree of
commitment to "the revolutionary cause of black liberation." [10]

Proponents of the black aesthetic urge total destruction of white
Western artistic and cultural norms for the building of a new black
art on black philosophical, moral, and racial foundations. The black
arts movement, as described by its founder, Larry Neal, would re-
place "white ideas, and white ways of looking at the world" with
"a separate symbolism, mythology, critique, and iconology." The
goal, writes Don L. Lee, is to develop a total black consciousness
that will strengthen the race's self-respect and lead Afro-Americans
to identify with and love black peoples throughout the world.[11]

9. Darwin Turner, "Afro-American Literary Critics," *Black World*, 19 (July,
1970), 61.

10. *Ibid.*, pp. 54–67 *passim*.

11. Arthur P. Davis, "The New Poetry of Black Hate," *CLA Journal*, 13
(June, 1970), 382–91; Larry Neal, "The Black Arts Movement," *The Drama
Review*, 12 (Summer, 1968), 29–39; Don L. Lee, "Directions for Black Writ-
ers," *The Black Scholar*, 1 (December, 1969), 53–57. For a variety of modern
critical viewpoints, see also two anthologies edited by Addison Gayle, Jr., *Black
Expression* and *The Black Aesthetic* (New York: 1969, 1971); Cecil M. Brown,
"Black Literature and Leroi Jones," *Black World*, 19 (June, 1970), 24–31;
Francis and Val Gray Ward, "The Black Artist—His Role in the Struggle,"
The Black Scholar, 2 (January, 1971), 23–32.

Common

    Rivers of love and mercy here,
    In a rich ocean join.
    Salvation in abundance flows
    Like floods of milk and wine.

One hymn of five stanzas, "Of the Christian's Barbarity," departs from the pattern to condemn slavery:

    Was stolen and sold from Africa,
    Imported to America:
    Like the brute beasts at market sold,
    To stand the heat and bear the cold.
    When will Jehovah hear our cries!
    And free the sons of Africa.
            . . . .
    But He that rides upon the storms,
    Whose voice in thunder rolls along:
    In his own time will make a way
    To relieve the oppressed of Africa.
    O, Prince of Glory be their friend!
    And keep them faithful to the end.

When this poem was reprinted in the *A.M.E. Church Review* in January, 1885, a headnote claimed that the New York Conference of the A.M.E. Church had proscribed Cannon's book in 1834 and forbidden its sale; therefore, it was a very rare book.[1] *The Rock of Wisdom* concludes with "The Ark," a lively thirty-two-line summons to praise God and pray for one another as did the biblical heroes:

    There Joshua and Joseph, Elias and Moses,
    Who pray'd and God heard from his throne.
    There was Abram, and Isaac, and Jacob, and David,
    And Solomon, Stephen and John.
    There was Simeon and Anna—I don't know how many,
    Who pray'd as they journey'd along;
    Some cast among lions—some bound with rough irons;
    Yet praises and glory they sung.

Cannon ends the poem and his book with a farewell quatrain and a hearty "Amen."

1. Daniel Murray says Cannon was twice "hauled up before the assembled theologians in conference and forced to renounce the theology advocated in his book." "Bibliographia-Africana," *VN*, 1 (May, 1904), 189.

SELECTED SOURCES

Loggins, 105–7.
Singleton, George A. *The Romance of Methodism: A Study of the A.M.E. Church.* New York: Exposition, 1952. Pp. 28, 108, 115.
Wayman, Alexander W. *My Recollections of African M.E. Ministers.* Philadelphia: A.M.E. Book Rooms, 1881. Pp. 7–10.

GEORGE MOSES HORTON
1797?–1883?

The "Colored Bard of North-Carolina" was the first slave to pro-
test his bondage in verse and the first Southern black man to pub-
lish a volume of poetry in America. Horton was born in 1797 in
Northampton County, North Carolina, four miles from the Roanoke
River on the small tobacco farm of William Horton. He was the
sixth of ten children. His mother had five girls, "not of one father,"
followed by George, another boy, and three girls "by her second
husband." [1] When George was six his master, William Horton,
moved to Chatham, 100 miles southwest of Northampton, where
by 1806 he owned over 400 acres of farmland planted mainly in
corn and wheat. Here, George recalls, he was a "cow-boy" for
ten years, an occupation he found "disagreeable." Very early he had
discovered his "extraordinary appetite for singing lively tunes," and
now he took pleasure in music and in hearing people read. With
his brother, "both remarkable for boys of color," George deter-
mined to read and write. Every Sabbath he went outdoors and
studied an "old black and tattered spelling book," persevering at
night by bark or brush light despite the heat and smoke. Neither
these hardships nor the taunts and temptations of his companions
deterred him; rather, he says, "Those obstacles had an auspicious
tendency to waft me, as on pacific gales, above the storms of envy
and the calumniating scourge of emulation, from which literary
imagination often sinks beneath its dignity, and instruction lan-
guishes at the shrine of vanity." George's extraordinary vocabulary
developed as he passed from spelling to reading lessons in the New

1. Horton's autobiography in *Poetical Works* is the source of most data to
1845 and of all quotations not otherwise noted. Additional biography is largely
from Walser. Date of birth is given as 1797 in *Hope of Liberty*, Weeks, Farri-
son, and Walser; 1798 in Cobb and *DLC Catalogue*; 1794 in Banks's "Sketch"
in *Naked Genius* (whose dates are generally unreliable).

Testament and Wesley's hymnals, and soon he was composing verses and hymns in his head.

In 1814 William Horton divided some of his property among his sons. By cast of lots, George fell to James Horton, who also farmed in Chatham. About 1817 George began his weekly Sabbath walks of eight miles to the Chapel Hill campus of the University of North Carolina to sell fruit to the students. In keeping with the custom of the time, the collegians put the slave on display. Having "discovered a spark of genius in him," George writes, they urged him to deliver extemporaneous orations for their diversion. He complied, although he was fully aware that the pranksters played on his "vain egotism." Soon, however, he abandoned these "foolish harangues" and won the students' awed admiration by composing love verses and acrostics on ladies' names to order. During the week, "at the handle of the plough," he made up a dozen poems, dictated them to the courtiers the next Sabbath, and collected twenty-five cents a verse for most, fifty to seventy-five cents for his more complicated efforts. Thus the "Colored Bard of North-Carolina" began his career. The collegians aided their bard's education by giving him books: Murray's *English Grammar*, Johnson's *Dictionary*, poetry of Milton, Thompson, Homer, Virgil, Shakespeare, Byron, and others, as well as geography, history, and oratory texts. During the 1820's Horton's fame spread through Chapel Hill. He won the patronage of University President Joseph D. Caldwell and devoted attention from Caroline Lee Hentz, author of many antebellum novels, notably *The Planter's Northern Bride*.[2] Mrs. Hentz, wife of a University professor, transcribed Horton's verse (he could not write until about 1832), tutored him in prosody, and sent his poems to the *Lancaster* (Mass.) *Gazette*, which published "Liberty and Slavery" and "On Poetry and Music" in 1828. For five years (1826–31) Mrs. Hentz encouraged Horton, and when she left Chapel Hill, he says, "She left behind her the laurel of Thalia blooming on my mind, and went with all the spotless gaiety of Euphrosyne with regard to the signal services which she had done me." To this tribute Horton added a poetic eulogy for the "immortal dame." Mrs. Hentz, President Caldwell, Dr. James Henderson, a local physician, and an unidentified philanthropist initiated the first of several campaigns to purchase Horton's freedom. Through their efforts the *Raleigh Register* printed a sketch of Horton's life, several of his

2. Mrs. Hentz records her impressions of Horton in her novel, *Lovell's Folly* (1833).

poems, and an account of the Manumission Society's interest in his case (July to October, 1828). Simultaneously in the North *Freedom's Journal*, in five issues from August 8 to October 31, 1828, appealed for funds—one penny from each Afro-American in New York—to buy the slave poet. Contributions did not flow in, however, and George Horton remained in bondage. In his oration, "The Stream of Liberty and Science" (1859), Horton notes that the governor of North Carolina, John Owen, had also tried to help by offering to pay his master $100 more for George than any person should say he was worth, but James Horton decided his property was too valuable to sell. Publication of Horton's *Hope of Liberty* in the summer of 1829 launched a second manumission campaign. This twenty-two-page pamphlet of twenty-one poems was only the third book of poetry by an Afro-American in the nation's history, following the volumes of Phillis Wheatley and Jupiter Hammon by some fifty years. The preface, probably written by the publisher, Weston R. Gales, urged contributions of a sum sufficient for George's emancipation, "upon the condition of his going in the vessel which shall first afterwards sail for Liberia. It is his earnest and only wish to become a member of that Colony" (Horton never expressed this wish in print). Gales's preface also disclosed that James Horton knew nothing of his slave's poetry, that George could now read and was learning to write, and that the poet "has been ever a faithful, honest and industrious slave."

Despite such assurances, *Hope of Liberty*'s fund-raising drive failed, and interest in Horton's manumission slacked off as events of 1830–31—David Walker's *Appeal* and Nat Turner's rebellion—terrified Southerners and prompted severe repressive legislation. At this time Horton was earning over three dollars a week from Sabbath sales of his love lyrics, and in about 1833 he arranged to hire his time from James Horton at twenty-five cents a day. His master probably stood to gain from this arrangement, for Horton's biographers claim that his literary aspirations made him "worthless as a farm hand, since his Pegasus resolutely refused to be harnessed to a plow" (Weeks, 574). In fact, Collier Cobb wrote, all his life George had "made a pretense of working on the farm," while actually spending winters hunting and fishing and summers going to camp meetings (Cobb, 4). In the early 1830's, then, Horton became full-time bard, handyman, hotel waiter, and servant to the students and staff at Chapel Hill. When his patron, President Caldwell, died in 1835, according to Cobb, Weeks, and Walser, the poet gave himself up to drink, squandered the proceeds from *Hope of Liberty*, and begged for money by declaiming his sad verses from room to room at the college. Horton was aware of his weakness for liquor, which he traced to childhood days when William Horton, a hard-drinking man, freely indulged his slaves and convinced them it was "an honor to be intoxicated." In those days, Horton recalls, "Bacchus was honored far more than Ceres" in North Carolina: "All christendom seemed to be relapsing into dissipation; and libertinism, obscenity and profanation were in their full career; and the common conversation was impregnated with droll blasphemy. . . . Hence it was inevitably my misfortune to become a votary to that growing evil [of drinking]." Moreover, later at Chapel Hill the collegians plied Horton with whiskey, flattering him into the belief "that it would hang me on the wings of new inspiration, which would waft me into regions of poetical perfection." By 1845, when he wrote these words, Horton had experienced the destructive consequences of intemperance and vowed total abstinence.

For over thirty years George Horton was a daily fixture at the University, prodigiously writing poetry, seeking publication, and at times actively appealing for his freedom. Through the efforts of Joshua Coffin, the Philadelphia abolitionist, Horton's *Hope of Liberty* was reprinted by Lewis Gunn in 1837 as *Poems by a Slave*. A year later Isaac Knapp, publisher of Garrison's *Liberator*, issued a third edition of it in Boston, appended to Phillis Wheatley's *Memoir and Poems*. In 1843 James Horton died, and in the auction of his effects George became the property of Hall Horton, a tanner, who raised the slave's daily hire-fee to fifty cents. The poet had on hand a large manuscript volume of poetry, "The Museum" (PW, xxi),[3] which he was anxious to publish. On September 3, 1844, Horton appealed to William Lloyd Garrison for "assistance in carrying my original work into public execution." "Sir," he wrote, "I am not alone actuated by pecuniary motives but, upon the whole, to spread the blaze of African genius and thus dispel the sceptic gloom so prevalent in many parts of the country."[4] The poet's impassioned plea that Garrison help "open to the world a volume, which like a wild bird has long been struggling in its shell" received no answer, for

3. Horton's published volumes are abbreviated in the text as follows: (HL), *Hope of Liberty* (1829); (PW), *Poetical Works* (1845); (NG), *Naked Genius* (1865).

4. Letter quoted in full in Walser, pp. 64–65.

Horton had naively entrusted the letter to the new University president, David Swain, who never mailed it. Shortly afterward, however, by his own efforts Horton collected ninety-nine subscribers' signatures from Chapel Hill students and dignitaries. These names, plus an autobiography of the "Colored Bard of North-Carolina," appear in his *Poetical Works,* published in the autumn of 1845. Sales at fifty cents a copy were very slow, and in 1852 volumes were available at half price.

Although Horton always had "several manuscript volumes" at hand ready to publish (Walser, 75), almost nothing of his appeared in print during the next twenty years.[5] Two poems from the ill-fated "Museum" had been published in the *Southern Literary Messenger* (April, 1843); the *Raleigh Register* (December 29, 1849) printed Horton's letter in defense of an American literature; and a poem, "What Is Time?" appeared in the *Chapel Hill Weekly Gazette* (May 9, 1857). There is no trace of either new editions of his poems or the short stories and essays Cobb says he published in the 1850's (Cobb, 7). From this period there exist in manuscript Horton's twenty-nine-page grandiloquent oration, "The Stream of Liberty and Science," delivered at Chapel Hill in 1859, and three letters testifying to his continued desire for manumission.[6] In 1852 Hall Horton agreed to sell his fifty-five-year-old slave for $250. George Horton wrote two letters to David Swain proposing that the University president buy him, in return for which the poet would give two-thirds of the proceeds from his new book plus "obligatory service to you for life." This offer was not accepted, and on September 11, 1852, Horton wrote to Horace Greeley "for some assistance to remove the burden of hard servitude":

> By favoring me with a bounty of 175 dollars, I will endeavor to reward your generosity with my productions as soon as possible. I am the only public or recognized poet of color in my native state or perhaps in the union, born in slavery but yet craving that scope and expression whereby my literary labor of the night may be circulated throughout the whole world.

5. Horton's poetry had previously appeared in many periodicals, including *Freedom's Journal, Emancipator, North Star, Liberator,* and *National Anti-Slavery Standard.*

6. Oration quoted in part, letters to Swain and Greeley in full in Walser, pp. 83–84, 76, 78–81. I am indebted to Carolyn A. Wallace, Manuscripts Curator, Southern Historical Collection, NcU, for her letters to me locating Horton's prose and poetry in manuscript.

To the letter Horton added a poem, "The Poet's Feeble Petition,"
which begins:

> Bewailing mid the ruthless wave,
>   I lift my feeble hand to thee.
> Let me no longer live a slave
>   But drop these fetters and be free.

The sincerity of Horton's words to Greeley, ending, "Let hearts of
petrification melt/ And bid the gifted Negro soar," contradicts
Cobb's assertion that "George never really cared for more liberty
than he had, but he was fond of playing to the grand-stand" (Cobb,
6). Once again, however, the poet's hope of aid from the North
was thwarted by David Swain, who buried the Greeley letter with
the one to Garrison among his presidential papers.

It was not until the Union troops occupied Raleigh in April, 1865,
that Horton, emancipated and adrift, found a patron in Wil-
liam H. S. Banks, a twenty-eight-year-old captain in the 9th Michi-
gan Cavalry Volunteers. Banks "adopted" George Horton, and to-
gether they traveled to Concord, North Carolina, on April 30, 1865.
In Concord, on the road to Lexington (where Banks was mustered
out of service on July 21), and until the summer's end, Horton com-
posed dozens of new poems commemorating Northern and South-
ern leaders, events of camp life, dying and homesick soldiers, as
well as a substantial batch of verses on love, slavery, religion, and
the art of poetry. Banks selected ninety of these poems, added forty-
four from *Poetical Works* and a "Sketch of the Author" to form
Horton's final volume, *Naked Genius,* published in Raleigh proba-
bly in September, 1865. Banks's motive was "to show that God in
his gifts was in no wise partial to the Uuropean [*sic*], but that he
gave genius to the black as well as the white man." On the title
page of *Naked Genius* Banks promises another volume, *The Black
Poet,* for "about the 1st of October, 1865," and he invites sales agents
to contact him in Lawton, Michigan (pp. 159–60).[7]

Horton traveled North in 1866, but without Banks or *The Black*

---

7. The subtitle of *Naked Genius* identifies Horton as author of "The Black
Poet . . . a work being now compiled and revised" by Banks. "This work will
contain a concise history of the life of the author, written by the compiler, and
will be offered to the public as one of the many proofs that God, in his infinite
wisdom and mercy, created the Black man for a higher and nobler purpose than
to toil his life away under the galling yoke of slavery." Some bibliographies in-
clude for Horton: *The Black Poet* (1865) and *Poems of an Exile* (Indianapolis:
Bobbs-Merrill, 1931). The former was never published; the latter, held at
Princeton University Library, is by another George Horton, born 1859.

Poet, arriving sometime that year in Philadelphia, where he probably resided for the seventeen years until his death. Life in Philadelphia was difficult and lonely for the aging poet. While in North Carolina, perhaps in the 1830's, he had married a slave of Franklin Snipes, a farmer in the Chatham neighborhood. Horton's son, known as Free Snipes, died in Durham in 1896, and a daughter, Rhody, married to Van Buren Byrum, was living in Raleigh in 1897 (Weeks, 576). It is unlikely that Horton's wife or children ever saw him after he left the South. Little is known about his activities in Philadelphia. Minutes of the Banneker Institute, a fraternity of educated black men, record a special meeting held on August 31, 1866, "to receive Mr. George Horton of North Carolina, a poet of considerable genius." The Institute discussed publishing a volume of his poetry but found the cost prohibitive (Weeks, 576). Cobb's claim that Horton wrote and published many short stories based on biblical themes as well as poetry during this "most productive period" of his life is unsubstantiated (Cobb, 10). Likewise, there is widespread opinion but no evidence that Horton was despised and rejected by the Philadelphia Negroes who found him "overbearing, conceited, and offensive" (Walser, 104) or "naively selfish and stuffed with the vanity of a child" (Redding, 16). Perhaps the only facts about Horton's later years, recorded in Cobb's letter of 1929, are that the poet worked for Cobb's father, his uncle, and great-uncle, and that Cobb visited Horton in Philadelphia in 1883, "the very year in which he died." The year 1883 is generally accepted for Horton's death, although neither date nor place can be corroborated. It is probably true that Horton, after sixty-six years in slavery, found freedom difficult, and that the snobbish black community of Philadelphia received this rustic who called himself poet with coolness, or worse. Yet somehow Horton survived as he always had, working when necessary and exercising his native guile, wit, and keen intelligence in freedom as in bondage for eighty-five years.

Horton's Poetry

Hope of Liberty (1829) is a monument to the remarkable mind and spirit of George Moses Horton. Deprived of intellectual enrichment by his bondage, Horton taught himself to read; he read widely but could not write until about 1832. Therefore, in 1828–29 the thirty-two-year-old slave dictated from memory, to some unknown amanuensis, all twenty-one selections in *Hope of Liberty.*

This feat alone gives the collection unique status in American liter-
ature. Horton's achievement becomes more extraordinary when his
poetry's artistic merit is considered, for he displays unusual skill
with meter and rhyme, firm control over content, and sensitivity
to language. Moreover, a joyous sense of life, originating in Horton's
naive enthusiasm for nature and for his Muse, enlivens many poems.

When *Hope of Liberty* appeared, Horton had been marketing
love pieces to Chapel Hill students for over ten years. His acrostics
and verses praising ladies' charms or bemoaning their obstinacy
became formulaic by 1829, for Horton found that with a few minor
adjustments his basic verses could be sold again and again. Of the
love poems extant—none from before 1828—there is one acrostic,
to Julia Shepard, "An Acrostic on the Pleasures of Beauty" (MS,
n.d.):

> Attracting beauty must delight afford,
> Sought of the world and of the Bards adored;
> Her grace of form and heart-alluring powers
> Express her more than fair, the queen of flowers.

Horton's language in the five love poems of *Hope of Liberty* is sim-
ilarly all-inclusive hyperbole, but his perfectly precise rhythms and
rhymings occur in pleasing varieties. In "Love" he uses a favorite
device, repetition with minor word change of the last line in each
stanza:

> Whilst tracing thy visage, I sink in emotion,
> For no other damsel so wond'rous I see;
> Thy looks are so pleasing, thy charms so amazing,
> I think of no other, my true-love, but thee.

"I fancy no other," "I pine for no other," follow. It seems that Hor-
ton's customers frequently failed at romance, for the love verses,
early and late, are largely "farewells," differing only in the ladies'
names. For example, "To Eliza" (HL) and "Farewell to Frances"
(PW) utilize Byron's couplet (from "Fare Thee Well," 1816).

> (1)   Eliza, tell thy lover why
>   Or what induced thee to deceive me?
>   Fare thee well—away I fly—
>   I shun the lass who thus will grieve me.

> (4)   Eliza, I shall think of thee—
>   My heart shall ever twine about thee;
>   Fare thee well—but think of me,
>   Compell'd to live and die without thee,

> "Fare thee well, and if forever,
> Still forever fare thee well."
>
>   .   .   .
>
> (1) Farewell, if ne'er I see thee more,
>   Though distant calls my flight impel
>   I shall not less thy grace adore,
>   So friend, forever fare thee well.
>
> (7) I leave thee, but forget thee never,
>   Words cannot my feeling tell,
>   "Fare thee well, and if forever,
>   Still forever fare thee well."

Such love pieces spouted to order are the weakest verse in *Hope of Liberty*, and Horton's later effusions on the theme are marked by hackneyed and bombastic diction, obscure allusions, and careless thought. Two exceptions, "Lines to My—" (1843?) and "Early Affection" (PW) share merits of rhythmic repetition, melodious phrasing, and elegantly simple language woven with tender tones into a classic morning to night pattern of imagery:

> I loved thee from the earliest dawn,
>   When first I saw thy beauty's ray;
> And will until life's eve comes on,
>   And beauty's blossom fades away;
> And when all things go well with thee,
> With smiles or tears remember me.
>
> I'll love thee when thy morn is past
>   And wheedling gallantry is o'er,
> When youth is lost in age's blast,
>   And beauty can ascend no more;
> And when life's journey ends with thee,
> O then look back and think of me. (PW)

Horton's other concerns in *Hope of Liberty* are religion, nature, the art of poetry, and slavery. "On the Truth of the Savior," in ten neatly crafted stanzas, hails the powers of Jesus, with an occasional fine image: "At his command the water blushed,/ And all was turned to wine." Here, in "The Gad-Fly," and in later poems such as "Pride in Heaven" (PW), "Death of a Favorite Chambermaid" (PW), and "The Close of Life" (NG), Horton neither preaches Christian ethics nor merely versifies the New Testament as Hammon and Wheatley did. Rather, he discards dogma and humanizes faith, God, and death as natural extensions of life. Religion, in fact, is of far less concern to Horton throughout his works than his bondage, his Muse, and everyday events, including the Civil War. Horton's

attitude toward death is consistently, "I'm here today, but gone to-
morrow/ To my long repose."

> Let me die without fear of the dead,
> No horrors shall my soul dismay,
> And with faith's pillow under my head
> With defiance to mortal decay,
> Go chanting away.
> ("Close of Life")

His easy synthesis of simple piety, poetic aspiration, and love of
nature emerges in "Praise of Creation" (HL), where the poet sum-
mons eagles, lions, thunders, mountains, volcanoes, cataracts, him-
self and his Muse to acclaim God's work with roars, yells, and
songs:

> Creation fires my tongue!
> Nature thy anthem praise;
> And spread the universal song
> Of thy creator's praise.

Horton's best nature poems are also in *Hope of Liberty*. The trio,
"On Spring," "On Summer," "On Winter," each in a different verse
form, draw on common rural sights and sounds to catch the mood
and movement of these seasons: "Thou noisy insect start thy drum;/
Rise lamp-like bugs to light the train"; a "weary plough horse
droops his head"; "The cattle all at noon retreat,/ And ruminate
beneath the shade" in summer. Later nature poems, sprinkled gen-
erously with mythological beings, sink heavily into eighteenth-
century diction, as "A Beautiful Moonlight Night in April" (NG),
in 120 lines of blank verse, suggests:

> Prolific queen, whilst wilt thou take thy leave,
> To dot thy rays on dark Hesperian wilds;
> The wanderers of the night would court thy stay
> And languish in the absence of thy smile.

Horton's antislavery poems cannot be dismissed as "selfish and
unimpassioned" (Walser, 70). The poet naturally concentrates on
his bondage, unlike Mrs. Harper, a prolific antislavery poet who,
being free, lavishes anathemas on the whole peculiar institution.
Moreover, Horton omits blood-curdling details of rack, whip, and
hairbreadth escapes—perhaps because these were alien to his own
minimally oppressive experience, and because he hoped to publish
the poems in a slave state. His three appeals for freedom in *Hope
of Liberty* and the "Petition" to Horace Greeley are honest and

moving verses, uniquely George Horton's in their identification of physical liberty with creation of poetry. The ten-stanza "On Liberty and Slavery," dictated to Mrs. Hentz in 1828, appeared in many newspapers and is most frequently anthologized:

> Alas! and am I born for this,
> To wear this slavish chain?
> Deprived of all created bliss,
> Through hardship, toil, and pain!
>
> . . . .
>
> Come, Liberty, thou cheerful sound,
> Roll through my ravished ears,
> Come, let my grief in joys be drowned,
> And drive away my fears.
>
> Say unto foul oppression, Cease:
> Ye tyrants rage no more,
> And let the joyful trump of peace,
> Now bid the vassal soar.
>
> . . . .
>
> Oh, blest asylum—heavenly balm!
> Unto thy boughs I flee—
> And in thy shades the storm shall calm,
> With songs of Liberty!

An equally popular poem, "The Slave's Complaint," begins:

> Am I sadly cast aside,
> On misfortune's rugged tide?
> Will the world my pain deride
> Forever?

"Forever" tolls a solemn conclusion to each of seven stanzas. "On Hearing of the Intention of a Gentleman to Purchase the Poet's Freedom" was Horton's response to the manumission campaign waged on his behalf in 1828. There is nothing primitive about the poem's structure and versification, and its exuberant tone soars through thirteen stanzas. Horton tells how his early delight in poetizing had vanished along with hope for freedom as his bondage endured. The prospect of freedom, however, released his Muse:

> With frantic joy she chaunted as she flew,
> And kiss'd the clement hand that bore her through;
> Her envious foes did from her sight retreat,
> Or prostrate fall beneath her burning feet.

The Muse's song was like that of sinners forgiven, like the "salutation of the dove" when spring returns, "like the evening of a nuptial pair," and "like fair Helen's sweet return to Troy."

> The silent harp which on the osiers hung,
> Was then attuned, and manumission sung;
> Away by hope the clouds of fear were driven,
> And music breathed my gratitude to Heaven.

The poet offers thanks to the "philanthropic souls" who "with pity strove to break the slavish bar" and concludes:

> Thus on the dusky verge of deep despair,
> Eternal Providence was with me there;
> When pleasure seemed to fade on life's gay dawn,
> And the last beam of hope was almost gone.

It is not surprising that Horton wrote very few antislavery poems in later years, and that these, like "Division of an Estate" (PW) and "The Slave" (NG), are unremarkable. By 1845, when *Poetical Works* appeared, Horton had been in bondage almost half a century, had failed in several attempts to gain freedom, and had apparently become resigned to the futility of further protest.

With resignation came a diminution of freshness and simplicity in his verse on all subjects. Among 135 poems in the 1845 and 1865 collections, only about a dozen are genuinely successful. There is evidence of increased technical experimentation and sophistication in such poems as "The Retreat from Moscow" (PW). Here metrical variation in alternate stanzas, concrete imagery, and a refrain ("The whirlwinds, the smoke, and the fire") convey the swift destructiveness of a great fire. Horton compares the conflagration to the battle of Troy and to Gomorrah, reaching a personal moral:

> O heaven, when earth is no more,
> And all things in nature expire,
> May I thus, with safety, keep distant before
> The whirlwinds, the smoke, and the fire.

In "To Miss Tempe" (PW) he makes effective use of alliteration and imagery as Hope, a bright bird and a glowing lamp, survives the flight of Time, personified as a young girl. New to *Poetical Works* are four delightful personal and earthy folk verses. "Troubled with the Itch and Rubbing with Sulphur" begins: "'Tis bitter, yet 'tis sweet;/ Scratching effects but transient ease";

> In fine, I know not which
> Can play the most deceitful game,
> The devil, sulphur, or the itch;
> The three are but the same.

> The devil sows the itch,
>   And sulphur has a loathsome smell,
> And with my clothes as black as pitch,
>   I stink where'er I dwell.

To such colloquial and homely detail Horton adds wry wit and a lively ballad refrain in "The Creditor to His Proud Debtor":

> My duck bill boots would look as bright,
> Had you in justice served me right;
> Like you I then could step as light,
>   Before a flaunting maid;
> As nicely could I clear my throat,
> And to my tights my eyes devote;
> But I'd leave you bare without that coat,
>   For which you have not paid.
>   Then boast and bear the crack,
>   With the sheriff at your back;
>   Huzza for dandy Jack,
>   My jolly fop, my Joe.

The same hearty spirit and truth to experience invigorate "The Tippler to His Bottle," "The Woodman and the Money Hunter," and an occasional verse in *Naked Genius* like "Death of an Old Carriage Horse."

Most of the ninety new poems in *Naked Genius* have more historical or biographical interest than aesthetic value. Very likely a majority of them were dashed off in about four months at the request of Captain Banks to give the volume contemporary relevance. Among the Civil War verses are several eyewitness accounts, such as "Execution of Private Henry Anderson" (a looter and murderer executed in Lexington) and "The Late Thunder Storm in Camp at Concord, N.C. June 20, 1865." Many are sentimental doggerel rhymes on homesickness, like "The Thought of Home in Battle," "Aspiring Home," "The Southern Refugee," and "The Friends Left at Home." There are tributes to Liberty, Union, the bravery of dying soldiers, and to the heroes, martyrs, and anti-heroes of the War like Generals Grant, Sherman, and Kilpatrick, Lincoln and Mrs. Lincoln, and Jefferson Davis. These tedious verses with rare exceptions consist of scarcely differentiated panegyrical clichés:

(Grant) What more has great Napoleon ever done,
         Though many battles in his course he won?
         What more has Alexander e'er achieved,
         Who left depopulated cities grieved?

To him we dedicate the whole in song,
The verses from our pen to him belong,
To him the Union banners are unfurled,
The star of peace the standard of the world.

(Lincoln)   We never shall forget his name,
             Which must be sculptured in his tomb,
             And flourish in eternal bloom,
           The seal of everlasting fame!
             Eternal peer forever soar
             In light, when nature is no more.

More honest and interesting are a group of verses on women, wives, and marriage like "Freedom," "Peace at Home," and "Rachael or Virtue." Horton plays the misogynist with relish, warning against foolish, demanding, and emancipated women, urging man to preserve his freedom or, if he must marry, to "Subdue your wife's destructive wave/ Nor let her bear you down a slave." Better still, if she gets pushy, "Leave her alone herself to shift,/ And vanish from her sight." In "New Fashions" Horton recalls with nostalgia the days when people were serious and cautious about death, weddings, paying debts, and keeping women in their place.

There was a time when ladies swore not,
   Teasing their husbands for a dram,
Draughts of gin their bosoms bore not,
   Effusing from their lips a damn;
Now they swear, they drink and boast,
And the fairest drink the most.

Naked Genius has its share of "farewell" love pieces, verses on religion, nature, and the poetic art. "The Obstruction of Genius" begins well with an angry, almost paranoiac plaint for lost opportunities, but discontent dwindles into a conciliatory "Let us the evil now forget." "The Art of a Poet" counsels that skill with rhyme and meter and inspiration from nature are not enough; the poet must attune his mind and inner eye to catch "things concealed" beneath the surface and reveal them in his poetry.

"George Moses Horton, Myself" (NG) returns to the simple diction and heartfelt tone of regret that gave his early antislavery pieces appealing individuality. This monody of a frustrated poet sums up Horton's life-long conviction that he was born to sing and that his Muse and he were wrongfully imprisoned. The poem discloses that sixty-eighty years of bondage could not dim Horton's spirit and aspiration:

> I feel myself in need
> Of the inspiring strains of ancient lore,
> My heart to lift, my empty mind to feed,
> And all the world explore.
>
> I know that I am old
> And never can recover what is past,
> But for the future may some light unfold
> And soar from ages blast.
>
> I feel resolved to try,
> My wish to prove, my calling to pursue,
> Or mount up from the earth into the sky,
> To show what Heaven can do.
>
> My genius from a boy,
> Has fluttered like a bird within my heart;
> But I could not thus confined her powers employ,
> Impatient to depart.
>
> She like a restless bird,
> Would spread her wing, her power to be unfurl'd,
> And let her songs be loudly heard,
> And dart from world to world.

In 1883, Collier Cobb visited the eighty-six-year-old Horton in Philadelphia. "I called him 'Poet' which pleased him greatly," Cobb recalled, "and he told me that I was using his proper title." So it was, because all his life "Poet" was synonymous with "George Moses Horton." He struggled for literacy to write poetry; he begged for manumission to write poetry; he earned modest freedom of movement and a livelihood by writing poetry and continued to write despite the failure of his three volumes and the certainty that untold numbers of poems in manuscript would never be published. Historically, the "Colored Bard of North-Carolina" is a major nineteenth-century poet, the only one to publish volumes of poetry while in bondage, and the first black man to publish any book in the South. From the first, Horton showed a natural talent for capturing the rhythms of verse, a perfect ear for rhyme, and a sensitive, often cynical awareness of what life, and thus poetry, was all about. His *Hope of Liberty* and occasional later folk verses are admirable, and in the context of his life they are superb. Overall, his greatest triumph was to be always Poet Horton.

SELECTED SOURCES

Adams, Raymond. "North Carolina's Pioneer Negro Poet." *New York Age,* December 21, 1929. Rpt. from *Greensboro* (N.C.) *Daily News,* November 24, 1929.

Brawley, *ENAW,* 110–22. Includes preface from *Hope of Liberty* and poems.

Brawley, Benjamin. "Three Negro Poets: Horton, Mrs. Harper, and Whitman." *JNH,* 2 (October, 1917), 384–92.

°Cobb, Collier. "An American Man of Letters." *The University* [*of North Carolina*] *Magazine,* OS 40, NS 27 (October, 1909), 3–10.

———. Letter to Victor Palsits, January 10, 1929. NNSch.

Farrison, W. Edward. "George Moses Horton." *North Carolina Authors.* Chapel Hill: University of North Carolina Library, 1952. Pp. 64–65.

°Horton, George Moses. "Life." In *Poetical Works.* Pp. iii–xx.

Loggins, 107–17.

Redding, 13–18.

°Walser, Richard. *The Black Poet: being the remarkable story (partly told my* [sic] *himself) of George Moses Horton a North Carolina slave.* New York: Philosophical Library, 1966.

Weeks, Stephen B. "George Moses Horton: Slave Poet." *Southern Workman,* 43 (October, 1914), 571–77.

ELYMAS PAYSON ROGERS
1815–61

In the early eighteenth century a slave ship from Africa was shipwrecked off the coast of Madison, Connecticut. From the few survivors the Reverend Jonathan Todd bought several children whom he raised as his family. Most of them died young, but one woman, Old Tamar, lived to a great old age, and to her and her descendants the Reverend Mr. Todd gave most of his property. Old Tamar's son Cesar was a farmer who worked for the Todds; Cesar's son Abel, "an honest, faithful, hardworking man, of great physical strength and endurance," was the father of a boy "unusually bright from his infancy"; the boy was Elymas Payson Rogers. This rare genealogy reaching back to an African ancestor appears in a testimonial to Rogers from the Reverend Jonathan Todd's great-nephew, who had lived with all the principals in his boyhood.[1] Elymas Payson Rogers, a third-generation Afro-American, was born in Madison on February 10, 1815, to Abel and Chloe (Ladue) Rogers. His biographer in the *Presbyterian Historical Almanac* stresses the piety of Rogers's parents and the fervid desire of the child to become a minister and preach the gospel in Africa. At the age of nine Elymas was sent by his impoverished parents to live with strangers in a distant town. He returned home at fifteen to labor on a farm with his father, and in the early 1830's Rogers moved to Hartford, where he worked for his board in the home of a Major Caldwell. In Hartford he attended school and in 1833 became a communicant of the Talcott Street congregation.

1. Testimonial and biographical sketch of Rogers are in Wilson. Photocopy courtesy of Gerald W. Gillette, Research Historian, Presbyterian Historical Society, Philadelphia. I am also indebted to Charles Willard, Acting Librarian, Speer Library, Princeton Theological Seminary, and to Norman A. Burgess, Director of Teacher Personnel, Rochester, N.Y., for their efforts to locate information on Rogers.

Determined to become a minister, in 1835 Rogers enrolled at a school for young men established by the reformer-philanthropist Gerrit Smith in Peterboro, New York. After studying there for eighteen months Rogers needed money to continue his education and was hired on the strong recommendation of Smith to take charge of a public school for black children in Rochester. Through the winter of 1836–37 Rogers taught in Rochester, and that spring he enrolled at Oneida Institute in Whitesboro, New York, to prepare for the ministry. For the next five years as the seasons changed he alternated teaching in Rochester and studying in Whitesboro until his graduation from Oneida in the spring of 1841. A testimony by Rogers in the autobiography of Jermain Wesley Loguen recalls their meeting in Rochester in the early winter of 1838. Rogers was teaching there when Loguen, an illiterate fugitive slave about Rogers's age, arrived in the city. Rogers took him on as a pupil, they became friends, and in the spring he convinced Loguen to enter Oneida Institute with him. Loguen credits his teacher with procuring his admission to Oneida, from which he rose to fame as an abolitionist and A.M.E. bishop.[2]

Rogers became principal of the public school for black children in Trenton, New Jersey, immediately after his graduation from Oneida. In August, 1841, he married Mrs. Harriet E. Sherman of Rochester; they settled in Trenton, where Rogers continued to teach and study theology until 1844. On February 7, 1844, he was licensed by the New Brunswick Presbytery, and that fall he took charge of the Witherspoon Street Church in Princeton, New Jersey, where he remained for two years, having received full ordination to the ministry in 1845.

Rogers became a member of the Newark Presbytery on October 20, 1846, and for the next fourteen years he was pastor of the Plane Street Church in Newark. Under his zealous and industrious care the church grew from 23 members to 140 communicants and 130 Sabbath scholars by 1857. The Plane Street Church, in a building worth $5,000, was one of only two churches evaluated as "Prosperous" in the *Minutes* of the Presbyterian and Congregational Convention of 1857. Rogers delivered the opening sermon at this con-

---

2. *The Rev. J. W. Loguen, as a Slave And as a Freeman* (Syracuse: J. G. K. Truair, 1859), pp. 351, 445–50. A poem by Rogers, "Loguen's Position," is included here. As if spoken by a fugitive slave, it justifies his bold and vengeful demeanor, recounts the evils of slavery, and prays for emancipation of all in bondage.

vention in Philadelphia—he had been moderator of the 1856 meeting—and on a motion by him, the convention denounced the Dred Scott decision as a sin against God and a crime against humanity, while it praised the two dissenting Supreme Court Justices. During his ministry in Newark Rogers published his two abolitionist satires, *A Poem on the Fugitive Slave Law* (1855) and *The Repeal of the Missouri Compromise Considered* (1856).

Rogers never abandoned his childhood desire to proclaim the gospel to his brothers in Africa. He became an active member of the African Civilization Society, and, after many years of labor on its behalf, he sailed from New York on November 5, 1860, arriving in Freetown, Sierra Leone, after a calm passage of twenty-seven days. The homeland of Old Tamar, his great-grandmother, moved him deeply:

> Oh how my heart leaped within me yesterday when for the first time I trod upon African soil. When I gazed upon the rich green mountains which overlook Freetown and the beautiful shrubbery which adorns them, and considered how much there is on every hand which is good for food as well as pleasant to the eye in this great garden of nature, I put the interrogation to myself which I had often put before, why is it that this pleasant land, as lovely as any which the sun ever looked upon, should for centuries be only the hunting ground of the merciless slave trade[r]. Why is it that adverse winds and waves have not sunk every slave ship that has come to these shores to rob Africa of her sons and daughters?

The answer, Rogers writes, is that God's ways and thoughts are different from ours; but "God is about to visit and redeem his people," and "there is a bright future for poor Africa." After writing this letter to the Reverend George Whipple (December 2, 1860), Rogers sailed the West African Coast for five weeks and visited Monrovia, Bassa, Sinoe, and Cape Palmas. He found a multitude of "idolatrous and superstitious" tribesmen, many of whom had learned from seamen "to cheat and to blaspheme" and to keep the Sabbath by drinking rum. In his second letter to Whipple (January [13], 1861) Rogers prays that many more missionaries will come from America to Africa and labor to bring both the arts of civilized life and the gospel of Christ to the benighted land. Rogers writes that he will leave Cape Palmas for Lagos on January 16 "and shall soon be at our Journey's end." His prophecy proved sadly ironic, for a day or two later he fell ill and died "of disease of the heart" on the eve-

ning of January 20, 1861.[3] Just fifty days after he had stepped on
African soil, Elymas Rogers lost his childhood dream. But, as he had
written to Whipple, missionaries "may fall at their posts as hundreds
of Christian men and women have already done, but they may de-
rive consolation from the thought that if they lose their lives they
shall find them again."

Rogers's Poetry

The Repeal of the Missouri Compromise Considered is a politi-
cal argument of some 925 lines in octosyllabic couplets. The poem
is unique in antebellum black poetry not only for its length, but
also because such effective topical satire was a courageous ven-
ture for a black poet of the 1850's. Rogers's verse is precise and at-
tractive, and the well-structured satire shows notable intellectual-
ity. The poet reviews the history of legislation as well as popular
arguments for and against slavery from enactment of the Com-
promise of 1820 to the Kansas-Nebraska Act of 1854. Through a
loosely structured dialogue between "Freedom" and "Slavery,"
white America, South and North, is condemned for sacrificing the
country's honor to material advantage and nationalistic expediency.
In 1820 Northerners had "bowed to Slavery," saying:

> 'Tis wisdom to convey a slice
> Of territory, thus to save
> The Union from a dismal grave.
>
> .   .   .   .
>
> We must support the Constitution
> And if we sin seek absolution.

Slavery boasted of this 1820 victory,

> And, as he turned to take his leave,
> He laughed immoderate in his sleeve,
> And said he'd surely call for more
> In eighteen hundred fifty-four.
>
> .   .   .   .
>
> I always have high heaven defied,

3. Letter from Stephen Douglass, Rogers's assistant, to George Whipple
(Cape Palmas, February 20, 1861); another letter from Rogers's colleague,
Henry B. Stewart, to Whipple (Sinoe, February 7, 1861) states that Rogers
had "the fevers." Photocopies and transcriptions of these and of Rogers's letters
from the American Missionary Association Archives are courtesy of Dr. Clif-
ton A. Johnson, Director, and Mrs. H. M. Perry, Assistant Secretary, Amistad
Research Center, New Orleans.

And man's authority denied;

. . . .

And presidents I nominate
For confirmation by each State,
And no Chief-Magistrate is made
Without my all-sufficient aid.

Slavery, vaunting his great influence in churches, schools, and press, gloats over his plans to subdue the North, Cuba, Haiti, and Mexico. But he is balked by Canada:

Inhabited by blacks and whites
Enjoying equal legal rights,
And where the whites will intermarry
With Susan, Tom and Dick, and Harry,—
Is not indeed the place for me;
It shocks my spotless purity.

Not monarchies, he says, but "Republics are the home for me." Freedom merely sighs at all this, and Slavery, true to his word, returns in 1854 with the "hocus-pocus measure" championed by Stephen Douglas, "Captain of the reckless band." The Missouri Compromise, honored for thirty years, now lies in ruin so that the Western planter may, "whene'er he votes,/ Take of his human chattels ten/ And make six Anglo-Saxon men." The poet compliments those lofty minds who "endured temptation" and fought against the bill, but most others, including the President and his cabinet, are damned as tyrants:

But all the blind Nebraskaites
Who have invaded human rights,
Will at the North in every case
Be overwhelmed in deep disgrace.

. . . .

But soon their names will be forgot,
The memory of them shall rot.
And let their burying places be
Upon the coast beside the sea;
And let the ever-rolling surge
Perform a constant funeral dirge.
And when the stranger shall demand
Why these are buried in the sand,
Let him be told without disguise:
They trod upon the Compromise.

Rogers's moral indignation, neatly balanced by wit and logic, gives power to his convincing satire.

He views the Kansas-Nebraska Act as a codicil to the Fugitive Slave Law and treats that "bloody code" of 1850 with equal contempt in the shorter poem, *On the Fugitive Slave Law* (1855). In the same verse form as his *Repeal*, it is a reasoned exposition on law. The poet insists that rules for right living laid down by such men as Blackstone, Witherspoon, and Cicero are subservient to "the Eternal code of laws." Even Lucifer claims that the Fugitive Slave Bill is "a complete gewgaw,/ Unworthy of the name of law," although it had been manufactured under his auspices in Hell. It will be defied by every right-thinking man:

> That bill is law, doughfaces say;
> But black men everywhere cry "Nay":
> We'll never yield to its control
> While life shall animate one soul
>
> . . . .
>
> Will any then the Act obey?
> Both male and female answer, Nay;
> For he who heeds it must withdraw
> His reverence for the Higher Law.
> Whatever human laws may say
> God's law we dare not disobey.
>
> . . . .
>
> We've leaders of the royal pith,
> Like Seward, Hale, and Gerrit Smith,
> Sumner and Wilson, who've no lack
> Of bony substance in the back.
> Led on by such a fearless band
> Securely trusting in God's hand,
> Soon slave laws will be obsolete,
> And victory will be complete.

Rogers's erudite satires remain significant attacks against two major restrictive bills which fanned the fires of abolitionism in the 1850's.

SELECTED SOURCES

Brown, *BM*, 272–74.

Loggins, 239–41.

The Minutes and Sermon of the Second Presbyterian and Congregational Convention. New York: Daly, 1858. 20 pp. Rogers's address, paraphrased, pp. 15–19. NNSch.

Rogers, Elymas P. Letters to the Reverend George Whipple, Secretary, American Missionary Association, December, 1860 and January, 1861. AMA Archives, Amistad Research Center.

*Wilson, Joseph M. *The Presbyterian Historical Almanac . . . for 1862.* Vol. 4 of 10 vols. (1858/59–1868). Philadelphia: Joseph M. Wilson, 1862. Pp. 191–95.

CHARLES LEWIS REASON
1818–93

An educator, reformer, poet, and essayist, Charles L. Reason was born on July 21, 1818, in New York of West Indian parents. His father, Michiel, was from Martinique and his mother, Elizabeth, from Port-au-Prince, Haiti.[1] Reason attended the African Free School in the city with his younger brothers Elwer and Patrick, the illustrator-engraver. Other classmates were Henry H. Garnet, Alexander Crummell, James McCune Smith, and Ira Aldridge.[2] Reason was considered a brilliant student, and at the age of fourteen he became an instructor at the school under the Lancastrian (monitorial) system (Mayo). As a young man he studied for some time to prepare for the Theological Seminary of the Protestant Episcopal Church in New York. However, he was barred from the seminary because of his race by the diocesan bishop "except as a listener," and Reason, rejecting such "sham Christianity," resigned from St. Philip's Church, whose vestry had chosen him for seminary training.[3]

Reason continued his education and began his teaching career in McGrawville, New York. He graduated from McGrawville College[4] and in 1849 became professor of belles lettres, Greek, Latin, and French, and adjunct professor of mathematics at New York Central College. Reason taught for one year at this strongly aboli-

1. Death certificate, New York, N.Y.
2. *The Negro in New York,* eds. Roi Ottley and W. J. Weatherby (New York: New York Public Library, 1967), pp. 87–88; Charles C. Andrews, *The History of the New-York African Free-Schools* (New York: Mahlon Day, 1830), *passim.*
3. Simmons, p. 1107; Payne, p. 118. Reason was never a student at Columbia University "Medical College," as suggested in some sources. I am indebted to Mary D. McGuire, Director of Alumni Office, College of Physicians and Surgeons, Columbia University, for checking several records.
4. Conyers, p. 112. Copy of pages relevant to Reason courtesy of A. R. Reddy, Reference Librarian, Cheyney State College.

tionist school, founded in 1849 by the American Baptist Free Mission Society for men and women of both races.[5] In 1852 he was appointed principal of another new school, the Institute for Colored Youth in Philadelphia. The Institute, founded and financed by Quakers, prospered under Reason's direction. It opened with six students in 1852, and when Reason resigned in 1855, 118 pupils of both sexes were enrolled in the primary school (under the direction of Sarah Douglass), the high school for teacher training, and the night school which Reason had developed along with a good library and a popular lecture series for the public.[6]

While at the Institute Reason worked with the General Vigilance Committee of Philadelphia from its inception in December, 1852.[7] This aid to fugitive slaves was not his first contribution to race welfare. From the 1830's and throughout his later New York City teaching career, Reason fought for civil rights and black suffrage. In 1837 he was secretary of the Political Improvement Association, campaigning for repeal of voters' property qualifications in New York. He was a secretary of the 1840 New York State Convention for Negro Suffrage; of the National Negro Convention in Rochester in July, 1853; and of the Citizens Civil Rights Committee which lobbied and won a civil rights bill in New York under Governor John A. Dix. A versatile reformer, Reason lectured on behalf of the Fugitive Aid Society, drafted convention calls, and presented papers in favor of industrial education. Alongside his friends Robert Purvis, Charles Remond, Charles B. Ray, and Frederick Douglass, Reason wrote resolutions and spoke against the American and African Colonization Societies.[8] His major poems, "The Spirit Voice" and "Free-

5. Reverend Edward C. Starr, Curator, American Baptist Historical Society, Rochester, N.Y., in a letter to me. New York Central College was one of three precursors of Cornell University. It went bankrupt in 1858, was sold to Gerrit Smith and reopened briefly in 1860, and closed in 1861. See Kenneth R. Short, "New York Central College," *Foundations*, 5 (July, 1962), 250–56.

6. Conyers, pp. 112–21; "Institute for Colored Youth, Annual Report, 1859," *Anglo-African Magazine*, 1 (October, 1859), 332. The Institute moved to Cheyney, Pa., in 1902 and became a normal school with Leslie Pickney Hill as principal. It is now Cheyney State College.

7. William Still, *Still's Underground Rail Road Records*, rev. ed. (1872; Philadelphia: William Still, 1886), p. 612.

8. Charles H. Wesley, "The Negroes of New York in the Emancipation Movement," *JNH*, 24 (1939), 93, 95; William E. Farrison, *William Wells Brown* (Chicago: University of Chicago Press, 1969), pp. 311–12; Quarles, pp. 172, 219; Herbert Aptheker, *Documentary History* (New York: Citadel, 1951), pp.

dom," written in the 1840's, are powerful appeals for abolitionism and black enfranchisement.

For about thirty-eight years Charles L. Reason served as a teacher and principal at several colored schools in New York City, notably No. 6, whose first building was described by Charles Ray as "a dwelling house leased and fitted up for a school, in which there is always four feet of water in the cellar." [9] Ray and Reason were founders of the Society for the Promotion of Education among Colored Children. When the last colored schools were absorbed into the city system in September, 1884,[10] Reason continued as teacher and principal at P.S. 80. He became chairman of the Committee on Grammar School Work of the Teachers Association in 1887 (Simmons, 1106). Although he was partially paralyzed during his later years, Reason refused to resign, and as late as June, 1892, he was driven to school daily. When he died in 1893, he was "the oldest teacher in point of service" in the New York school system (Mayo).

Nothing is known of Reason's private life except that he was married three times, last to Mrs. Clorice Esteve, whom he survived (Brawley, 250). His literary contemporaries described him as a personable, modest, respected citizen, beloved by his pupils and colleagues. Simmons commended Reason's knowledge of literature, history, and theology, as well as his poetic talent; Brown and Delany called him a "high-souled gentleman" of "superior intelligence"; and Bishop Daniel A. Payne, who had met Reason in New York in 1835, praised his generosity, his teaching ability, and said he was "too upright to be a politician, but not lacking in the spirit of a patriot." [11] Charles Reason was a handsome youth, recalled by Payne "as noble in his *physique* as a prince of the blood royal," while a portrait of 1854 shows a light-complexioned man with an aquiline nose, deep-set eyes, and wavy hair, his lips set in a faint,

341–42, 353–57; *Douglass' Monthly*, June, 1859, January, 1863, pp. 87, 782; *National Anti-Slavery Standard*, August 6, 20, and September 3, 1870.

9. "Communication from the New York Society for the Promotion of Education among Colored Children," *Anglo-African Magazine*, 1 (July, 1859), 223. Brawley, Ray, and Mayo mention different schools, including nos. 3, 6, and 80, at which Reason taught. John E. Ramsay, Bureau of Teachers Records, New York City Board of Education, in a letter to me finds that Reason taught on Saturdays in Colored School No. 1 on Mulberry Street.

10. *42nd Annual Report of the Board of Education* (New York: Board of Education, 1884), pp. 8, 35–36.

11. Simmons, pp. 1105–8; Brown, p. 187; Delany, pp. 114–15; Payne, pp. 47–48.

mysterious smile. The only other clues to Reason's personality are his clear, dashing handwriting and elaborate signature.[12] Charles Lewis Reason died at age 75 on August 16, 1893, of nephritis and heart disease in his New York home, and he was buried in Greenwood Cemetery.[13] In private and public life he had avoided the publicity given to his notable friends, but with quiet perseverance he served his race for fifty years and left a few important poems to posterity.

Reason's Poetry

It is unfortunate that we now have only four poems by Reason, although many more, as Simmons suggests, may have been published in newspapers during his long life.[14] "Silent Thoughts" (1841) is a thirty-six-line ode in regular iambic pentameter. The poem lacks consistency of tone and clarity of expression, and it is not until the twenty-fifth line that its subject emerges:

> 'Tis thought alone, creative fervent thought!
>   Earnest in life, and in its purpose bent
> To uphold truth and right, that rich is fraught
>   With songs unceasing, and with gleamings sent
> Of sure things coming from a brighter world.

"Hope and Confidence" (1854) similarly cautions the heart to trust not in transient glories but in "the shapes of the purified mind." The poet philosophizes in a romantic setting of "dimliest shadows" and "full-laden zephyrs" where the heart pursues phantoms,

> Well knowing, that certain, there soon must come,
> An end to the visions, that so gladsome,
>   It bewilder'd has eagerly sought.

Reason's "The Spirit Voice" (1841) is a stirring summons to the disfranchised blacks of New York State "To vow, no more to sleep, till raised and freed/ From partial bondage, to a life indeed." In the eighty-six-line ode, the voice of liberty resounds in the peal of

12. *Autographs for Freedom*, portrait facing p. 226; Reason's letter to Crummell, May 12, 1873 (MS 297, NNSch). Reason was a witness at Crummell's wedding in 1880 (MS 316, NNSch).

13. Death certificate. Reason's home was at 242 East 53rd Street. His occupation is given as "schoolteacher," his color as "white," and marital status, "widowed."

14. P. 1108. Simmons also mentions Reason's "beautiful translations made from the French of Lamartine in his 'Retirement.'"

bells, mountain echoes, and in "each breeze that blows o'er Hudson's tide," calling to those who suffer "under legal sin" to honor their beloved homes, mothers, friends, and sires who died for freedom:

> Why can ye not, as men who know and feel
> What most is needed for your nation's weal,
> Stand in her forums, and with burning words
> Urge on the time, when to the bleeding herds,
> Whose minds are buried now in polar night,
> Hope shall descend; when freedom's mellow light
> Shall break, and usher in the endless day,
> That from Orleans to Pass'maquoddy Bay,
> Despots no more may earthly homage claim,
> Nor slaves exist, to soil Columbia's name.

The poet's sincere dedication to reform, expressed in such direct, passionate language, intensifies and sustains the appeal for full manhood and freedom. A forty-eight-stanza apostrophe, "Freedom" (1846), recounts Freedom's victories in historical campaigns from Egypt to Greece and Rome, through modern Europe and Toussaint's Santo Domingo, until her banner was raised by Thomas Clarkson, the English abolitionist whom the poem commemorates. Grandiose language sometimes makes Freedom hobble rather than march through the "crimson-dyed" battlefields of the world. However, at the end, when the poet pleads for her return to his native soil, his angry voice is eloquent in denunciation and in hope:

> God's civil rulers cringing bow
> To hate, and fraud, and customs vile!
>
> The *church,* to her great charge untrue,
> Keeps Christian guard, o'er slavery's den!
> Her coward laymen, wrong pursue,
> Her recreant priesthood, say—amen.
>
> O! purify each holy court!
> The ministry of law and light!
> That man, no longer, may be bought
> To trample down his brother's right.
>
> We lift imploring hands to Thee!
> We cry for those in prison bound!
> O! in thy strength, come! Liberty!
> And 'stablish right the wide world round.

Reason's militant "Spirit Voice" and "Freedom" are significant examples of antebellum protest verse which inspired free blacks to struggle for racial justice.

SELECTED SOURCES

Brawley, *ENAW*, 250–51.

Brown, *BM*, 187–90.

Conyers, Charline H. "A History of the Cheyney State Teachers College, 1837–1951." Dissertation, New York University, 1960. Pp. 112–21.

Delany, Martin R. *The Condition, Elevation . . . of the Colored People of the United States.* 1852; rpt. New York: Arno, 1968. Pp. 114–15.

*Mayo, Anthony R. *Charles Lewis Reason, Pioneer New York Educator and Leader of the Movement to Secure Equal Opportunities for Negroes in the New York Public School System: A Brief Sketch of His Life. Commemorating the Fiftieth Anniversary of his Death August 16th, 1893.* N.d., n.p. 12 pages. Copy: NNSch.

*Payne, Daniel A. *Recollections of Seventy Years.* 1888; rpt. New York: Arno, 1968. Pp. 46–48, 118, 327.

Quarles, Benjamin. *Black Abolitionists.* New York: Oxford University Press, 1969. Pp. 142, 145, 172, 218–19.

*Simmons, 1105–8.

ANN PLATO
1820?–?

"My authoress is a colored lady, a member of my church, of pleasing piety and modest worth." With these words Ann Plato is introduced to the reader of her slim volume of essays and poetry (1841) by James W. C. Pennington, pastor of the Colored Congregational Church of Hartford, Connecticut. Her pastor stresses Miss Plato's youth and devotion to Christianity. He compares her to Phillis Wheatley in her passionate fondness for reading and asks that her poetic efforts "to accomplish something for the credit of her people" be encouraged. After all, he concludes, not all the Greeks were Homers or Platos, "But as Greece had a Plato, may we not have a Platoess?" The Reverend Mr. Pennington reveals nothing more about the Hartford Platoess, and except for scattered hints in her poetry there appears to be no information on her life. Two poems in *Essays* suggest that she was in her teens. In "Advice to Young Ladies" she hopes "To try to please young ladies minds/ Which are about my age," and she urges them to embrace the Lord as she did at age thirteen. In "Lines on Examination for a Teacher" she states, "Now fifteen years their destined course have run,/ In fast succession round the central sun." In "The Infant Class" we learn that she was a teacher of young children. In two other poems Miss Plato mourns a dead brother, Henry, and suggests that her father tell the story of how his "Indian fathers dwelt."

Miss Plato's sixteen essays, four biographies, and twenty poems are the pious, moralistic effusions of a Puritan girl. She counsels emulation of her heroes, Columbus, Demosthenes, Benjamin Franklin, and Robert Bruce, urging adoption of such virtues as obedience to parents, "order, industry, and perseverance," integrity, "benevolent and humane affections," and, above all, love of God. Miss

33

Plato's verse form is neat iambic tetrameter, and her attempts at variation, as in "The Natives of America," are not successful:

> Oh! silent the horror, and fierce the fight,
> When my brothers were shrouded in night;
> Strangers did us invade—strangers destroy'd
> The fields which were by us enjoy'd.

Her favorite subjects, death and religion, are blended in several consolatory verses to the memory of departed friends and children. In these the young author's faith in heaven's glories seems tempered by her fear of death. In "Christ's Departed" she tells of those who have reached the abode of the blest by trusting in God:

> They wake no more with greeting smile,
>   Gay voice or buoyant tread;
> And yet some voices say the while,
>   Of sleepers,—they are dead.
>
> The bless'd in Christ, 'tis true do sleep,
>   They sleep, but are not dead;
> Angels around their beds do keep,
>   They lightly, softly tread.

Miss Plato's collection includes an unexceptional tribute to British emancipation, "To the First of August," and one love poem, "Forget Me Not," of eight stanzas and refrain:

> Then when in silence thou doest walk,
> Nor being round with whom to talk;
> When thou art on the mighty deep,
> And do in quiet action sleep;
> If we no more on earth do meet
>
>   Forget me not.

Miss Plato's book is just what the Reverend James Pennington claimed: "It contains the pious sentiments of a youth devoted to the glory of God, and the best good of her readers."

SOURCE

Loggins, 248–49.

JOSHUA McCARTER SIMPSON
1820?–76

The poet of poignant and witty antislavery songs is the primary source of his own biography,[1] which often sounds as apocryphal as the names given him by other writers, like Joshua C. McSimpson, John McCarty Simpson, and J. S. McCarter. Simpson was freeborn in Morgan County, Ohio, about 1820. When he was three years old, his impoverished widowed mother apprenticed him to Isaac Kay, an English stonemason (and/or farmer). Kay soon died, his wife remarried, and their nephews, now in control of the farm and Simpson, starved and beat the boy so fearfully that at the age of ten he was removed from the place by law. Subsequently Simpson was bound out to another farmer until he was twenty-one. During these years he received only three months of schooling, but with his own books he studied by candlelight. On gaining his majority Simpson determined to educate himself and become a teacher. After rejection by several local schools he entered "the so-called Abolition school" at Big Bottom, Ohio, for a year or two.

As soon as he could write, when past twenty-one, Simpson was moved by a "spirit of poetry" to envision the horrible condition of his people, and a voice urged, " '—you can sing what would be death to speak.' " He wrote his first poem and sang it in public for the "School Exhibition on 'Big Bottom' " in 1842. About a year later, with the desire to make himself "useful to his brethren," the penniless poet left home and friends, "took my old clothes in a knapsack on my back, and tramped one hundred and fifty odd miles through rain, snow and deep mud, to reach" Oberlin College. Oberlin's rec-

1. "Note to the Public," "How I Got My Education," *The Emancipation Car*, pp. iii–iv, 128–38; anonymous article, "Dr. J. McC. Simpson—The Poet of Freedom," *AMECR*, 33 (October, 1916), 78–81, includes biography from *The Emancipation Car* and five songs.

ords do show that Simpson came from Windsor, Ohio, to Oberlin
in 1844 and remained a student in their preparatory department
until 1848. During his stay, on August 14, 1847, Simpson was mar-
ried in Zanesville.[2] According to the poet, he spent only two years
and six months at Oberlin, studying hard and avoiding all college
sports, recreations, and luxuries: "Swinging the axe and maul, scythe
and cradle, and other implements common to farming, from three
to nine hours per day, was gymnastics enough for as poor a man as
I was." Faith in God's providence and abstemious living—"I slept
on straw summer and winter"—saw the poet through his Oberlin
years, but the eminence he had sought, the opportunity to be a
teacher, he never achieved.

The voice of poetic inspiration had come to Simpson in 1842, but
his first published poem was probably "The First of August in Ja-
maica," dated Zanesville, May 25, 1848, and appearing in the *North
Star* on July 28 of that year. In 1852 his song "Away to Canada" was
printed in the *Liberator* (December 10) with Garrison's headnote:
the selection was from "a small pamphlet, entitled 'Original Anti-
Slavery Songs, by Joshua McSimpson, a Colored Man'—printed at
Zanesville, Ohio." Although no copy of this pamphlet has been
found, it was surely circulating before Simpson's known volume of
songs, *The Emancipation Car*, was published in 1874, for in 1863
Harriet Beecher Stowe reported hearing Simpson's "Away to Can-
ada" sung joyfully by Sojourner Truth.[3] In addition to his verse and
autobiography, Simpson's *Emancipation Car* contains two notable
essays. "The Colonization Society" is a weighty, fervid denunciation
of emigration schemes, supported by facts and figures. Simpson in-
sists that black men are rightfully Americans and must establish
their identity in America. A remarkable witty parody, "A Consistent
Slaveholder's Sermon," purports to be the Sabbath address of Rt.
Rev. Bishop Policy to his slaves. The sermon begins: "Well, Darkies,
I am happy to see so many shining eyes and greasy faces to-day. It
speaks two great truths—first, that you are all awake to your own
welfares; and secondly, that your Masters treat you well, and gives
you meat. You have come out to-day to hear the word of God."

However, the word of God, he says, is not from "the white man's

2. W. E. Bigglestone, Archivist, Oberlin College, in a letter to me. I am also
indebted to Mr. Bigglestone for a newspaper clipping from the *Zanesville*
(Ohio) *Times-Signal* which largely repeats material in *The Emancipation Car*.
3. "Sojourner Truth, the Libyan Sibyl," *Atlantic Monthly*, 11 (April, 1863),
479.

Bible" but *your* Bible: "The text is recorded in the laws of Maryland, A.D.:, 1715. Chapter 44: Section 22," and it "declares positively, you will all be slaves during your natural lives." Bishop Policy preaches that out of "pity and compassion" white men rescued Africans from idolatry, cannibalism, ignorance, and soulless "Orang-Outang" existence to tenderly transport them to America. Here "through much toil, on the part of the white man, you are becoming quite intelligent." Moreover, "through amalgamation," the fortunate Africans have acquired their benefactors' "straight hair, high nose, blue eyes, thin lips and perfect form" as well as the possibility of salvation: "This is better than a thousand lives in Africa." Bishop Policy assures the slaves that God has favored them with robust constitutions and superior capacity for hard and dirty work in the hot sun, while the puny, pale bishop is fit only to think, preach, and make laws. The sermon continues with a lengthy list of violations, from arson to cock-fighting, for which punishment is "thirty-nine lashes." After taking up a collection to pay for his breath spent "in prayer for negroes," the bishop concludes: "Watch over these negroes during holiday; let them not fall into the wicked and ungodly hands of the Abolitionists, nor into the cars of the Under-Ground Railroad; may they all return safely to their masters and mistresses, for Jesus' sake—Amen."

This "Slaveholder's Sermon," written perhaps as early as 1850, keenly satirizes the theological, biological, and psychological "truths" perpetuated by slavery's advocates. Unlike most of the black poets, Simpson artfully clothes his angry race protest in sardonic humor, and without didactic shrillness he creates powerful literary propaganda. The same tone of sly ridicule enlivens many of Simpson's poems and is perhaps what made them so popular among fugitives on the Underground Railroad.

In 1874, when *The Emancipation Car* was published, Simpson lived in Zanesville, Ohio, where he served as elder in charge of the Zion Baptist Church and reputedly was a practicing herb doctor as well.[4] Simpson died in Zanesville in 1876.[5] A fellow poet, Albery A. Whitman, wrote a eulogy, "The Lute of Afric's Tribe," to the "man of song and soul,/ And stalwart energies," a poet whose "soaring vision" and zeal for liberty broke the silence that the lute of Afric's tribe had kept.

4. *Zanesville* (Ohio) *Times-Signal,* August 13, 1950.
5. Date of death from Oberlin College files.

But hushed the bard, his harp no longer sings
The woes and longings of a shackled mind;

. . . . .

Of him, whose harp then lies by death unstrung—
A harp that long his lowly brethren cheered,
May'nt we now say that, sainted choirs among,
An everlasting theme inspires his tongue,
Where slaves ne'er groan, and death is never feared?[6]

Simpson's Poetry

The fifty-three selections in *The Emancipation Car* share quali-
ties of simple diction, repetition of phrases and refrains, topicality,
and humorous, pathetic, or militant tones. The verses are written
to be sung to familiar hymns, to popular folksongs like "Old Folks
at Home," "Dan Tucker," and "Lily Dale," or to patriotic airs like
the "Marseillaise" and "Hail Columbia." Many of them resemble
folk ballads in their narration of a single dramatic episode or de-
velopment of a theme through dialogue, closing with a summary
statement. The poet's subject is the black man, his slavery and free-
dom: the painful lot of captives, slaves' true feelings toward their
masters, their shrewd trickery and escapes to Canada and England.
Simpson celebrates the doom of slaveholders, the Fifteenth Amend-
ment, the Underground Railroad, West Indian and American eman-
cipation; he denounces colonization plans.

Occasionally Simpson's choice of tunes for his lyrics is shrewdly
ironic. His "Warning to the White People of America," which cau-
tions them that judgment is coming, is sung to "Massa's in the Cold,
Cold Ground"; a condemnation of brass bands, roaring cannon, and
speeches celebrating July Fourth in Alabama takes the tune of
"America." The militant "Song of the Aliened American" is like-
wise set to "America":

(1)   My country, 'tis of thee,
        Dark land of slavery,
          In thee we groan.
        Long have our chains been worn—
        Long has our grief been borne—
        Our flesh has long been torn,
          E'en from our bones

6. The full title is "The Lute of Afric's Tribe: To the memory of Dr. J.
McSimpson, a colored Author of Anti-Slavery Ballads. Written for the Zanes-
ville, O., Courier." Whitman's poem appears in his *Not a Man, and Yet a Man*
(Springfield, Ohio, 1877) in the "Poems on Miscellaneous Subjects" section.

(4) No! no! the time has come,
    When we must not be dumb,
    We must awake.
    We now "Eight Millions Strong,"
    Must strike sweet freedom's song
    And plead ourselves, our wrong—
    Our chains must break.

The black man is "aliened" not only in America but in the universe. In "The Twilight Hour," with finely organized detail, Simpson has Nature boast of her freedom, as in a series of stanzas the stream, fish, nightingale, breeze, lightning, and finally the white man say, "I am free." Only the bondsman is unfree, but his day is coming.

Several verses ridicule the slaveholder's naive underestimation of their chattels' intelligence and feelings. "No, Master, Never!" tells of a slave whose master is so certain of his loyalty that he takes Jack on a trip to Cleveland. There Jack runs off, singing about his adventure to the tune of "Pop, Goes the Weasel":

The next day in Malden town,
    Who should I see but master,
He says, Jack you must go home,
    You'll starve and freeze to death sir.
Says I, you are a nice old man;
    Very kind and clever;
But think I'll wear my chains again?
    "No, master, never!"

Simpson refutes the myth that slaves love their masters in "The Slaveholder's Rest," where bondsmen rejoice over their cruel owner's death: "He will no more trample on the neck of the slave,/ For he's gone where the slaveholders go." The slaves' quest for freedom, especially in Canada, is the theme of some two dozen songs, including "The Fugitive's Dream," "The Bondman's Home," "The Fugitive in Montreal," "The Little Maid on Her Way," the title poem, "The Emancipation Car," and Sojourner Truth's favorite, "Away to Canada" (to the tune, "Oh, Susannah"):

I'm on my way to Canada,
    That cold and dreary land;
The dire effects of slavery,
    I can no longer stand.
My soul is vexed within me so,
    To think that I'm a slave;
I've now resolved to strike the blow
    For freedom or the grave.

O righteous Father
   Wilt thou not pity me?
And aid me on to Canada,
   Where colored men are free.

In another stanza of "Away to Canada," Queen Victoria, the per-
sonification of freedom in many songs, welcomes the fugitives as she
does in "Queen Victoria Conversing with Her Slave Children." This
poem of eleven stanzas employs the dialogue form for an effective
ballad.

Slaves

Our masters we fear will blight our undertaking,
   Our very eyes
   They'll advertise,
   We can't come away.
The northern States though free by name,
Have negro dogs in every range,
Who linger for pocket change;
   We can't come away.

Queen

O come, come away, why will you longer tarry,
   The Lord will stand
   At your right hand,
   O come, come away.
You'll meet with many a northern friend
Who will his best endeavors lend
To speed you on to freedom's land;
   O come, come, away.

Combining his two favorite subjects, Canada and Queen, with a
beloved hymn, "Come to Jesus, Just Now," Simpson offers "A Par-
ody," one of many poems which lend support to interpretation of
the spirituals' imagery as secular rather than otherworldly. Jeru-
salem, Zion, Canaan, and Heaven are kingdoms of *this* world, the
"happy land" of Canada or New England to which slaves can "come
home" or "come to freedom" by means of Jacob's ladder, a chariot,
train, or ship: their "emancipation car." This majestic car of liberty
rolls through the nation as slaves sing, "We're travelling home to
Heaven above;/ Will you go, will you go? . . . I'm going to see
the old North Star,/ Will you go, will you go? . . . I'm going to
see Victoria's face . . .

I've many friends to Chatham gone,
And many more will follow on—
To master, lash and "Negro Gong,"
   Fare you well, fare you well.
            ("Albert Morris")

Victoria, not Jesus, seems to have been the slaves' savior, and much-admired Britain gave them and the black poets a "holy" day, August 1, 1834, the day of emancipation in the British West Indies. Simpson glorifies the Queen and Liberty in "The First of August in Jamaica" (1848), a stirring hymn to the tune of "Hail Columbia": [7]

> Wake the psaltry, lute and lyre,
> And let us set the world on fire.
>> And may Jehovah blow the flame,
>> Till all mankind shall see the light
> Of knowledge, liberty and right!
> Our hands are clear of human blood;
>> We bought our liberty from God.
>> Love, joy and peace are now combined
>> With freedom's golden chain entwined,
> Firm united may we stand,
> A happy, free and social band;
>> Each brother feels his brother's care.
> And each his brother's burthen [*sic*] bear.

Universal freedom from bondage is anticipated or commemorated in most of Simpson's songs, and the ultimate promised land he envisions is America. Like a majority of the black poets, and Afro-Americans in general, Simpson rejects the colonizationists' offer of a "goodly land,/ Where milk and honey flows":

> Give joy or grief—give ease or pain,
>> Take life or friends away;
> I deem this as my native land,
>> And here I'm bound to stay,
> "I have a mind to be a man
>> Among white men and free;
> And OLD LIBERIA!
>> Is not the place for me!"
>>> ("Old Liberia is not
>>> the Place for Me")

Joshua McCarter Simpson was not the first composer of popular freedom songs. In subject and tunes his work resembles the forty-six anonymous songs in William Wells Brown's compilation, *The Anti-Slavery Harp* (Boston, 1848), which includes Brown's own verse, "Fling out the Anti-Slavery Flag." But Simpson's *Emancipation Car* is the largest single collection by a black man. His compositions are strong folk poetry which vividly convey, as the best slave narratives do, the slaves' ardent desire for liberty and the freedmen's pride in race.

7. *Emancipation Car* version given. Title in the *North Star*, July 28, 1848, is "A Voice from Jamaica on the First of August," and lines also vary.

JAMES MONROE WHITFIELD
1822–71

One summer day in 1850 Frederick Douglass visited the basement barber shop of James Whitfield in Buffalo, New York. Douglass was deeply grieved to find "this sable son of genius" in so lowly a position: "That talents so commanding, gifts so rare, poetic powers so distinguished, should be tied to the handle of a razor and buried in the precincts of a barber's shop . . . is painfully disheartening," he wrote. Douglass hoped that Whitfield would rouse his dormant energies, raise himself in society, and become "the most brilliant" racial leader: "Come out of that cellar, Whitfield! and let your bugle blasts of liberty career [*sic*] over our Northern hills. You are implored to do so by your enslaved and slandered people." [1] Like Douglass, William Wells Brown and Martin R. Delany felt that the barber "was intended by nature for a higher position in life." Delany, to whom Whitfield dedicated his volume of poetry, *America*, considered him "one of the purest poets in America," who could be the equal of Whittier and Poe if he tried. Whitfield's friends urged him upward, but, as Douglass put it, "the malignant arrangements of society" chained him in the barber shop. [2]

Whitfield was born in New Hampshire on April 10, 1822. [3] Little is known about his family and education, except that he was a descendant of Ann Paul, sister of Thomas Paul, an Exeter, New Hampshire, clergyman, and that he had a sister, in later years Mrs. Elizabeth P. Allen, whose daughter, Annie Pauline Pindell, became

1. *Anti-Slavery Bugle*, August 24, 1850, p. 1. I am greatly indebted to Floyd J. Miller, Oberlin College department of history, for photocopies of this and many other periodical references to Whitfield, for a photocopy of *Poem*, and for his informative letters to me.
2. Brown, *BM*, p. 152; Delany, *The Condition, Elevation . . . Colored People of the United States* (1852; rpt. New York: Arno, 1968), p. 132.
3. Death certificate, San Francisco, Calif.

a famous singer.[4] John E. Bruce, the New York journalist, reported that Whitfield attended the "District School of his neighborhood" and had a wife, two sons, and a daughter.[5] Whitfield worked as a barber all his life and devoted his spare time and talents to two avocations: writing poetry and championing the cause of black separatism.

From 1849 to 1852 Whitfield frequently contributed poems to the *North Star* and *Frederick Douglass' Paper,* and in 1853 he published the collection *America and Other Poems.* The bitter tone of much of Whitfield's verse reflects his abortive attempts to become a man of letters while obliged to earn a living as a barber. Soon after *America* appeared, he expressed his frustration and yearning for financial independence to an anonymous correspondent of the *Pennsylvania Freeman.* This gentleman sent a copy of *America* to the *Freeman,* explaining that he met Whitfield in his barber shop on board the steamer *Bay State* while traveling from Dunkirk to Detroit and was greatly impressed by the unassuming barber, "a man of nearly pure African blood," who asked him to purchase a copy of his book. The poet, he wrote, hoped to earn enough money from the book to support himself and devote time "to the cultivation of his mind, and to writing." [6] Whitfield's literary ambitions were not realized, however, and, returning to work in his Buffalo barber shop for the next five years, his concern shifted from poetry to emigrationism.[7]

Whitfield is linked with James T. Holly and Delany as the foremost champions of colonization activities during the 1850's; but Whitfield dates his interest in emigration to 1838, when as a boy of sixteen he had prepared an address for a Cleveland convention urging black settlement on the borders of California. However, his preparatory work for the 1854 National Emigration Convention in

4. James T. Abajian, Bibliographer, Martin Luther King, Jr., Special Collection, San Francisco Public Library. I am grateful to Mr. Abajian for his letters to me and many references to Whitfield's poetry in Douglass's papers and *San Francisco Elevator* and *Pacific Appeal.*

5. MS 1946 (May 1, 1922), pp. 2–3, Bruce Collection, NNSch.

6. *Pennsylvania Freeman,* September 29, 1853, p. 154.

7. From 1854 to 1859 Whitfield's Buffalo residence was on South Division Street (fronting Lake Erie) at numbers 192, 194, 195, and 294. His barbershop was at 30 East Seneca Street in 1858 and probably in his home in previous years. Buffalo directory (1854–59) references courtesy of H. Sass, Senior Librarian, Buffalo and Erie County Historical Society. I am also indebted to Ridgway McNallie, history department, Buffalo and Erie County Public Library, for his efforts to assist me.

Cleveland first brought him public recognition. This convention's call, signed by Whitfield, prompted an exchange of letters in the *North Star* with Douglass and William J. Watkins. With factual and logical argumentation Whitfield supports separatism while refuting his opponents' emotional appeals to patriotism, patience, and faith in God's justice. "The American government, the American churches, and the American people, are all engaged in one great conspiracy to crush us," Whitfield writes. A scattered, oppressed minority, chained from birth to a sense of inferiority, will never be integrated equals in American society, for all avenues to education, higher employment, and political power will remain closed to them. And it will always be true that "while the negro *servant* is viewed with a certain degree of complacency, the negro *gentleman* is regarded with unmitigated hatred." Whitfield argues that whites will never relinquish their hegemony; he has "NO faith left in the justice of this country" nor in God's deliverance, for, he says, "He helps those who help themselves."

Moreover, Whitfield writes, it is the destiny of the black race "to develop a higher order of civilization and Christianity than the world has yet seen" and "to possess all the tropical regions" of the American continent and adjacent islands. Here, where blacks are already numerically superior, they must establish independent, politically powerful black nations whose successful self-rule would be "ocular proof" of the race's "physical, moral, and mental" superiority. Such achievement would command the world's respect (and fear) and usher in equality and elevation of the race everywhere. Emigration, Whitfield insists, would not be *en masse*, but limited to that minority of American blacks who refuse to "lick the dirt from the foot that kicks" them and to labor for the enrichment of their oppressors. These few must place themselves where they "*can help* strike an effective blow against the common foe" for the benefit of the entire race.[8]

Although Whitfield lacked the opportunity to implement these proposals until 1859, he remained active in the colonization movement. At the 1854 convention, whose call had initiated the letters, Whitfield and others urged establishment of a quarterly periodical to publicize the emigration cause as well as "all questions connected with the welfare, progress and development of the Negro race." Whitfield was designated editor of this *Afric-American Repository*, and its prospectus, signed by Whitfield, appeared in the *Provincial*

8. *North Star,* September 25, November 15, December 30, 1853.

Freeman of December 6, 1856. The first issue was to appear in Buffalo in July, 1858, but no evidence of its publication has been found.[9]

The Buffalo directory lists Whitfield for the last time in 1859, and his name does not appear anywhere until 1861 on a "Memorial" from "free colored persons of California" to Congress, asking for "means for their colonization." Whitfield's activities from 1859 to 1861 remain vague, but it is commonly assumed that he was traveling in the "tropical regions" of the Americas seeking land for a black colony. The 1854 convention had sent James T. Holly to Haiti for this purpose, but when plans for a Haitian settlement failed, interest shifted to Central America. A proposal to acquire territory there or in South America was offered to the House of Representatives by Frank P. Blair, Jr., of Missouri, and Whitfield enthusiastically supported the project. Although no details of his journey are recorded, Whitfield was probably sent as fact-finding commissioner to Central America in 1859.[10]

When he returned to California in 1861, Whitfield's separatist sentiments were less militant than they had been in 1853 when he wrote to the *North Star*, "A *black patriot* in this country must be more fool than knave. The fact is, I have no country, neither have you, and your assumption that you are an *integrant* part of *this* nation, is not true." In the second year of the Civil War, Whitfield wrote to the *Pacific Appeal* (August 9, 1862) urging a concerted effort by all Americans "of the loyal states" to put down the rebellion. "The U.S. Government must make an alliance with their own people, i.e. the people of color. . . . Also, abrogate or nullify the odious Dred Scott decision, which takes from every colored man his rights as a man and a citizen." Let slavery be ended, he writes, and the President will have at his command "the greatest and most valiant army the world ever saw."

Whitfield had nothing further to say in support of emigration;

9. *Proceedings of the National Emigration Convention of Colored People . . . 1854* (Pittsburgh: A. A. Anderson, 1854), pp. 12, 28–31; Penelope L. Bullock, *The Negro Periodical Press in the United States, 1838–1909*, dissertation, University of Michigan, 1971 (facsimile rpt., Ann Arbor: University Microfilms, 1972), pp. 59–62, 353.

10. Misc. Doc. 31, U.S. House of Representatives, 37 cong., 2 sess., courtesy of James T. Abajian; Howard H. Bell, "Negro Nationalism: A Factor in Emigration Projects, 1858–1861," *JNH*, 47 (January, 1962), 42–45; James M. Whitfield, letter to James T. Holly (February 1, 1858) in *The Mind of the Negro*, ed. C. G. Woodson (Washington: Association for the Study of Negro Life and History, 1926), pp. 500–502, and letter to Frank Blair in Frank P. Blair, Jr., *The Destiny of the Races of This Continent* (Washington: Buell and Blanchard, 1859), pp. 37–38.

rather, for the nine years from 1862 until his death, he worked as a barber and wrote more poetry. California became Whitfield's home except for the interval from June, 1863, to 1865, when he barbered in Portland, Oregon, and in Placerville and Centerville, Idaho. In 1867 (and until 1869) he had a hairdressing shop in San Francisco.[11] In this city on New Year's Day, 1867, the poet delivered a major "bugle blast of liberty," his *Poem* written for the fourth anniversary of the Emancipation Proclamation. He dedicated *Poem* to Philip A. Bell, editor of the *San Francisco Elevator*, in which many of Whitfield's poems and letters appeared from 1867 to 1870.

The poet left San Francisco in May, 1869, for a year's sojourn in Nevada. A resident of Elko, he participated in literary and political activities of the Elko Republican Club and was chosen to sit on a jury in Elko County, thus becoming, with three other black men, one of the first jurors of his race in Nevada. Whitfield traveled to Virginia City, Nevada, at least twice: in August, 1868, he had come from California, where he was Grand Master of that state's Prince Hall Masons (from 1864 to 1869), to install the Masonic Ashlar Lodge of Virginia City; and in April, 1870, when he read a poem commemorating ratification of the Fifteenth Amendment.[12]

Sometime after July, 1870, Whitfield returned to San Francisco. On April 23, 1871, at age forty-nine, he died of heart disease and was buried in the Masonic Cemetery.[13] Although the humble barber never reached the heights predicted for him by Douglass, Brown, and Delany, he became a major propagandist for black separatism and racial retributive justice through his impassioned prose and poetry.

11. *Pacific Appeal*, 1863, May 9: 2, 4; June 6: 2, 3; 1864, January 9: 3; George Owens, *General Directory . . . of the Principal Towns East of the Cascade Mountains* (1865), p. 96. In San Francisco, Whitfield's barbershop was at 916 Kearny Street, his home at 918 and 1006 Washington Street. San Francisco *Directory* and *Pacific Appeal* references courtesy of Floyd J. Miller. I am also indebted to Marian Marquardt of San Francisco for her help in locating data on Whitfield's California years.

12. *San Francisco Elevator*, August 21, 1868, p. 1; May 14, 1869, p. 2; July 8, 1870, p. 3. Other references to Whitfield are in the *Elevator* for 1869: July 30, p. 2; August 30, p. 2; September 3, pp. 2–3; and December 31, p. 2. For information on Whitfield's stay in Nevada and for a copy of his 1870 poem, I am indebted to Elmer R. Rusco of the University of Nevada. Whitfield's term as Grand Master is recorded by William H. Grimshaw, *Official History of Freemasonry Among the Colored People in North America . . .* (1903; rpt. New York: Negro Universities Press, 1969), p. 218.

13. Death certificate. Whitfield died at 111 Prospect Place.

Whitfield's Poetry

The anonymous writer of the introduction to *America and Other Poems* (1853)[14] justifiably claims that the volume "would be creditable to authors of greater pretensions than the humble colored man, who hath wrought it out amid the daily and incessant toil necessary for the maintenance of a family. . . . There is in it the fire of a genius which, under more favored circumstances, would have soared high, and obtained no mean place in the world's estimation." Among black nineteenth-century poets, Whitfield is outstanding not only for his metrical smoothness and breadth of classical imagery, but even more for the biting cynicism of his antislavery tirades and the bitter pessimism of his self-portraits.

Two long poems, "America" (160 lines) and "How Long?" (238 lines), written in iambic tetrameter with varying rhyme schemes, are typical of Whitfield's protest poetry. "America" begins:

> America, it is to thee
> Thou boasted land of liberty,—
> It is to thee I raise my song,
> Thou land of blood, and crime, and wrong.

This land, the poet says, was drenched with tears of black women and blood of black soldiers shed "in freedom's cause"; but their patriotic sacrifices are repaid with deceit, shame, and slavery. "How Long?" denounces the world's oppression of men who claim "the right to speak, and think, and feel," to labor for humanity, responsible only to God.

> The same unholy sacrifice
> Where'er I turn bursts on mine eyes,
> Of princely pomp, and priestly pride,
>   The people trampled in the dust,
> Their dearest, holiest rights denied,
>   Their hopes destroyed, their spirits crushed.

More reprehensible than devastations by European tyrants he finds

14. *America* is poorly edited and printed. "The Arch Apostate" listed in the table of contents is not in the text; "The North Star" is in the text but not in the table of contents. Three poems are printed twice with pagination repeated, one poem ends with a page from another, and one is left incomplete. A "Volume of Poems, 1846" is listed for Whitfield in George W. Williams, *History of the Negro Race* (New York: Putnam's, 1885), II, 554. This entry, repeated in bibliographies through 1916, was probably in error. Volume not located.

the "scenes of rapine, lust, and shame" that beset America, where
everyone learns

> That conscience must not only bend
>   To everything the church decrees,
> But it must also condescend,
>   When drunken politicians please
> To place their own inhuman acts
> Above the "higher law" of God.

The poet lashes church and state for sanctioning the "monstrous
wrong" of slavery, and with unusual sensitivity he perceives the
insidious plague of moral corruption infecting the nation:

> Blasting with foul pestiferous breath
>   The fountain springs of mortal life,
> And planting deep the seeds of death,
>   And future germs of deadly strife;
> And moral darkness spreads its gloom
>   Over the land in every part,
> And buries in a living tomb
>   Each generous prompting of the heart.

Both long jeremiads demand heavenly vengeance for America's
"heinous guilt" and end with anguished cries for justice and "glori-
ous liberty" for all mankind. The same sentiments are less effectively
expressed in several shorter poems, including "Prayer of the Op-
pressed," "To Cinque," and "Stanzas for the First of August."

America also includes hymns for Christmas, New Year's, and
church dedications which are conventional in all respects. Four love
poems addressed to anonymous or initialed ladies are serious, ten-
der tributes, generally well structured and musical. In spite of heavy
eighteenth-century poetic diction, the poems achieve a pleasingly
simple and sincere tone. In "To A. H.," for example, the poet muses
on ancient days and summons a pantheon of Greek, Persian, and
Mohammedan mythological beings to pay homage to his beloved.
She, of course, surpasses them all:

> Thy form, high o'er the rest upraised,
>   Appeared, with brighter splendor crowned,
> And every eye was turned on thee,
>   Of Houri, Peri, Goddess, Grace,
> As, bright in peerless majesty,
>   You mounted to the highest place.

With classical restraint he praises each charm and talent of Miss
A. H. by comparison with the traditional attributes of the fabled

beauties. A fifth love poem, similarly unsentimental, is a discourse, "Love." The nature of love is known neither by the "brainless youth" who "twines a wreath, or plucks a flower" nor by the "gallant gay,/ With witty jest, and jibe, and jeer." The poet concludes, simply, "God is love."

Whitfield's most compelling poems are dark imprecations against a world "disjoint and out of frame" in which men, women, religion, love, and the gentler aspects of nature seem as corrupt and meaningless to him as they did to the melancholy Dane. Four such poems—"Self-Reliance," "Delusive Hope," "Yes, Strike Again That Sounding String," and "The Misanthropist"—recall in their tone, imagery, and ideas the worlds of Hamlet, Faust, and Byron's fatal men. But their setting is unmistakably America, and their protagonist Whitfield himself. Although the order of composition of these soliloquies is unknown, a possible sequence may be conjectured based on their progressively darker attitudes of pessimism and despair.

A youthful enthusiast speaks in "Self-Reliance":

> I love the man whose lofty mind
>   On God and its own strength relies;
> Who seeks the welfare of his kind,
>   And dare be honest though he dies;
>
> Who cares not for the world's applause,
>   But, to his own fixed purpose true,
> The path which God and nature's laws
>   Point out, doth earnestly pursue.

These ideals, like the promises of "lasting friendship, holy truth,/ And steadfast love" in "Delusive Hope," are shattered by life's misery and hypocrisy. In both poems, however, the speaker hopes to transcend adversity by turning to God, "Whose word is truth, whose name is love." No such solution brightens "Yes, Strike Again" or "The Misanthropist," where all is "dark and cheerless night,/ Without one ray of hopeful light." In the latter a poet refuses to sing of virtue, beauty, and love because his heart has become calloused "like a rude and rugged rock" from battling "with the ills of life." Having lived in "life's darkest, deepest shade" from childhood, he searches for emotional and spiritual experiences to dispel the gloom. The poet is moved by Nature, but only "in her sternest moods" of "Fire and tempest, storm and flood." Her primeval force wakens deep echoes in his soul, quickens his blood with uncontrollable destructive impulses, and kindles his "seething brain" to "wilder

horrors." Likewise, he finds "a fierce and fitful pleasure" from books,
but only from those which tell of "foul and dark intrigue,"

> Where the grim-visaged death-fiend drank
>   His full supply of human gore,
> And poured through every hostile rank
>   The tide of battle's awful roar. . . .

Not for this outcast is the one true way of religion or love: religion
proved "but a false and empty name" used by "senseless bigots" to
justify devastation by fire and steel of unbelievers; and a passionate,
truthful love he once knew "was blighted in its opening bloom."
All avenues of redemption from the dark night of his soul being
closed, the poet consigns himself to eternal doubt, isolation, and
doom:

> To bare my breast to every blow,
> To know no friend, and fear no foe,
> Each generous impulse trod to dust,
> Each noble aspiration crushed,
> Each feeling struck with withering blight,
> With no regard for wrong or right,
> No fear of hell, no hope of heaven,
> Die all unwept and unforgiven,
> Content to know and dare the worst
> Which mankind's hate, and heaven's curse
> Can heap upon my living head,
> Or cast around my memory dead;
> And let them on my tombstone trace,
> Here lies the Pariah of his race.

Whitfield's 204-line "Misanthropist" is a harmonious, sustained
dramatization of estrangement, futile aspiration, and defeat, a
unique poetic portrait of the Afro-American artist.

Fourteen years after *America*, in 1867, the poet sounded a "bu-
gle blast of liberty" with his 400-line *Poem* celebrating the Eman-
cipation Proclamation. With sure metrical control Whitfield surveys
two hundred years of American history, building on a farming meta-
phor with its imagery of sowing, blooming, harvesting, and blight-
ing. "Two sails, with different intent,/ Approached the Western
Continent."

> New England's cold and sterile land
> Gave shelter to the pilgrim band;
> Virginia's rich and fertile soil
> Received the dusky sons of toil.

Pilgrims and slavers planted seeds. In the North, future generations reaped

> Abundance of the glorious fruit—
> Freedom of thought, and of the pen,
> Free schools, free speech, free soil, free men.

But from germs sown in Virginia grew the bloody strife of Civil War. War "purged the moral atmosphere" and Lincoln, "Our real Moses," led four million slaves to freedom; but a second crop ripens from the seeds of slavery: "Such fiendish murders as of late/ Occur in every rebel State." Once again the moral air is tainted, and the poet summons everyone to purge the nation of its poison, inequal-

> Wipe out the errors of the past,
> Nursed by the barbarous pride of caste
> And o'er the nation's wide domain,
> Where once was heard the clanking chain,
> And timorous bondsmen crouched in fear,
> Before the brutal overseer,
> Proclaim the truth that equal laws
> Can best sustain the righteous cause;
> And let this nation henceforth be
> In truth the country of the free.

Whitfield's verse history of slavery and its effects does not comment on African traders' responsibility for the enslavement of their countrymen. It is uncertain whether ignorance or black chauvinism lies behind such omissions, but all black poets, militant and conciliatory, condemn slavery as exclusively the white man's burdensome sin.

Whitfield's last known poem, which he read in Virginia City, Nevada, in April, 1870, was a 152-line paean to "order, law, and liberty." Its antislavery sentiments and language generally echo his previous verse; but Whitfield's earlier antipathy toward America has mellowed into bounteous sentimental praise for the "One favored land," leader of the world in arts, riches, commerce, and Freedom for all.[15]

Whitfield's poems are among the most robust and convincing of their time. No poet so forcefully, with such anger and pathos as well as artistry, described the crippling of a creative soul by race prejudice and the destructive self-hatred engendered. Whitfield's

15. Published as "Poem by J. M. Whitfield" in the *San Francisco Elevator,* April 22, 1870, p. 3.

poetry of protest and despair, like his own unfulfilled aspirations, remains a vivid testament to the alienation of Afro-Americans in the nineteenth century.

SELECTED SOURCES

Brawley, *ENAW*, 228.
Loggins, 241–45.

GEORGE BOYER VASHON
1824–78

The first black graduate of Oberlin College and the first black lawyer in the state of New York, George Vashon was driven by America's race prejudice into self-exile in Haiti. He was a brilliant student, teacher, attorney, and writer, born on July 25, 1824, in Carlisle, Pennsylvania, the only son (there were two older daughters) of the eminent free-born Virginian, John Bethume Vashon. John Vashon, son of a mulatto woman and a prominent white Indian agent, fought in the War of 1812. He organized the African Education Society of Pittsburgh (1832) and that city's first Anti-Slavery Society (1833); he also served as committeeman of the first (1844) and succeeding Annual Conventions of People of Color. Vashon's anti-colonization stance and generous financial and moral support for Garrison's *Liberator* initiated a warm, lasting friendship between the two abolitionists.[1]

John Vashon moved his family from Virginia to Carlisle, and then to Pittsburgh in 1829, where George attended local schools. In July, 1838, a Juvenile Anti-Slavery Society, the first in the United States, was formed in Pittsburgh with fourteen-year-old Vashon as secretary.[2] Two years later the precocious boy entered Oberlin College, and in 1844 he earned the first bachelor of arts degree conferred on

1. Vashon's date of birth from Walter C. Worthington, friend of the Vashon family, in a letter to me; William C. Nell, *The Colored Patriots of the American Revolution* (Boston: Wallcut, 1855), pp. 181–88 (Nell credits M. R. Delany for this account). John Vashon's middle name, "Bathan" in Nell, is "Bethume" in *Frederick Douglass' Paper* (February 3, 1854); Quarles, pp. 20–21, 24, 108 *et passim;* "Letters of William Lloyd Garrison to John B. Vashon," *JNH,* 12 (January 1927), 32–40.

2. Quarles, p. 30; Letter from the Society (November 14, 1839) donating five dollars to the *Colored American,* signed Peck and Vashon, rpt. *The Black American,* eds. Leslie H. Fishel, Jr., and B. Quarles (New York: Morrow, 1970), pp. 196–97.

a black man.[3] During his junior year at Oberlin, Vashon had taught school in Chillicothe, Ohio, where he earned the respect and admiration of the community and the gratitude of John Mercer Langston, his pupil. Vashon personally enrolled Langston at Oberlin in March, 1844, settled him into college life, and found a family to board the future congressman and minister to Haiti.[4]

From Oberlin Vashon returned to Pittsburgh, where for about two and a half years he studied law under Judge Walter Forward. Late in 1847, with Forward's full support, Vashon applied for examination for admittance to the bar; but, as Martin R. Delany put it, the "colorphobites" of Pittsburgh refused to examine him. Vashon filed a show cause suit before Judge Walter H. Lowrie of the District Court, demanding that he be examined. Lowrie rejected the suit, citing a ruling by Chief Justice Gibson of Pennsylvania that colored people were not citizens. This blatant discrimination and Vashon's subsequent announcement that he would leave for Haiti enraged his friends and raised protests such as this from the *Pittsburgh Telegraph*: George B. Vashon has been "driven from home, friends, and family by the bitter, vulgar, and unnatural prejudice against color, which prevails in all parts of this boasted republic. . . . A few drops of African blood flowed in his veins," and this alone "stamps him with the brand of reprobation, and compels him to be an outcast from the land of his birth." En route to Haiti, however, Vashon stopped in New York. Here, reported William C. Nell, "for the first time in the history of the State of New York . . . a colored man was yesterday [January 11, 1848] admitted after due examination as Attorney, Solicitor, and Counsellor of the Supreme Court of the State." [5]

George B. Vashon, now Esquire, spent thirty months in Haitian exile teaching at College Faustin in Port-au-Prince. He returned to the United States in the late summer of 1850, practiced law for four years in Syracuse, and wrote the remarkable epic poem, "Vincent

3. W. E. Bigglestone, Archivist, Oberlin College, in a letter to me. There is no record of an M.A. degree mentioned by Brawley. I am also indebted to Mr. Bigglestone for a copy of Vashon's obituary in the *Oberlin Review*.

4. John M. Langston, *From the Virginia Plantation to the National Capitol* (1894; rpt. New York: Bergman, 1969), pp. 74–81 *et passim*.

5. Accounts of Vashon's legal studies, Pittsburgh rejection, and New York bar admission were reprinted from various papers by the *North Star*. Vashon's law preceptor the Honorable Walter Forward served as secretary of the treasury, chargé d'affaires to Denmark, and president of the bench of the District Court of the Western District of Pennsylvania, according to Delany.

Ogé" (1853). In the fall of 1854 Vashon became professor of belles lettres and mathematics at New York Central College in McGraw-ville, New York.[6] He was an outstanding teacher, wrote William Wells Brown, whose students would try to stump him with "phrases and historical incidents" from Greek, Latin, and Hebrew. But Vashon always knew the answers, and they concluded "he was the best-read man in the college." After three years Vashon left Mc-Grawville for Pittsburgh, which was to be his home until 1867. Here in 1857 he married Susan Paul Smith of Boston, a teacher who was fourteen years his junior. They had seven children, and Mrs. Vashon survived her husband by thirty-four years.[7]

Vashon did not reapply for admission to the Pennsylvania bar but served as a principal and teacher in Pittsburgh, in the colored public schools from 1858 to 1863, and at Avery College from 1864 to 1867.[8] According to the *Oberlin Review,* Vashon was a solicitor for the Freedman's Bureau in Washington in the fall of 1867, held "other responsible positions at the Capitol," and subsequently became professor of mathematics, Greek, and modern languages at Alcorn University in Mississippi.[9] In 1869 Vashon participated in the national convention of the Colored Men of America held in Washington. Leading activists of the century, representing twenty-two states, attended. Frederick Douglass, Henry H. Garnett, J. Sella Martin, and F. G. Barbadoes led the convention; among the delegates were John Langston, George Downing, Charles and Robert Purvis, and William Whipper. Vashon joined this distinguished company as delegate from Rhode Island and served as chairman of the committee on credentials, member of the committee on rules and of the group sent to congratulate Grant on his election. He prepared and read an appeal for universal suffrage, urging all black men to send petitions and memorials to Congress. Vashon continued to work with this organization, joining its national executive committee in 1870. That year, in a burst of literary activity, he con-

6. See "Charles L. Reason," note 5, for New York Central College.

7. Sylvia Dannett, "Susan Paul Vashon," *Profiles of Negro Womanhood* (Yonkers: Negro Heritage Library, 1964), p. 319; death certificate, State of Missouri (1912).

8. Pittsburgh *City Directories,* references courtesy of Mrs. George S. Cunningham, Librarian, Pennsylvania Division of the Carnegie Library of Pittsburgh. Vashon's name appears for the last time in the *Directory* of 1867/68.

9. No record of Vashon's affiliation with Alcorn exists in either the college or the state Department of Archives records, according to Walter Washington, President, Alcorn A. & M. College, in letters to me.

tributed regularly to *New Era*. In addition to letters and poems, Vashon wrote learned disquisitions on the history, geography, and mythology of the Nile River, on legal and historical grounds for black citizenship, on the missionary potential of Africa, and on civilizing benefits of poetry from ancient to modern times. Vashon's activities from 1870 until his death are as yet unknown. It is commonly thought that he died in Mississippi in October, 1878, probably of yellow fever, which was epidemic there at the time.[10]

A gentleman and a scholar by all accounts, Vashon, said Brown, was "a man of few words." Regrettably, he left few words, especially in poetry, to posterity. His "Vincent Ogé" burns with race pride and bittersweet yearning for retributive justice. "A Life-Day" (1864) decries the spiteful cruelty of Southern whites, and his "Ode on the Proclamation of the Fifteenth Amendment" (1870) celebrates the enfranchisement Vashon had fought for. In an eloquent letter to President Lincoln (1862) confuting the proponents of federally sponsored black emigration, Vashon shows keen intelligence and fine literary skills. His weapons in this respectful but never humble rebuttal are logical, legal, and historical arguments delivered with masterful irony. He argues that compulsory emigration is neither just, expedient, nor feasible, and concludes:

> President of the United States, let me say in conclusion, that the negro may be "the bone of contention" in our present civil war. He may have been the occasion of it; but he has not been its cause. That cause must be sought in the wrongs inflicted upon him by the white man. The white man's oppression of the negro, and not the negro himself, has brought upon the nation the leprosy under which it groans. The negro may be the scab indicative of the disease but his removal, even if possible, will not effect a cure. Not until this nation, with hands upon its lips, and with lips in the dust shall cry repentantly, "Unclean! unclean!" will the beneficent Father of all men, of whatever color, permit its healing and purification.[11]

With his own career blasted by prejudice, Vashon continued to seek a better life for his race. Measured by such labors, his academic achievements, learned essays, and masterful "Vincent Ogé," George Vashon was a man of extraordinary courage and talent.

10. Brawley, p. 261, gives October 5, 1878, at Rodney, Miss.; *Oberlin Review*, October, 1878, at Alcorn University, Miss.; the state of Mississippi has no record of Vashon's death.
11. *Douglass' Monthly*, 5 (October, 1862), 727–28.

Vashon's Poetry

The 391 lines of "Vincent Ogé" tell a simple story. Inspired by
the French Revolution, mulattoes of Haiti rise against white author-
ity (in 1790–91); they are slain or captured, tortured, and executed.
This real event of insurrection becomes not only a metaphor for
universal racial conflict and mankind's resistance to tyranny, but
also a symbol of disequilibrium, of a world in perpetual chaotic
motion. The vision of "Vincent Ogé" is Heraclitian: "All things
flow," and, more specifically, "War [of contraries] is the father of
all, the king of all; and some he shows as gods, some as men; some
he makes slaves, some free" (Heraclitus). Vashon sustains an am-
bience of unstable activity throughout the poem with an image
pattern of flickering light, storms, blood, and warfare; by shifts from
classical to prosaic to metaphorical diction; by abrupt changes in
metrical and stanzaic form; by intermittent use of descriptive, nar-
rative, and subjective voices; by movement in temporal and spatial
scene; and by direct statement of theme such as, "Life is a change-
ful thing." In addition, "Vincent Ogé" as we have it (only in *Auto-
graphs for Freedom*) consists of eight fragments of uneven length,
divided from one another by asterisks—a form which may possibly
be deliberate.

The following adjacent fragments on the effects of the French
Revolution illustrate the design of the poem and several techniques
suggested above:

> The loud shouts from the distant town,
> Joined in with nature's gladsome lay;
> The lights went glancing up and down,
> Riv'ling the stars—nay, seemed as they
> Could stoop to claim, in their high home,
> A sympathy with things of earth,
> And had from their bright mansions come,
> To join them in their festal mirth.
> For the land of the Gaul had arose in its might,
> And swept by as the wind of a wild, wintry night;
> And the dreamings of greatness—the phantoms of power,
> Had passed in its breath like the things of an hour.
> Like the violet vapors that brilliantly play
> Round the glass of the chemist, then vanish away,
>
>   .   .   .   .
>
> And a flame was there [Haiti] kindled which fitfully shone
> Mid the shout of the free, and the dark captive's groan;

As, mid contrary breezes, a torch-light will play,
Now streaming up brightly—now dying away.

* * * * *

The reptile slumbers in the stone,
   Nor dream we of his pent abode;
The heart conceals the anguished groan,
   With all the poignant griefs that goad
      The brain to madness;
Within the hushed volcano's breast,
   The molten fires of ruin lie;—
Thus human passions seem at rest,
   And on the brow serene and high,
      Appears no sadness.
But still the fires are raging there,
Of vengeance, hatred, and despair;
And when they burst, they wildly pour
   Their lava flood of woe and fear,
And in one short—one little hour,
   Avenge the wrongs of many a year.

* * * * *

Although such poetry serves the thesis of disorder, the epic as a
whole is structurally stable: chaos reigns within a traditional dra-
matic framework with its beginning, middle, and end. The first
four lines of the poem set the image pattern and theme in motion:

There is, at times, an evening sky—
   The twilight's gift—of sombre hue,
All checkered wild and gorgeously
   With streaks of crimson, gold and blue;—
A sky that strikes the soul with awe . . .

The poet finds this motley, unquiet sky far more glorious than the
peaceful skies of sunrise or morning, and immediately he makes it
the metaphorical equivalent of human passion, of intense joy and
pain in the struggle for freedom, and of battlefield conflict itself.
However, the calm tone, slow pace, and melodious sound of these
lines contravene the imagery, making the stanza a microcosm of the
world of the poem.

The next large section of "Vincent Ogé" describes Haiti before
the insurrection. It is an island home of nymphs and fairies, a Satan-
less Eden, a painting, and a dream of heaven unspoiled by humanity
or by nature's demonic forces:

Basking in beauty, thou dost seem
A vision in a poet's dream!
Thou look'st as though thou claim'st not birth
With sea and sky and other earth. . . .

The regular iambic tetrameter and classical diction blend perfectly
with images of peace, immutability, purity, magic, radiance, and
artistic creation to convey an insular ideal, as insubstantial as Pros-
pero's isle. Thus Vashon's "beauteous whole" the world can never
be is this pre-revolutionary Haiti which floats through the poem as
the contrary and foil of reality, linked to all succeeding places and
events by imagery. For example, the island's "bright-winged birds"
which sing of "pure and constant love" later become a simile for
Ogé, "the lorn and mateless bird/ That constant mourns"; the is-
land's radiant sunshine recurs as the fitful glare of Freedom's torch,
the flash of cannon "like the swift fires of a northern light," the
quivering flames of lightning, and the gleam of rebels' eyes.

The tale of Vincent Ogé begins on this heavenly isle, follows
Ogé's preparation and heroic battle, and ends in a hellish prison.
Again, Vashon adapts the poetry to the context, painting in tones
of despair and horror an abode of darkness, serpents, and fiends; of
rack and wheel, mortified flesh, and passions extinguished in death:

> Grim powers of death all crusted o'er
> With other victims' clotted gore.
> Frowning they stand, and in their cold,
> Silent solemnity, unfold
> The strong one's triumph o'er the weak—
> The awful groan—the anguished shriek—
> The unconscious mutt-rings of despair—
> The strained eyeball's idiot stare—
> The hopeless clench—the quiv'ring frame—
> The martyr's death—the despot's shame.

And the sun no longer shines on Haiti:

> The sunbeams on the rack that play,
> For sudden terror flit away
> From this dread work of war and death,
> As angels do with quickened breath,
> From some dark deed of deepest sin,
> Ere they have drunk its spirit in.

Death does not bring an end to chaos in the world of "Vincent
Ogé." Like grim tigers returning after a kill, human killers gloat
over the martyrs, but "Quail neath the flashing of the eye,/ Which
tells that though the life has started,/ The will to strike has not de-
parted." The martyrs' will to strike for freedom now passes into the
liberator of Haiti, Toussaint L'Ouverture. It does not die even with
him but in all "times of blood,/ Will live to be the tyrant's fear—/
Will live, the sinking soul to cheer!" As long as the "quivering glare"

of lightning illumines our earth and streaked twilight skies beautify
it, passion for freedom will fire men's hearts and gleam from their
dying eyes. The war is eternal; today's gods may be tomorrow's
slaves:

> A thousand hearts are breathing high,
> And voices shouting "Victory!"
>   Which soon will hush in death;
> The trumpet clang of joy that speaks,
> Will soon be drowned in the shrieks
>   Of the wounded's stifling breath,
> The tyrant's plume in dust lies low—
> Th' oppressed has triumphed o'er his foe.
> But ah! the lull in the furious blast
> May whisper not of ruin past;
> It may tell of the tempest hurrying on,
> To complete the work of the blast begun.

After the major achievement of "Vincent Ogé," Vashon's "A Life-
Day" (1864) is disappointing. However, in conception and execu-
tion this 126-line poem surpasses most denunciations of race perse-
cution. Vashon's headnote claims the poem is based on an event of
1864: a judge declared illegal the marriage between a white South-
erner and his black slave, and at the man's death returned the
widow and their two children to slavery. In 1866 this judge became
"a provisional governor in President Johnson's plan of reconstruc-
tion." "A Life-Day" is an allegory of Southern history divided into
three sections titled "Morning," "Noon," and "Night." A white
Southerner rises from a sickbed where he has been deserted by all
but a faithful slave to greet a beautiful summer morning and this
loving black woman. In "Noon" they have been married twelve
years and have two lovely children. "Night" brings death to the
husband and re-enslavement to his anguished family. Several direct
statements on the precariousness of human happiness and life echo
"Vincent Ogé." But Vashon's major concerns in "A Life-Day" are
to vilify vicious whites who come "like vultures to the dead," and
to point out the perversion of human and national ideals in Amer-
ica's treatment of its blacks. The poet's pity and bitter anger rise to
this conclusion:

> Shades of the heroes, long since gone!
>   Was this your glory's end and aim?
> Was it for this, O Washington!
>   That, welcoming the rebel's name,
> Halter and battle you defied?
>   For this! O Warren! that you died?

Vashon read his "Ode on the Proclamation of the Fifteenth Amendment" at Israel Church (Washington, D.C.) on April 13, 1870. In 108 lines of irregular length, the ode offers a variety of stanzaic patterns and rhyme schemes. In other respects it resembles dozens of other commemorative odes in well-worn rhetoric. Nevertheless, George Vashon's unique status is assured by his "Vincent Ogé," surely the most imaginative poem by a black man of his century.

SELECTED SOURCES

Brawley, *ENAW*, 261–78 ("Vincent Ogé" and "A Life-Day").
Brown, *BM*, 223–27 (with an excerpt from "Astronomy").
Delany, Martin R. *The Condition, Elevation . . . of the Colored People of the United States.* 1852; rpt. New York: Arno, 1968. Pp. 119–20.
*———. "Letter to Frederick Douglass, Pittsburgh, January 14, 1848." *North Star*, January 28, 1848.
*"George B. Vashon." *Pittsburgh Telegraph*, n.d. Rpt. *North Star*, January 21, 1848.
Loggins, 129, 235–38.
*Nell, William C. "George B. Vashon" ("New York letter of the Philadelphia *Inquirer*," January 12, 1848). Rpt. *Pittsburgh Telegraph*, n.d.; extract in *North Star*, January 28, 1848.
Oberlin Review, November 20, 1878. Obituary notice, rpt. from *People's Advocate*, Washington, D.C., n.d.
Proceedings of the National Convention of the Colored Men of America, Held in Washington, D.C., January 13, 14, 15 and 16, 1869. Washington, D.C., 1869. 42 pp.
Quarles, Benjamin. *Black Abolitionists.* New York: Oxford University Press, 1969.

FRANCES ELLEN WATKINS HARPER
1824–1911

In an 1859 essay, "Our Greatest Want," Miss Watkins declared that neither gold, intelligence, nor talent were the most pressing needs of her people; rather, "We want more soul, a higher cultivation of all spiritual faculties. We need more unselfishness, earnestness and integrity. . . . We need men and women whose hearts are the homes of a high and lofty enthusiasm, and a noble devotion to the cause of emancipation, who are ready and willing to lay time, talent and money on the altar of universal freedom."[1] No sounder description of the virtues Miss Watkins herself possessed was ever written, although journalists from Maine to Alabama, fellow abolitionists, and contemporary historians acclaimed her unsparing dedication to humanity and honored her as the equal of Bishop Daniel Payne and Frederick Douglass in her contributions to race advancement.[2]

Frances Ellen Watkins was born in Baltimore in 1824,[3] the only child of free parents. When her mother died in 1828 she went to live with her aunt and soon became a student in the academy of her uncle, William J. Watkins.[4] Here daily Bible readings, composition practice, and Watkins's zealous abolitionist teachings shaped her young mind. At the age of fourteen Miss Watkins left school to

1. *Anglo-African Magazine*, 1 (May, 1859), 160.
2. See Bragg, Brown, Daniel, Frazier, Majors, and Still; prospectus for 2nd edition of *Iola Leroy*, NNSch; *Liberator*: September 8, 1854, p. 143; January 11, 1856, p. 7; October 28, 1864, p. 175; March 3, April 21, 1865, pp. 35, 62; December 29, 1865, p. 208; *National Anti-Slavery Standard*, July 4, 1857; June 5, 1869.
3. Dates and places of birth, death, and burial are from Mrs. Harper's death certificate, Pennsylvania Department of Health, Harrisburg.
4. Biography, unless otherwise noted, is from Still, Daniel, and newspaper articles in note 2, above. Quotations in the text are from Mrs. Harper's letters to Still in his *Records*.

work as housekeeper and seamstress in the home of a Baltimore bookstore proprietor. She continued her education in his library and wrote poems and articles that were published in local newspapers during the 1840's. Miss Watkins left Baltimore in 1850 for Union Seminary, a vocational school near Columbus, Ohio, founded by the African Methodist Episcopal Church and later absorbed into Wilberforce University. Here she instructed classes in embroidery and plain sewing until 1852, when for a year she taught fifty-three "unruly children" in Little York, Pennsylvania.

In Little York Miss Watkins was deeply moved by "the poor, half-starved, flying fugitive[s]" traveling the Underground Railroad (757) and by the story of a free Maryland black man who was kidnapped and sold into slavery in Georgia. She now pledged herself to the antislavery cause, "to use time, talent, and energy in the cause of freedom" (758). In 1854 Miss Watkins lived at the Underground Railroad Station in Philadelphia. That summer she visited the antislavery office in Boston and there published her first volume of poems, *Poems on Miscellaneous Subjects* (with a preface by William Lloyd Garrison).[5] In August at a public meeting in New Bedford, Miss Watkins delivered her first lecture, "The Elevation and Education of Our People," and in September, 1854, the Maine Anti-Slavery Society hired her to lecture throughout New England for the next eighteen months. After a visit to the fugitives in Canada in September, 1856, Miss Watkins added Ohio and New York to her lecture circuit and was soon engaged by the Pennsylvania Anti-Slavery Society as lecturer and agent for eastern Pennsylvania and New Jersey from October, 1857, to May, 1858.[6] From 1854 until 1860 Miss Watkins took to the podium in more than eight states, usually daily but often two or three times a day, in the cause of emancipation. She attracted large, enthusiastic audiences, for her

5. Still (p. 756) and later biographers mention a verse pamphlet, *Forest Leaves* (also called *Autumn Leaves*), privately published by Miss Watkins in Baltimore, around 1851. No one has seen a copy. James P. Boyd, in his biographical introduction to Still's *Records,* says that Still arranged an appearance for Miss Watkins in Philadelphia's Assembly Building in 1853 to gain literary recognition for "a little book written in verse and prose" which she had brought along (p. xxxi). *Eventide. A Series of Tales and Poems* (1854) by Effie Afton has been attributed to Miss Watkins (see Loggins, p. 397n). *The Library of Congress Catalog of Printed Cards,* II (1942), 90, identifies Effie Afton as Mrs. Sarah Elizabeth (Harper) Monmouth (1829–87).
6. See Still for detailed itinerary; Quarles, p. 179; William E. Farrison, *William Wells Brown* (Chicago: University of Chicago Press, 1969), pp. 287–88.

fragile, dainty figure and dignified manner belied her power to kindle abolitionist fervor in the hearts of both races. Piercing black eyes dominated her dark African features, and her handsome face radiated the vitality and resolute passion of a charismatic orator. She recited her poetry, demanded liberty for the slave and right-eousness from the nation with graceful gestures and in a strong, clear, musical voice. Her wit, reason, sincerity, and eloquence im-pressed every auditor. In short, she was "a magnificent type of woman, physically and mentally." [7]

Miss Watkins's sympathetic identification with the bondsmen and her tragic sense of the impending crisis grew steadily. She wrote to William Still, "I have lived in the midst of oppression and wrong, and I am saddened by every captured fugitive in the North; a blow has been struck at my freedom, in every hunted and down-trodden slave in the South; North and South have both been guilty; and they that sin must suffer" (763). In letters to Still, with whom she corresponded from 1854, Miss Watkins sent money for the fugitives and pleaded for more work of any kind that she might do for their welfare. She lived in Still's Philadelphia home with Mrs. John Brown for the two weeks preceding Brown's execution in 1859, and afterward she wrote letters and sent packages to the martyrs still in prison.

Miss Watkins retired from public life for a few years when she married Fenton Harper, a widower, in Cincinnati on November 22, 1860, and bought a small farm near Columbus for their home. They had a daughter, Mary, who became a Sunday School teacher and volunteer social worker. Mary never married, but lived with Mrs. Harper and died about two years before her. Fenton Harper died on May 23, 1864, and in October Mrs. Harper returned to the lecture circuit with a speech on "The Mission of the War." Until 1865 she lectured in New England; then, except for a few months in Phila-delphia (fall, 1867), she traveled until 1871 at her own expense through thirteen Southern states. In the South Mrs. Harper lived with the freedmen in "the old cabins of slavery" and spoke at Sun-day schools, day schools, churches, town meetings, in homes and village squares, on the same daily and two-a-day schedule as before the War. Her only income was from sparse collections taken at

7. John Edward Bruce, "Noted Race Women I Have Known and Met" (1923), pp. 14–15, MS 2007, Bruce Collection, NNSch; letters in Bruce Col-lection mentioning Mrs. Harper are MSS 1139, 1685, 1735. See also *Frederick Douglass' Paper*, October 31, 1865, and newspaper notices, note 2, above.

FRANCES ELLEN WATKINS HARPER. *Atlanta Offering* (1895).

REV: N.C.W. CANNON.

The true Ministers are Instruments indeed, in order to spread the Cement of Brotherly Love which unites us in one Sacred Band, and so let us all agree and work in peace. Ps. 133.—*And so remember me, this denotes the Angel in the bush, and the Star in the East.* Exod. 3rd. Ch. 2nd. Ver.—Mat. 1st. Ch. 7th. & 10th. Ver.—Rev. 1st. Ch. 16th. & 20th. Verse.

F. M. Gore. Sc.

THE

ROCK OF WISDOM;

AN EXPLANATION OF THE SACRED SCRIPTURES.

BY THE

REV. N. C. CANNON,

A MAN OF COLOR.

TO WHICH ARE ADDED SEVERAL

INTERESTING HYMNS.

——

1833.

The Rock of Wisdom by Noah C. W. Cannon.

LES CENELLES.

Choix de Poésies indigènes.

Et de ces fruits qu'un Dieu prodigue dans nos bois
Heureux, si j'en ai su faire un aimable choix!

A. MERCIER.

NOUVELLE ORLEANS.

Imprimé par H. Lauve et Compagnie.

1845.

Les Cenelles by A. Lanusse, P. Dalcour, V. Séjour, C. Thierry, et al.

THE HOPE

OF

LIBERTY.

CONTAINING

A NUMBER OF POETICAL PIECES.

BY

GEORGE M. HORTON.

RALEIGH:
Printed by J. Gales & Son.
1829.

The Hope of Liberty by George Moses Horton.

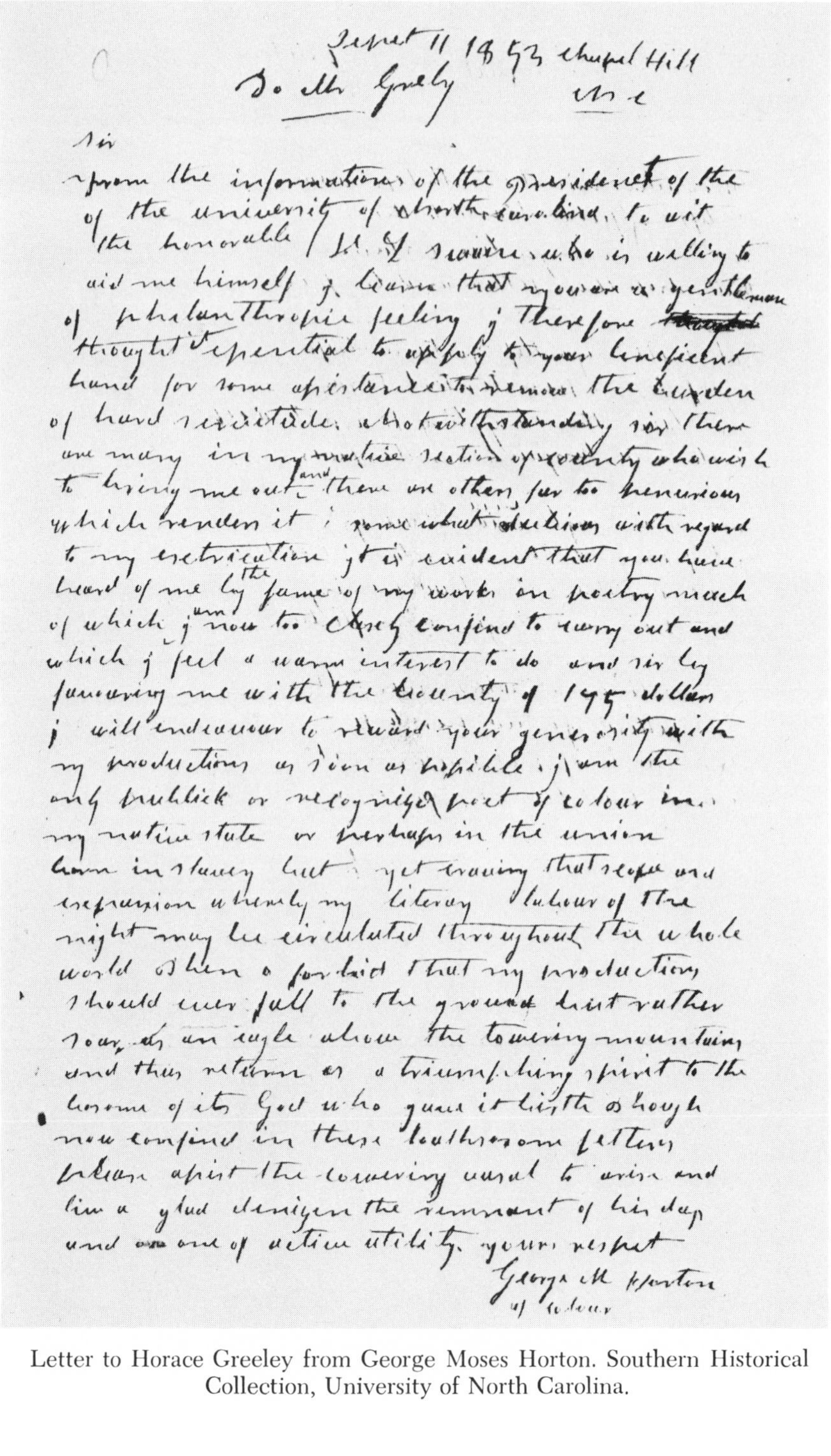

Sept 11 1853 Chapel Hill
To Mr Greely
N C

Sir

from the informations of the president of the
of the university of North carolina to wit
the honorable D. L. swain who is willing to
aid me himself I learn that you are a gentleman
of philanthropic feeling I therefore thought
thought it essential to apply to your beneficent
hand for some assistance to remove the burden
of hard servitude. notwithstanding sir there
are many in my native section of country who wish
to bring me out and there are others far too penurious
which renders it somewhat dubious with regard
to my extrication it is evident that you have
heard of me by the fame of my works in poetry much
of which I am now too closely confined to carry out and
which I feel a warm interest to do and sir by
favoring me with the bounty of 175 dollars
I will endeavour to reward your generosity with
my productions as soon as possible. I am the
only publick or recognized poet of colour in
my native state or perhaps in the union
born in slavery but yet craving that scope and
expression whereby my literary labour of the
night may be circulated throughout the whole
world. then o forbid that my productions
should ever fall to the ground but rather
soar as an eagle above the towering mountains
and thus return as a triumphing spirit to the
bosom of its God who gave it birth though
now confined in these loathsome fetters
please assist the cowering vassal to arise and
live a glad denizen the remnant of his days
and one of active utility. yours respect

George M Horton
of colour

Letter to Horace Greeley from George Moses Horton. Southern Historical Collection, University of North Carolina.

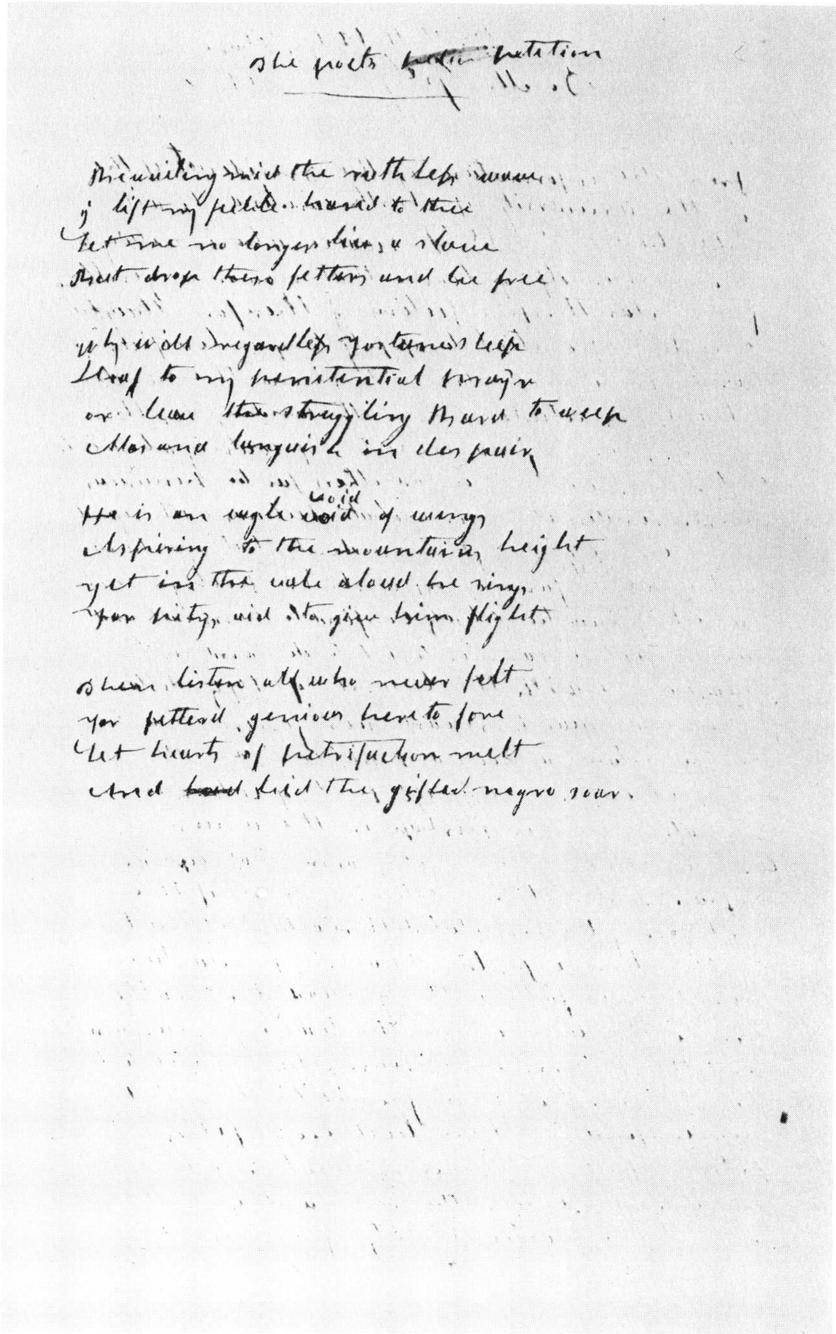

The poets ~~feeble~~ petition
H. G.

Bewailing mid the ruthless wave
I lift my feeble hand to thee
Let me no longer live a slave
But drop these fetters and be free

Why will regardless fortune sleep
Deaf to my penitential prayer
Or leave the struggling bard to weep
Alas and languish in despair

He is an eagle ~~void~~ void of wings
Aspiring to the mountain height
Yet in the vale aloud he sings
For pity's aid to give him flight

Then listen all who never felt
For fettered genius heretofore
Let hearts of petrifaction melt
And ~~bend~~ bid the gifted negro soar.

Poem by Horton to Greeley on reverse of letter.

CHARLES LEWIS REASON. *Autographs for Freedom*, ed. J. Griffith (1845).

JAMES MADISON BELL. *The Poetical Works* (1901).

DANIEL ALEXANDER PAYNE.
Recollections of Seventy Years (1888).

GEORGE HANIBAL TEMPLE. *The Epic of Columbus' Bell* (1900).

MARY E. TUCKER LAMBERT.
Poems (1867).

ISLAY WALDEN. Gardner A. Sage Library, New
Brunswick Theological Seminary.

GEORGE CLINTON ROWE. *Thoughts in
Verse* (1887).

meetings and from sales of new poetry, *Moses, A Story of the Nile* (1869) and *Poems* (1871), and reprints of *Poems on Miscellaneous Subjects*, which reached a twentieth edition in 1871. Speaking in an Alabama brush arbor or before the legislature of South Carolina, Mrs. Harper exhorted the freedmen to be independent, responsible citizens, to gain education and land, to build strong families and homes based on mutual respect and Christian morality. Her lectures were broad in scope: "National Salvation," "Enlightened Mother-hood," "The Colored Man as a Social and Political Force," "Racial Literature," "The Mission of the War and the Demands of the Col-ored Race in the Work of Reconstruction." Although in poor health and often depressed by the ignorance and indifference of the freed-men, Mrs. Harper labored for six years with a crusader's zeal, with infinite compassion and faith to bring about the elevation of the race. "After all," she wrote in 1870, "whether they encourage or discourage me, I belong to this race, and when it is down I belong to a down race; when it is up, I belong to a risen race" (773).

After 1871 Mrs. Harper also wrote and lectured in support of many nationwide social and moral reform movements, for it was a "privilege," she said, to be "sister to the human race." For forty years after making Philadelphia her permanent home in February, 1871, she worked with a dozen organizations on behalf of educa-tion, women's and children's rights, and temperance. In 1872 she organized and was assistant superintendent of a YMCA Sabbath school in Philadelphia. She served as lecturer and officer in the National Association of Colored Women, the National Council of Women of the United States, the American Association of Educators of Colored Youth and Author's Association. From about 1875 to 1882 Mrs. Harper was superintendent of the Philadelphia and Penn-sylvania chapters of the National Women's Christian Temperance Union, Colored Branch. Without remuneration she headed the Northern United States WCTU activities from 1883 to 1890 and continued as an organizer, field worker, and lecturer for them until 1896. For this service her name was placed on the Red Letter Cal-endar of the World WCTU in 1922. In addition, Mrs. Harper wrote and worked for the African Methodist Episcopal Church, which "adopted" her—she was a Unitarian—and frequently paid homage to her selfless labors.[8]

8. Details and bibliography of organizations are in Daniel; see also Gertrude B. Mossell, *The Work of the Afro-American Woman*, 2nd ed. (Philadelphia: George S. Ferguson, 1908), pp. 13–14; Still, p. 778; Brown, p. 103; Fannie C.

During these busy years, Mrs. Harper published new poetry in *Sketches of Southern Life* (1872) and in three verse pamphlets, *Light Beyond the Darkness, The Sparrow's Fall and Other Poems,* and *The Martyr of Alabama,* all of which were later included in *Atlanta Offering* (1895). Mrs. Harper was the first woman of her race to publish a short story, "The Two Offers" (1859), and a novel, *Iola Leroy* (1892). Her celebrity as an author, lecturer, and reformer was virtually unsurpassed in her day; however, like other black poets and most race leaders, soon after her death her volumes of poetry were out of print and her deeds all but forgotten. She died of heart disease at the age of 87 on February 20, 1911, and, after a funeral service at the First Unitarian Church, she was buried in Eden Cemetery, Philadelphia, on February 24. For her contributions to literature and human welfare Mrs. Harper deserves to be honored anew among the healers and builders of nineteenth-century America.

Mrs. Harper's Poetry

As the most popular black poet before Dunbar, Mrs. Harper earned enough from sales of twenty-five-cent pamphlets and slim volumes of verse to support herself and to buy the three-story house at 1006 Bainbridge Street, Philadelphia, from which her later works were published.[9] Although most of her poetry, and the best of it, was written by 1872, new titles and reprints continued to appear at least until 1901.[10] She shifted the thematic emphasis of her poetry from volume to volume; nevertheless, from 1854 through 1901 her

---

L. Bentley, "The Women of Our Race Worthy of Imitation," *AMECR*, 6 (April, 1890), 476; Harper, "The WCTU and the Colored Woman," *AMECR*, 4 (April, 1888), 313–16; *The Negro Year Book,* ed. Monroe N. Work (Tuskegee Institute, Ala., 1925), VII, 282. An account of her work as vice-president of the Universal Peace Union is Alfred H. Love, "Memorial Tribute to Mrs. Frances E. W. Harper," *The Peacemaker,* 30 (June–July, 1911), 118–19 (DHU).

9. The house is mentioned in a letter to Mrs. Harper from William Still, who, while the poet was on the road, paid her taxes, collected a tenant's rent, and provided custodial service (letter of November 3, 1873, William Still Letterbook, Historical Society of Pennsylvania).

10. From 1853 until 1901 her poems and essays appeared in periodicals such as *Liberator, National Anti-Slavery Standard, AMECR, Frederick Douglass' Paper, New National Era, Alumni Magazine* (Lincoln University), *Southland,* and *Howard's American Magazine;* see also *Colored American Magazine* (1900–1909).

subjects remain religion, race, and social reform. Mrs. Harper's verse is frankly propagandist, a metrical extension of her life dedicated to the welfare of others. She believed in art for humanity's sake:

> Let me make the songs for the people,
>   Songs for the old and young;
>   Songs to stir like a battle-cry
>   Wherever they are sung.

Her poems were "songs to thrill the hearts of men/ With more abundant life," "anthems of love and duty" for children, and songs of "bright and restful mansions" for the "poor and aged" ("Songs for the People," 1894).[11] Except for *Moses* (1869) and *Sketches of Southern Life* (1872), which will be considered later, Mrs. Harper's lyric and narrative poetry varies little in form, language, or poetic technique.

Her numerous religious poems embrace both New and Old Testament ideologies and imagery, honoring their respective God heroes, a gentle Redeemer and a fiery Jehovah. The former brings "comfort, peace and rest," "changes hearts of stone/ To tenderness and love" through grace, and offers a "crown of life" hereafter to all who trust in him. This God of light and mercy appears in several early poems like "That Blessed Hope" and "Saved by Faith" (1854), in poems of the middle years when, following the loss of her husband in 1864, Mrs. Harper seems preoccupied with death (twelve of the twenty-six selections in *Poems* [1871] concern dying or life after death), and in the 1890's the same God of love dominates some two dozen poems such as "The Refiner's Gold," "The Sparrow's Fall," "The Resurrection of Jesus," and "Renewal of Strength." Mrs. Harper's fervid commitment to Christian virtues and her faith in a "gloryland" are moving, but poetically more interesting is her allegiance to a dynamic warrior God who "hath bathed his sword in judgement," who thunders in "whirlwinds of wrath" or swoops with a "bath of blood and fire" to redress injustice in *this* world. It is the God of the Israelites who will free her people, as in "Ethiopia" (1854):

> The tyrant's yoke from off her neck,
>   His fetters from her soul,

11. Earliest known date of a poem's publication is given in parenthesis. Symbols are used for two volumes of uncertain date: (SF) *Sparrow's Fall*, (LBD) *Light Beyond the Darkness*.

> The mighty hand of God shall break,
>   And spurn the base control.
>
>   .   .   .   .
>
> Secure by night, and blest by day,
>   Shall pass her happy hours;
> Nor human tigers hunt for prey
>   Within her peaceful bowers.
>
> Then, Ethiopia, stretch, O stretch
>   Thy bleeding hands abroad!
> Thy cry of agony shall reach
>   And find redress from God.

In poems like "Lines" (1857), "Retribution" (1871), and "The Martyr of Alabama" (1894), Mrs. Harper invokes the God of Moses not only as a militant redeemer, but also as the scourge of men and nations who "trample on His children." She wrote to John Brown in prison in 1859: "God writes national judgements on national sins." Thus when men of Cleveland returned a young fugitive girl to slavery to "preserve the union," Mrs. Harper prophesied the coming chaos in one of her best poems, "To the Union Savers of Cleveland" (1860). These are the last five of eleven stanzas:

> There is blood upon your city,
>   Dark and dismal is the stain;
> And your hands would fail to cleanse it,
>   Though Lake Erie ye should drain.
>
> There's a curse upon your Union,
>   Fearful sounds are in the air;
> As if thunderbolts were framing
>   Answers to the bondsmen's prayer.
>
> Ye may offer human victims,
>   Like the heathen priests of old;
> And may barter manly honor
>   For the Union and for gold.
>
> But ye can not stay the whirlwind,
>   When the storm begins to break;
> And your God doth rise in judgment,
>   For the poor and needy's sake.
>
> And, your sin-cursed, guilty Union
>   Shall be shaken to its base,
> Till ye learn that simple justice
>   Is the right of every race.

Mrs. Harper seldom shows such righteous indignation as gives power to this poem, and even less often is she bitter or cynical. However, these emotions do invigorate such poems as "The Bible

Defense of Slavery" (1854), "The Dismissal of Tyng" (1857), and "A Fairer Hope, A Brighter Morn" (LBD) in which the poet denounces white "prophets of evil" who weave phantom fears of miscegenation out of their own guilt in order to oppress the race they formerly enslaved.

In many other poems on racial themes, such as "Eliza Harris" (1853) and "The Slave Auction" (1854), Mrs. Harper describes the anguish of slave mothers, the heroism of black men, and the suffering of fugitives and captives. As in most abolitionist verse, emotions of fear, pain, and pity are generic, like the situations, detached from both poet and poetry. Without Mrs. Harper's dramatic recitations they remain superficial, sentimental period pieces. On the other hand, when the poet speaks in her own voice, as in "Bury Me in a Free Land" (1858), true passion is felt, and the poem succeeds:

> Make me a grave where'er you will,
> In a lowly plain, or a lofty hill;
> Make it among earth's humblest graves,
> But not in a land where men are slaves.
>
> . . . .
>
> I'd shudder and start if I heard the bay
> Of bloodhounds seizing their human prey,
> And I heard the captive plead in vain
> As they bound afresh his galling chain.
>
> . . . .
>
> I ask no monument, proud and high,
> To arrest the gaze of the passers-by;
> All that my yearning spirit craves,
> Is bury me not in a land of slaves.

More objective and intellectual than the abolitionist verses are Mrs. Harper's postwar appeals for freedmen's rights. Although often militantly urgent in tone, they express conciliatory sentiments. "Words for the Hour" (1871) is addressed to "Men of the North":

> 'Tis yours to banish from the land
> Oppression's iron rule;
> And o'er the ruin'd auction-block
> Erect the common school.
>
> To wipe from labor's branded brow
> The curse that shamed the land;
> And teach the Freedmen how to wield
> The ballot in his hand.

"An Appeal to the American People" (1871) reminds white Americans of the black soldiers' heroism, chides them for ignoring these "offerings of our blood," and appeals to their manhood, Christian principles, and honor to see justice done in the nation. There are no suggestions of black separatism in these poems; rather, the poet optimistically envisions racial brotherhood and national progress, as in "The Present Age" (SF):

> Blame not the age, nor think it full
> Of evil and unrest;
> But say of every other age,
> "This one shall be the best."
>
> The age to brighten every path
> By sin and sorrow trod;
> For loving hearts to usher in
> The commonwealth of God.

As black and white work together for mutual betterment, their souls must be pure and their hearts consecrated to Christian morality and social welfare. In some three dozen "reform" ballads Mrs. Harper weeps for families ruined by King Alcohol, and she gushes over innocent children and helpless women threatened or ruined by a sinful world. Her lecture audiences were captivated by these catalogues of human frailty which now seem maudlin. Nevertheless, such ballads on issues of national concern represent a unique and significant movement by a black poet, a breaking away from exclusively racial protest themes to write "more of feelings that are general . . . and delve into the heart of the world." [12] The "slavery of intemperance," Mrs. Harper wrote, "is a curse in the home, a menace to the Church, a blight to the State, a fretting leprosy in the national house," against which we must "consecrate, educate, agitate, and legislate." [13] In "The Drunkard's Child" (1854) a boy dies of neglect in his besotted father's arms. A ruined bride, mother, and child regain happiness through "the gospel and the pledge" in "Signing the Pledge" (1888); a dozen unsuspecting people are destroyed by drink in the melodramatic "Nothing and Something" (1888); and a typical alcoholic father repents at the sight of his child's empty Christmas stocking in "The Ragged Stocking" (1889):

> Stony drink is a raging demon,
>   In his hands are shame and woe,
> He mocketh the strength of the mighty
>   And bringeth the strong man low.

· · · ·

12. Harper, letter to Thomas Hamilton, ed. *Anglo-African Magazine* (1861), quoted in Redding, p. 39.
13. "Symposium-Temperance," *AMECR*, 7 (April, 1891), 373–74.

> Then I knelt by this little stocking
> And sobbed out an earnest prayer,
> And rose with strength to wrestle
> And break from the tempter's snare.

Mrs. Harper was also an outspoken champion of women's rights. In "A Double Standard" (SF) a deceived young girl speaks:

> Crime has no sex and yet today
> I wear the brand of shame;
> Whilst he amid the gay and proud
> Still bears an honored name.
>
> . . . .
>
> No golden weights can turn the scale
> Of Justice in His sight;
> And what is wrong in woman's life
> In man's cannot be right.

Other oppressed women are victims of economic injustice, as in "Died of Starvation" (1854), or martyrs to man's pride like Vashti, Queen of Persia. Occasionally Mrs. Harper projects her own moral and spiritual strength into biblical heroines, creating appealing individuals, warm, courageous, loving women who transcend the cause they espouse. In poems like "Rizpah, the Daughter of Ai" (1857), "Ruth and Naomi" (1857), "Mary at the Feet of Christ" (1871), and "Vashti" (1870), emotions tied to specific crises are conveyed in simple, direct language, giving the poems a vibrant immediacy as well as lasting human validity.

Most of Mrs. Harper's religious, racial, and reform verse resembles the typical nineteenth-century work in Rufus W. Griswold's *Female Poets of America* (1848, 1873), possessing by today's standards more cultural and historical than aesthetic value. Generally her diction and rhymes are pedestrian; the meters are mechanical and frequently dependent on oral delivery for regularity, and the sentiments, however genuine, lack concreteness and control. However, Mrs. Harper attains notable artistic success with *Moses: A Story of the Nile* (1869) and the Aunt Chloe poems in *Sketches of Southern Life* (1872). *Moses*, a forty-page narrative in blank verse recounting the career of Israel's leader, was no doubt inspired by the Emancipation and Lincoln's death.[14] Through a dramatic dia-

14. Mrs. Harper frequently praises Moses and compares the black people to the Israelites in bondage. Concerning Lincoln's assassination, she wrote, "Moses, the meekest man on earth, led the children of Israel over the Red Sea, but was not permitted to see them settled in Canaan. Mr. Lincoln has led up through another Red Sea to the table land of triumphant victory, and God has seen fit

logue of Moses and Charmian, the poet describes Moses' departure
from the Pharaoh's court. Then her narrative moves briskly through
the Old Testament story to Moses' death. Mrs. Harper handles the
blank verse skillfully, bringing the biblical events to life with vivid
imagery:

> Then Moses threw his rod upon the floor,
> And it trembled with a sign of life;
> The dark wood glowed, then changed into a thing
> Of glistening scales and golden rings, and green,
> And brown and purple stripes; a hissing, hateful
> Thing, that glared its fiery eye, and darting forth
> From Moses' side, lay coiled and panting
> At the monarch's feet.

In grisly detail, the ten plagues descend on Egypt: "every fountain,
well and pool/ Was red with blood, and lips, all parched with
thirst,/ Shrank back in horror from the crimson draughts/"; frogs
"crowded into Pharaoh's bed, and hopped/ Into his trays of bread,
and slumbered in his/ Ovens and his pans." The horrors continue,
until

> for three long days, nor saffron
> Tint, nor crimson flush, nor soft and silvery light
> Divided day from morn, nor told the passage
> Of the hours; men rose not from their seats, but sat
> In silent awe. That lengthened night lay like a
> burden
> On the air,—a darkness one might almost gather
> In his hand, it was so gross and thick.

The poet conveys Moses' complex emotions and strong personality
through his actions. In the final chapter she admirably evokes the
mingled sense of pride and sorrow felt by the Israelites, "reaching
out unconscious hands" to keep him. She portrays the solitude of
Moses and his mixed feelings of regret and joy as "He stood upon
the highest peak of Nebo,/ And saw the Jordan chafing through its
gorges . . . the ancient rocks/ That dripped with honey . . . the
vines opprest/ With purple riches, the fig trees fruitcrowned/ Green
and golden"—a scene of peace and beauty which prepares Moses'
"ransomed soul" for the even fairer land of "crystal fountains" to
which "a troupe of fair young angels" soon conveys him. The poem's
elevated diction, concrete imagery, and formal meter harmoniously

---

to summon for the new era another man. It is ours then to bow to the Chastener
and let our honored and loved chieftain go" (Still, 767).

blend to magnify the noble adventure of Moses' life and the mysterious grandeur of his death. Mrs. Harper maintains the pace of her long narrative and its tone of reverent admiration with scarcely a pause for moralizing. *Moses* is Mrs. Harper's most original poem and one of considerable power.

She shows a similar talent for matching technique and subject in the charming series of poems which make up most of *Sketches of Southern Life* (1872). Aunt Chloe, the narrator, is a wise, practical ex-slave who discusses the war and Reconstruction with earthy good humor, as Uncle Jacob, a saintly optimist, counsels prayer, "faith and courage." These poems are unique in Mrs. Harper's canon for their wit and irony; the colloquial expressions of Aunt Chloe's discourse form a new idiom in black poetry which ripens into the dialect verse of Campbell, Davis, and Dunbar in the last decades of the century. "The Deliverance" in sixty stanzas describes antebellum plantation life and the departure of young master for war:

> And I said to Uncle Jacob
>   'Now old Mistus feels the sting.
> For this parting with your children
>   Is a mighty dreadful thing.'
>
> Mistus prayed up in the parlor
>   That the Secesh all might win;
> We were praying in the cabins,
>   Wanting freedom to begin.

Among the slaves, great rejoicing and praise of Lincoln greet the Yankee victory,

> But when old Mistus heard it,
>   She groaned and hardly spoke;
> When she had to lose her servants,
>   Her heart was almost broke.

Aunt Chloe chides the freedmen for selling their votes for three sticks of candy and gloats over the man who "sold out for flour and sugar;/ The sugar was mixed with sand." But she is at last an optimist, admitting that most of the freedmen know "freedom cost too much" to be given away for profit or pleasure. In shorter sketches like "Learning to Read," antagonism of the "Rebs" to the freedmen's progress is quietly but firmly overcome by trickery or hard work. The Aunt Chloe series is successful because a consistent, personalized language and references to everyday objects give authenticity to the subjects while directly communicating the freedmen's varying attitudes of self-mockery, growing self-respect, and optimism without sentimentality. Serious issues sketched with a light touch are rare in Mrs. Harper's work, and it is unfortunate that Aunt Chloe's fresh and lively observations were not enlarged.

Mrs. Harper wrote a great quantity of poetry during half a century, all of it in moments snatched from her public life as lecturer and reformer. Possibly *Moses* and *Sketches* were composed during her brief marriage, only four years out of eighty-seven that might be called leisure time. Her race protest and reform verse, combined with her lectures, were effective propaganda; she takes honors as well for the originality and harmony of poetic form and language in *Moses* and the innovative monologues of Aunt Chloe. In short, Mrs. Harper's total output is the most valuable single poetic record we have of the mind and heart of the race whose fortunes shaped the tumultuous years of her career, 1850–1900.

SELECTED SOURCES

All biographical material in the following works, with the exception of Daniel, is condensed from Still with minor additions or none.

Bragg, George F., Jr. *Men of Maryland*. Baltimore: Church Advocate Press, 1925. Pp. 73–86.

Brawley, *ENAW*, 290–98.

Brown, Hallie Q., comp. *Homespun Heroines and Other Women of Distinction*. Xenia, Ohio: Aldine, 1926. Pp. 97–103.

*Daniel, Theodora Williams. "The Poems of Frances E. W. Harper, Edited with a Biographical and Critical Introduction, and Bibliography." M.A. dissertation, Howard University, 1937. 256 pp. Copy: DHU.

Dannett, Sylvia. *Profiles of Negro Womanhood*. Yonkers: Negro Heritage Library, 1964. I, 102–9.

Frazier, S. Elizabeth. "Some Afro-American Women of Mark." *AMECR*, 8 (April, 1892), 378–81.

*Loggins, 245–46, 324–26, 342–44.

Majors, Monroe. *Noted Negro Women*. Chicago: Donohue and Henneberry, 1893. Pp. 23–27.

Quarles, Benjamin. *Black Abolitionists*. New York: Oxford University Press, 1969. Pp. 75–76, 179 *et passim*.

*Redding, 38–44.

Sillen, Samuel. *Women against Slavery*. New York: Masses and Mainstream, 1955. Pp. 70–75.

*Still, William. *Still's Underground Rail Road Records*. Rev. ed., 1872; Philadelphia: William Still, 1886. Pp. 755–80.

ALFRED GIBBS CAMPBELL
1826?–?

Only two facts are known about the life of Alfred Gibbs Campbell: on September 2, 1852, he married Anne Hutchinson of Trenton, New Jersey, in that city; and in 1857 he was a vice-president of the American Anti-Slavery Society.[1] Campbell's published work reveals that he was a man of strong convictions with the courage and talent to express them well in poetry and prose. On July 4, 1851, in Paterson, New Jersey, Campbell published the first issue of his monthly newspaper, *The Alarm Bell*.[2] At the odd terms of twenty-five cents per year in advance, or five copies for a dollar, Campbell's four-page *Alarm Bell*—"Ring out the False—Ring in the True" —loudly pealed for temperance, abolitionism, women's rights, and liberal, nonsectarian Christianity, and against the death penalty, unmuzzled dogs, and tobacco. As publisher, editor, and almost sole writer, Campbell offered the paper at least until October, 1852, "to raise men to a higher standard of morality and virtue by exposing those evils and vices now so unhappily prevalent in society," and to establish "the Universal Brotherhood of Man" (4:2).

To combat the most pernicious vice, rum, Campbell printed the names of over 150 persons who had signed "recommendations for Tavern License" in Paterson; he reported on meetings of temperance societies throughout the country, including Paterson's, of which he was secretary; he commented on liquor laws of many

1. *Paterson Intelligencer,* September 8, 1852. Reference courtesy of J. D. Quackenbush, Jr., Passaic County Historical Society; *National Anti-Slavery Standard,* May 16, 1856.
2. Vol. I, nos. 1–9 appeared July–September, 1851, and May–October, 1852. No announcement of the paper's demise is in the last known issue. Agents for the *Alarm Bell* were John J. Campbell (Trenton) and J. Price Campbell (Bordentown), whose relation to the editor is unknown (5:2). Issue and page number of quotations are given in the text.

states, reviewed their enforcements, and lamented New Jersey's failure to prohibit rum traffic. Campbell's more literary articles like "The History of Alcohol" vividly plead for the cause. What do you gain by "tippling," he asks:

> You gain disease, vitiated appetite, clouded brain, inflamed passions, empty pockets, wretchedness at home and misery abroad. You gain the suspicion of your friends, the cold shoulder of your relatives, the contempt of yourselves. You gain the horror of forging and wearing shackles of the drunkard—of knowing that you are treading rapidly down the road that leads inevitably to ruin and death (9:1).

Campbell's antislavery, anti-government, anti–July Fourth celebration diatribes appear in every issue. He reports at length a first anniversary celebration of the Jerry rescue in Syracuse, where irate citizens defied the Fugitive Slave Law and rescued Jerry McHenry from federal marshalls (9:3). He denounces the government as "a stupendous slave-breeding, slave-catching, slave-holding organization" whose chief concern is to preserve "woman-whipping, cradle-plundering, and soul-crushing villainy" (5:2), and he vows to use every means to overthrow the pro-slavery Constitution (9:2). As ardent a women's rights advocate as Mrs. Harper, Campbell insists on perfect equality between the sexes before the law, in education, and in employment opportunities. Woman, he says, must have "the right to think and act and judge for herself" with the "free and unfettered use of all the faculties God has given her" (6:1). A major target of Campbell's wrath is authority, be it man (priest or king), book, or institution (church or state) which attempts to alienate man "from his only rightful ruler and lawgiver," God (5:4). Having been denounced as a Sabbath-breaker for selling *The Alarm Bell* at Sunday temperance meetings, Campbell devotes a whole issue to "the rights of conscience." He denies that there is any "peculiar sanctity about Sunday," the "harvest-day" of the hypocritical priesthood. His essay, "The Sabbath," is a learned discourse on Scripture vs. Mosaic law and inward vs. ceremonial religion (8).

Religion (twenty-six poems) and abolitionism (twenty poems) are the major subjects in Campbell's collection, *Poems* (1883). In "On the Deep" his simple, regular meter and tones of concern and despair changing to quiet confidence perfectly suit the tale. Although his subject is traditional—a floundering ship is saved by Jesus as man tossed in stormy night will be—Campbell's allegory is vivid, fast paced, and well constructed. "The Divine Mission," in rhymed couplets, compares pre-Christian "moral night" to modern dark times where priests are "gain-seeking" men in league with God's foes. The poet summons Jesus to once again vindicate his majesty and power. Other poems such as "Life's Pilgrimage," "Death's Death," and "Jesus, Give Me of Thy Spirit" are sincere expressions of Christian faith; so too is "God Shall Be All in All," which first appeared in *The Alarm Bell* (July, 1852):

> I deem they greatly err, who hold
>   That He who made the human soul,
>   Will not its destinies control
> For final good, but wrathful fold
>
> It in the shrouds of hopeless woe
>   Of deathless gloom, of quenchless fire,
>   The creatures of His vengeful ire,
> Whence it can never ransom know.

"The Lord Is Love," the poet concludes, and will preserve all souls forever.

"Cry 'Infidel' " is a satiric attack on dogmatic religionists, reiterating Campbell's spirited prose defense of "conscience and reason" in *The Alarm Bell*:

> What though his heart with love overflow
> To the victims of sin and want and woe,
>   Spare him not! Cry "Infidel!"
> What though, in the long-waged fearful fight,
> He is ever found on the side of Right,
>   Cry "Infidel!"
>   .   .   .   .
> What right has he to think other than you?
> To judge for himself what is false or true?
>   Spare him not! Cry "Infidel!"

Campbell brings versatility and fervor to the cause of abolitionism. Among several compelling antislavery poems is "Lines, July 4, 1855":

> *We are not free!* In every Southern State
> Speech and the Press are fettered;—and for him
> Who dares speak out, the martyr-fires await,
> Or Hangman's rope from tallest pine-tree's limb.
> *We are not free!* One man in every seven,
> Throughout our false Republic, groans beneath
> The vilest despotism under heaven.
> Which leaves no hope of freedom but in death.

"Warning," in blank verse, execrates supporters of the Fugitive

Slave Law. With sarcastic wit, "A Virginian's Appeal" unmasks Southerners who fear that teaching blacks their "A. B. C." will ruin them for service. We cannot be without our "niggers," they cry: who would cook dinner, till farms, and refill purses made fat from "nigger breedings"? The poet demands freedom, justice, and truth in "I Would Be Free," "The Slave's Prayer," and "A Battle-Cry"; in three tributes to John Brown; and in "The Doom of Slavery," a poem of thirteen stanzas from 1856:

> Slavery, Union, Compromise,
> (Foulest of all trinities)
> Throned upon a tower of lies,
> Are the nation's deities.
>
> Hurl these false Gods from their throne!
> Snatch from Slavery's brow the crown!
> Tear the blood-stained Union down!
> Trample Compromises down!
>   . . . .
> Till the morning dawn, whose rays
> Force and Fraud and Fear shall chase,
> And fair Freedom take her place,
> Empress of the Human Race!

Poems also includes consolatory and memorial verses; the uplifting "Go Ahead" which counsels work, play, prayer, and watchfulness; several trite album dedications; and a pleasing love poem, "To My Absent Wife."

> My dear, true wife,
>   Life of my life,
> And my heart's solace only,
>   Thou knowest not
>   How drear my lot
> Without thee, and how lonely!
>   . . . .
>   Love cannot die!
>   'Tis Deity!
> 'Tis bliss, pure, bright, supernal;
>   Though worlds shall fall
>   To ruin—all,
> Yes, all of Love's eternal!

None of the many temperance pieces in *Poems* is as original and witty as Campbell's tale of the old decanter, perhaps the first American "concrete" poem, in his *Alarm Bell* for June, 1852.

There was an old decan-
ter, and its mouth was
gaping wide; the
rosy wine had
ebbed away
and left
its crys-
tal side;
and the wind
went humming—
humming,
up and
down the
sides it flew,
and through the
reed like
hollow neck
the wildest notes it
blew. I placed it in the
window where the blast was
blowing free, and fancied that its
pale mouth sang the queerest strains to
me. "They tell me—puny conquerors! the
Plague has slain his ten, and War his hundred
thousand of the very best of men; but I"—'twas
thus the Bottle spake—"but I have conquered
more, than all your famous conquerors, so
feared and famed of yore. Then come, ye
youths and maidens all, come drink from

out my cup, the beverage that dulls the/ brain and burns the
spirits up;"—continues the decanter, as its sides slope gracefully to
contain fourteen more lines on the dire effects of drunkenness.

Alfred Gibbs Campbell is unduly modest in his preface to *Poems*.
Of the verses he composed from 1851 to 1883, he says, "For want of
a more distinctive name, I call them 'Poems,' which possibly, in a
minor sense, they may be. I claim for them no literary excellence."
The poet, however, does occasionally offer fresh and imaginative
treatments of well-worn subjects. No distance separates the man
and his causes from his verse, and such personalization, along with
lively imagery and metrical variety, give vitality to many poems.

JAMES MADISON BELL
1826–1902

The "Bard of the Maumee"[1] was one of the nineteenth century's most articulate witnesses to racial oppression and to the black man's struggle for equality. "The burden of all our songs shall be/ To Lincoln, God, and Liberty!" Bell wrote, and for forty years (1860–1900) his poetic orations dramatized the Afro-American view of slavery, Civil War, emancipation, and Reconstruction. Ohio's first native black poet[2] was born in Gallipolis on April 3, 1826. Bishop Benjamin Arnett's lengthy panegyrical sketch of Bell in *Poetical Works,* the source of all other published biographies, remains vague about many years of the poet's life.[3] Nothing is known about Bell's family or his first sixteen years, spent in Gallipolis. From 1842 to 1853 Bell lived in Cincinnati and worked as a plasterer with his brother-in-law, George Knight, who had taught Bell the trade.[4] They were skilled craftsmen, for in 1851 Knight and Bell "received a contract for plastering the public buildings of Hamilton County."[5] Bell attended a Cincinnati high school established for

1. Arnett, p. 11. All quotations in the text are from Arnett and will hereafter be followed by parenthetical page references to his sketch.
2. William Coyle, *Ohio Authors and Their Books* (Cleveland: World, 1962), p. 47. For copies of Coyle's paragraph and suggestions of other sources I am indebted to John Mullane, Librarian, Public Library of Cincinnati and Hamilton County and to the Library of the Ohio Historical Society, Columbus. Neither library held any additional material on Bell.
3. Biographies derived from Arnett include Benjamin Brawley, *DAB* (1929) and *ENAW,* 279; brief references to Bell are in *Who Was Who in America,* rev. ed. (Chicago: Marquis, 1967), p. 119, and W. Stewart Wallace, comp., *A Dictionary of North American Authors Deceased before 1950* (Detroit: Gale, 1968), p. 37.
4. Cincinnati directories list Bell as a plasterer from 1849 through 1853. References courtesy of Frances Forman, Assistant Librarian, Cincinnati Historical Society.
5. Peter H. Bergman, *The Chronological History of the Negro in America* (New York: Harper, 1969), pp. 198–99.

colored people in 1844. He studied full-time during the winter and at night in summer and fall when he worked as a plasterer.

On November 9, 1847, Bell married Louisiana Sanderlin in a civil ceremony in Cincinnati;[6] according to Arnett, they had "a number of children" (7). In 1854 Bell moved with his family to Canada West (Ontario), where for six years he worked at his trade. In Cincinnati, Bell had been indoctrinated "into the principles of radical antislaveryism" (7), and now he became a friend and ally of John Brown, "The Hero, Saint and Martyr of Harpers Ferry" to whom Bell later dedicated *The Day and the War*. Brown arrived in Chatham, Canada West, for his provisional convention on April 29, 1858, and made his headquarters in Bell's home, living with Bell during the convention, May 8–10, and possibly until he left Canada on May 29.[7] The journal of Brown's convention lists Bell as one of five men chosen to select candidates for officers and as a signer of the revolutionary "Provisional Constitution and Ordinances for the People of the United States," adopted there in great secrecy.[8] Subsequently Bell enlisted men and raised funds for Brown's fateful raid in October, 1859.

Leaving his family in Canada, Bell departed for California and arrived in San Francisco on February 29, 1860, after a month's journey. In this city for the next five years Bell worked as a plasterer,[9] agitated for black educational and legal rights, served as steward of the A.M.E. Church and as a prominent lay member of their convention (1863) on the finance, ministry, and Sabbath schools committees. Meanwhile he wrote, published, and gave public readings of poetry. From 1862 until 1869 (although he left California in 1866) Bell's poetry frequently appeared in the *San Francisco Elevator* and *Pacific Appeal*. These papers also reported his poetry readings at the first "literary entertainment" of the San Francisco Literary Institute (1860), at the Bethel A.M.E. Church (1863), and at later gatherings in Ohio, Illinois, and Indiana (1867).[10]

Bell's first poem in pamphlet form was probably the one called

6. Marriage certificate, Hamilton County, Ohio.

7. Oswald G. Villard, *John Brown, 1800–1859* (1910; rpt. Gloucester, Mass.: Peter Smith, 1965), pp. 330, 338.

8. Transcribed in "The Outbreak in Virginia," *Anglo-African Magazine*, 1 (December, 1859), 369–83.

9. San Francisco *Directories*, references courtesy of Marian Marquardt.

10. Data courtesy of James de T. Abajian, Bibliographer, Martin Luther King, Jr., Special Collection, San Francisco.

simply *A Poem*, which he read in San Francisco on August 1, 1862, commemorating the emancipation of slaves in the District of Columbia. Two years later he recited *The Day and the War*, published with an "Argument" by Philip A. Bell, the poet's friend and editor of the *Pacific Appeal*, at the first anniversary celebration of the Emancipation Proclamation. For the third anniversary Bell composed *The Progress of Liberty* and delivered it at Zion Church on New Year's Day, 1866. Bell celebrated the Fifteenth Amendment with another ode, *The Triumph of Liberty*, read at the Detroit Opera House on April 7, 1870.[11]

Early in 1866 Bell returned to Canada for his family and, after a short stay there, established them in Toledo, Ohio. Bell's day-to-day movements from 1866 are sketchy, but he remained a plasterer and poet and assumed the additional roles of itinerant lecturer and politician. Through the late 1860's Bell lectured and read his poetry to freedmen in Ohio (accompanied at times by Bishop Arnett, whom Bell first met in 1866). He toured "all of the large cities of the North and South," including St. Louis, Baltimore, Louisville, Atlanta, and Charleston (10). In 1867, at a series of poetical readings in Washington, D.C., Bell met William Wells Brown. Brown described Bell as a handsome mulatto "of fine physical appearance" and praised his oratory, his logical, acute reasoning, and his "soul-stirring appeals" which inspired "enthusiasm of admiration" in his listeners.[12] For several years Bell, "holding the trowel in one hand and his pen in the other" (11), followed the trade of traveling poet-plasterer, alternating roles in the same winter-summer pattern of his early Cincinnati years. In Toledo from 1870 to 1873 he also served as superintendent of the A.M.E. Sunday School under the pastorate of Bishop Arnett.

Bell entered politics in 1872 as elected delegate from Lucas County (Toledo) to the state Republican convention. This body elected him as delegate at large from Ohio to the national convention in Philadelphia which nominated Grant for President (1872). Bell may have received such recognition from the party for his satiric exposé of President Andrew Johnson, "Modern Moses, or

11. In one of only three references to black poets, Bell's *Poem* and *The Day and the War* are praised by Lorenzo D. Turner, *Anti-Slavery Sentiment in American Literature* (Washington, D.C.: Association for the Study of Negro Life and History, 1929), pp. 114n–15n, 117n.

12. *Rising Son*, p. 505.

'My Policy' Man" (1868?). In any case, Bell campaigned for Grant but seems to have progressed no further in a political career.

Abandoning his traveling life about 1890, Bell rejoined his family in Toledo. In 1901, at Bishop Arnett's insistence, Bell collected and published his life's poetry in *Poetical Works*. He was seventy-five years old, and a portrait in *Works* (the only one of Bell that has survived) shows a well preserved although bald and wrinkled old man, decidedly Anglo-Saxon in features and complexion, staring with grim severity at a turn-of-the-century America which had failed to heed his repeated appeals for liberty and justice for Afro-Americans. James Madison Bell died in 1902,[13] memorialized in his *Works*, "a collection of the man—a busy man, a God-fearing man, a race-loving man" (13).

Bell's Poetry

The Bard of the Maumee's poetry requires such spirited dramatic recitals as Bell gave it on his reading tours, for on the printed page his over-long discourses are uniformly soporific. In his three longest poems, typical of all his work, both emotional force and intellectual conviction languish in abstractions, clichés, and monotonously regular meter and rhyme. Occasionally amid the generalities references to specific events, persons, or places rouse momentary interest. Bell varies his stanza lengths among four-, eight-, and twelve-line forms, and at times he adds a fifth foot to his steady iambic tetrameter. Otherwise the poems are indistinguishable from one another.[14]

The Day and the War (1864) takes the reader from slavery days through the Civil War to Emancipation in about 750 lines.

> America! I thee conjure
> By all that's holy, just and pure,
> To cleanse thy hands from Slavery's stain,
> And banish from thy soil the chain.
> Thou canst not thrive, while with the sweat
> Of unpaid toil thy lands are wet,
> Nor canst thou hope for peace or joy
> Till thou Oppression doth destroy.

13. Brawley, *DAB*.

14. Although direct influence is unlikely, Bell's historical narratives strongly resemble such earlier poetry as John Trumbull's "Prospect of the Future Glory of America" (1770), Timothy Dwight's "Greenfield Hill" (1794), and Joel Barlow's "The Columbiad" (1807); and compare Bell's "Modern Moses" to Philip Freneau's "George the Third's Soliloquy" (1779, rev. to 1809).

. . . .
And though they fell, as has been seen,
Each slept his lifeless foes between,
And marked the course and paved the way
To ushering in a better day.
Let Ballaklava's cannons roar,
    And Tennyson his hosts parade,
But ne'er was seen and never more
    The equals of the Black Brigade!

. . . .
And when the Nation shall convene
In mass, as ne'er before was seen.
And render eulogistic meeds
To worthy heroes' noble deeds,
A lengthened train shall claim their boast,
But LINCOLN'S name shall lead the host!

The Progress of Liberty (1866) in about 850 lines reviews the
four years of war and peace from 1862, liberty's triumph, and
Lincoln's martyrdom:

Hail! hail! glad day! thy blest return
    We greet with speech and joyous lay.
High shall our altar-fires burn,
    And proudly beat our hearts today.

. . . .
Liberia has been recognized—
    Also the Haytian's island home;
And lo! a Negro undisguised
    Has preached within the Nation's dome! [15]

. . . .
For lo! Arkansas doth rejoice,
And Texas sings with cheerful voice,
And Mississippi's heart doth swell,
And hail with joy the rising knell
Now sounding on her gulf-bound coast—
The dirge of a departed ghost.

To discuss "the changes of the last decade," Bell's *Triumph of
Liberty* (1870) requires over 950 lines. Prefaced as "a statement
of facts—not fiction" (which suggests Bell's problem as a poet),
the poem takes us again through slavery, John Brown's triumph,
the Civil War and its black heroes, and the changing fortunes of
Liberty. Frequent variations in metrical and stanzaic form here
cannot redeem the narrative from dullness:

15. Bell refers to John Willis Menard, the first black man to address the
House of Representatives (1869).

> Lift up your hearts, ye long oppressed,
>   And hail the gladsome rising dawn,
> For Slavery's night, that sore distressed
>   And tortured you, has passed and gone!
>
>   . . . .
>
> Hail! hail mighty Land with thy proud destiny!
> Enduring as time, all chainless and free!
> Hail! hail to thy mountains majestic and high,
> Reclining their heads against the blue curtained sky.

The poet similarly hails valleys, prairies, streamlets, oceans, cities, and railroads of the land of liberty:

> And hail to thy Telegraph, thy glory and prime,
> Defying all distance, and outstripping Time,
> Extending its arms through the heart of the sea
> And binding all Realms to the Land of the Free. . . .

A dozen shorter poems in *Works* echo the sentiments and language of Bell's major salvos to liberty and racial justice. "The Dawn of Freedom" celebrates William Wilberforce and abolition of slavery in the British West Indies; two poems commemorate emancipation in the District of Columbia; and "The Death of Lincoln," "Triumphs of the Free," and two poems for the first of August follow suit. "Admonition" warns that men are lords of all creation but not of other men, and it urges humanitarianism and brotherhood. "The Black Man's Wrongs" appeals for consistency in judging men:

> Look on the face of men like Ward,
>   Day, Douglas [sic], Pennington, and then
> Tell me whether these should herd
>   With beasts of burden or with men.

In the same vein Bell champions the right of contrabands to fight "the war for Freedom"; and in "Sons of Erin" he warns Irish-Americans to remember O'Connell and refrain from oppressing blacks as the English had the Irish.

Very few of Bell's poems digress from racial themes. "Creation Light" recounts the world's creation from a "shapeless, hetero-geneous mass" through the events of Genesis, "Till reason's torch illumined the mind" of man. Night and chaos will return when the world ends, but "God, Jehovah, Deity" will remain changeless. The "Descriptive Voyage from New York to Aspinwall" is a tedious journey; Bell's account of the sea and of Aspinwall are typical of his nature description:

> O! Thou eternal mystery,
> Thou grand, sublime, though awful sea,
> Alas, how oft thy fury smothers
> The last fond hope of wives and mothers.
>
> . . . .
>
> For rarer fruits and fairer flowers
> Scarce ever bloomed in Eden bowers,
> Than bud and bloom and ripen here
> Through all the seasons of the year.

Two acrostics offer philosophical advice, this to Mary Jane Wilson:

> Wisdom, bless'd wisdom, she speaks unto all,
> In the summer of life, prepare for the fall.
> Like apples of silver, or pictures of gold,
> So prize the rich moments of youth as they roll.

Outstanding among Bell's poems is "Modern Moses, or 'My Policy Man,'" a daring, original, and lively satiric assassination of the character and policies of Lincoln's successor, Andrew Johnson. The reactionary ex-Democrat is lumped with those despised braggart knaves and brainless wights raised to power by other assassins' blows. Worse than the murderer Cain is "My liege of graceless dignity,/ The author of *My Policy.*"

> But choose we rather to discant,
> On one whose swaggish boast and rant,
> And vulgar jest, and pot-house slang,
> Has grown the pest of every gang
> Of debauchees wherever found,
> From Baffin's Bay to Puget Sound.

With wit and irony Bell catalogues the treacheries of Reconstruction and lays them at Johnson's door. This modern Judas, "with arrogant unworthiness," had sworn to be the bondsman's friend and Moses. Instead he vetoed the Freedman's Bureau bill:

> He next reversed the bill of rights,
> Lest all the girls—that is the whites—
> Should Desdemonias [*sic*] become,
> And fly each one her cherished home,
> And take to heart some sooty moor,
> As Fathers did in days before.
>
> . . . .
>
> Would give the matrimonial hand
> Unto some swarthy son or other
> And some, perhaps, might wed a *brother.*

Bell observes Johnson's "blooming nose," crimson either from drink or his Policy, and his playing "the *knave and clown*" on a national tour which was "the grandest burlesque of the age." Johnson is treasonous and disloyal for his switch to support of Southerners:

> For he, to use a term uncivil,
> Has long been mortgaged to the Devil;
> But the fact which no one knows,
> Is why the deuce he don't foreclose.
> Perhaps he entertains a doubt,
> And fears that Mose might turn him out;
> Hence, *His Satanic* Majesty's
> Endorsement of *My Policy.*

This memorable political satire draws its vitality from Bell's skillful combination of the rhymed couplet form, concrete topicality, and uninhibited personal (rather than corporate) emotion.

Bell's sincere dedication to Afro-American freedom and rights is unquestioned. Oral delivery of the massive Liberty odes surely stirred audiences to enthusiastic aspiration, as Bishop Arnett claimed. But it is only in recital and to such audiences of the last decades of the century that Bell's poetry could ever seem "like the flowing of the mountain spring . . . bubbling, sparkling, leaping, rolling, tumbling, and jumping down the mountain side" (10). Bell's poetry, read today, lacks the spontaneity, natural vigor, particularity, and compression of thought and feeling which communicate poetic experience without the poet's physical presence. Artistic merit aside, James Madison Bell was undoubtedly *the* verse propagandist for Afro-Americans in his century.

SELECTED SOURCES

*Arnett, Benjamin W. "Biographical Sketch." In Bell's *Poetical Works* (1901). Pp. 3–14.
Brown, William Wells. *The Rising Son.* Boston: A. G. Brown, 1874. Pp. 504–5.
Redding, 44–47.

CHARLOTTE L. FORTEN GRIMKÉ
1837–1914

The City of Brotherly Love was "old abominable Philadelphia," a stronghold of segregation, to Charlotte Forten, who was born there on August 17, 1837, into the leading black family of the city.[1] Her grandfather, James Forten, had risen from a powder boy in the Revolutionary War to a sailmaker-merchant with a personal fortune of over $100,000. During the first three decades of the nineteenth century James Forten won national acclaim as the opponent of colonization and the champion of racial equality, moral reform, and, above all, abolitionism. In 1831 Forten contributed large sums and gathered subscriptions to launch Garrison's *Liberator*. During the next ten years his Lombard Street home, in which Charlotte spent much of her youth, became Philadelphia headquarters for Garrison and American Anti-Slavery Society workers. After his death in 1842 Forten's five children carried on his crusades. While tutors educated Charlotte at home to avoid the segregated schools, her aunts and uncles, her father, Robert Bridges Forten, and their activist friends taught her by example to despise prejudice and fight for racial justice.

After her mother's early death, Charlotte lived for several years with her uncle, Robert Purvis, an ardent Garrisonian, president of the American Anti-Slavery Society, and founder of the Vigilance Committee of Philadelphia. Purvis's palatial home, Byberry, was a refuge for radical abolitionists at this time and in later years when Charlotte also took refuge there. At the age of sixteen she moved to Salem, Massachusetts, to live in another abolitionist haven, the

---

1. Biography is from Miss Forten's *Journal*—the manuscript diaries are in the Howard University Library, Negro History Division—including Billington's introduction and notes, and from Mrs. Cooper's two-volume study. Unless otherwise noted, quotations are Miss Forten's from her *Journal*.

home of Charles Lenox Remond. Here, in May, 1854, Miss Forten began her remarkable *Journal,* and she enrolled at the integrated Higginson Grammar School for Girls. During the next eight years, although she took furloughs in Philadelphia and Byberry to recover her always fragile health and visited her brother Henry in New York City, Miss Forten's mind and heart never left New England.

Many of the century's outstanding orators, statesmen, and authors became her friends and correspondents in Salem. In Remond's home she met William Wells Brown and his daughter Josephine, with whom Miss Forten joined the Salem Female Anti-Slavery Society. Brown lavishly praised her poetry and prose, crediting her with "genius of a high order." He described her as standing "between the Anglo-Saxon and the African, with finely-chiselled features, well-developed forehead, countenance beaming with intelligence, and a mind richly stored with recollections of the best authors." [2] In her daily rounds of anti-slavery fairs, sewing circles, lyceum lectures, and abolitionist rallies, Miss Forten gained the friendship of Garrison, Lydia M. Child, Maria Chapman, Wendell Phillips, Lucretia Mott, and Charles Sumner. With the historian William C. Nell she discussed spiritualism—but remained a skeptic —and visited the great library of Theodore Parker. Most thrilling and lasting was her friendship with John Greenleaf Whittier, who came to call "on a day to be marked by a white stone." "A great and sudden joy has completely dazzled—overpowered me," Miss Forten wrote in her diary; "Whittier! one of the few men whom I truly reverence for their great minds and greater hearts" (August 10, 1857). In her charming "Personal Recollections of Whittier," Miss Forten later reviewed the growth of their mutual respect and tender affection through her visits to Amesbury and Oak Knoll, their correspondence and exchange of gifts until Whittier's death.[3]

Charlotte Forten's intimacy with radical abolitionists strengthened her hatred of prejudice and hypocrisy as well as her ambition for personal excellence and race advancement. In her *Journal* she expresses outraged despair every time a fugitive slave is brutally captured, anguish when she and her friends are barred from ice

2. *Rising Son,* p. 475.
3. Despite the difference in their ages, Whittier and James Forten had enjoyed a warm friendship. Among Forten's papers Charlotte discovered Whittier's verse tribute to her aunts, Margaretta, Sarah, and Harriet ("To the Daughters of James Forten"), and she published it in *AMECR,* 23 (April, 1907), 370.

cream saloons, trains, and museums in Philadelphia or when she
is snubbed by white schoolmates in Salem. Assailed by the din
of July Fourth celebrations, she denounces the mockery of freedom
in a land of slaves, and cries:

> Oh! it is hard to go through life meeting contempt with contempt,
> hatred with hatred, fearing, with too good reason, to love and trust
> hardly anyone whose skin is white,—however lovable, attractive and
> congenial in seeming. In the bitter, passionate feelings of my soul
> again and again there rise the questions "When, oh! when shall this
> cease?" "Is there no help?" "How long oh! how long must we con-
> tinue to suffer—to endure?" (September 12, 1855).

Miss Forten did not give in to "ignoble" despair but vowed to ac-
quire knowledge and work earnestly for the eventual ascendancy
of "Liberty, Truth," and universal brotherhood. To the limits of
her strength she pursued this dual goal. In February, 1855, she
graduated from the Higginson School and, a month later, entered
Salem Normal School. After graduating with distinction in July,
1856, Miss Forten taught in the all-white Epes Grammar School
of Salem until her failing health forced her to resign in March,
1858. The *Salem Register* expressed the community's regret, noting
that she had earned the respect and affection of teachers, parents,
and pupils during her happy and most useful connection with the
school.

Although Miss Forten again taught in Salem in 1860 and 1861,
she found "a teacher's life not nearly as pleasant as a scholar's."
A program of self-education, begun in her teens, included studying
French, Latin, and German, and extensive reading—as many as
one hundred books a year—of authors like Macaulay and Rollins,
the Brontës, Dickens, Hawthorne, Phillis Wheatley, all the New
England poets, her "beloved *Liberator*," and a great favorite, Mrs.
Browning. In Salem she joyously imbibed music, art, Shakespearean
drama, and the wisdom of great orators like Parker Pillsbury (her
Luther), Lowell, Agassiz, and Emerson. Deeply impressed by these
intellectual riches and the achievements of noble men and women
around her, Miss Forten continually deplored her own ignorance
and "utter insignificance." With "sorrow, shame and self-contempt"
she mourned her lack of wit, beauty, talent, intelligence, and ac-
complishment. Although she did possess a greater than average
share of these attributes and many kind friends to encourage her,
Miss Forten was a lonely, love-starved girl, longing now for a
mother's love or a letter from her father, and later for "some great

emotion to rouse the dormant energies" of her nature. At twenty-one she expressed this need in a "forlorn old maid's reverie":

I am *lonely* tonight. I long for one earnest sympathizing soul to be in close communion with my own. I long for the pressure of a loving hand in mine, the touch of loving lips upon my aching brow. I long to lay my weary head upon an earnest heart which beats for me,—to which I am dearer far than all the world beside. There is none, for me, and never will be (November 15, 1858).

Three years later adventure and perhaps love entered Miss Forten's life. In August, 1862, with a letter of recommendation from Whittier, she asked the Boston Educational Commission to send her to the Sea Islands of South Carolina as a teacher. Here the Port Royal experiment to educate and acculturate recently emancipated slaves was in progress. Miss Forten was turned down in Boston, but J. Miller McKim, acting for the Philadelphia Port Royal Relief Association, gladly accepted her services, and on October 24, 1862, she sailed from New York for St. Helena's Island. The voyage seemed inauspicious, for she wrote: "Of all the doleful, dismal, desperate experiences, sea-sickness is certainly the dolefulest, dismalest, and desperate-est." However, from the landing at Hilton Head until May, 1864, Miss Forten, braving heat, fleas, and warfare, taught and succored contrabands of all ages, worked in their store and in the military hospital. She was among the first to appreciate and set down the hymns and shouts of the Sea Islanders, and she contributed a valuable record of the Port Royal experience in vivid letters to the *Liberator* and to Whittier, which he had published in the *Atlantic Monthly*. Among her many friends at Port Royal, Miss Forten most admired Edward L. Pierce, pioneer superintendent of the project, Colonel Thomas Wentworth Higginson,[4] commander of the valiant black regiment of First South Carolina Volunteers, and, above all, Dr. Seth Rogers, surgeon of the regiment. In 1860

4. An anonymous obituary of Mrs. Grimké says, "There is a tradition that she might have been Mrs. Higginson instead of Mrs. Grimké had she so desired." The writer suggests they had a love affair in the mode of Garrison–Susan Paul and Charles Redmond–Maria Weston (Chapman); "Death in the High Ranks of Afro-America," *AMECR*, 31 (October, 1914), 217–18. Edmund Wilson, "Northerners in the South: Charlotte Forten and Colonel Higginson," *Patriotic Gore* (1962; rpt. New York: Oxford University Press, 1969) remarks on Miss Forten's popularity and says her relations with Dr. Rogers "decidedly give us the impression of verging on a genuine love affair" (pp. 252–55). Wilson's "Charlotte Forten and Colonel Higginson," *The New Yorker* (April 10, 1954), pp. 120–31, is primarily a historical account of the Port Royal experiment and does not suggest a romance.

Miss Forten had been restored to health by Dr. Rogers's water cure at Worcester, and now, responding to "a magnetism about him impossible to resist," she found "unspeakable happiness" in their many romantic excursions through the semi-tropical islands.

On her return from Port Royal in June, 1864, Miss Forten lived for a time in Philadelphia and the Cambridge-Boston area, where she was assistant secretary of the teachers' committee of the Freedmen's Aid Society. When the Society disbanded, she moved to Washington, D.C. Here her childhood dream of finding "the friendship of a great, a truly noble *genius*" seems to have materialized. In 1877 she met Francis James Grimké, son of the South Carolina planter Henry Grimké—a brother of abolitionists Sarah and Angelina (Mrs. Theodore Weld) Grimké—and his slave Nancy Weston. Francis Grimké, an honors graduate of Lincoln University and Princeton Theological Seminary, would gain national renown as a race leader, writer, and distinguished pastor of Washington's Fifteenth Street Presbyterian Church. When they were married on December 19, 1878, Miss Forten was forty-one, thirteen years older than her husband. A daughter, Theodora Cornelia, born January 1, 1880, died six months later, and the marriage remained childless. Otherwise, their union of thirty-six years seemed ideally happy as they worked with equal vigor for racial equality and shared a love of music, art, and literature that made their home a social and cultural center.

Except for four years spent in Jacksonville, Florida (1885–89), the Grimkés lived in Washington, where for a time Mrs. Grimké worked as a clerk in the Treasury Department and served as trustee and secretary of the board of the Westborough Insane Hospital. During these years she wrote a few more poems, many well-informed fiery letters on racial issues to newspapers, essays on art, the Philadelphia Exposition (1876), and Washington events, and her moving tributes to Frederick Douglass and Whittier.[5] Intellectual and emotional maturity mark this late work, which reveals her fine talent for strong, succinct, and beautifully descriptive prose. Having suffered from "lung fever" all her life, Mrs. Grimké was an invalid from 1887. The Reverend Francis Grimké describes her terminal five-year illness, during the last thirteen months of which she was confined to bed, preceding her death on July 23,

5. Mrs. Grimké's poetry, letters, and prose are conveniently found only in Mrs. Cooper's volumes.

1914. Condolences and eulogies from their many friends expressed such sentiments as this, from a letter by Richard T. Greener:

> Her life was long and beloved, because she always gave so cheer-fully of herself, her thoughts, and her kind offices to all of her friends, without looking for return; always gracious, always natural, and al-ways smiling. Those of us who have had a long advantage of her ac-quaintance can never forget her. We shall miss her, as well as you, and her presence will be with us among the sweetest of life's mem-ories.[6]

To perpetuate her memory, Grimké endowed a scholarship in her name at Lincoln University. But the most valuable legacy remains Mrs. Grimké's *Journal* of the turbulent years 1854–64, both a chron-icle of great men and events and a categorical imperative of racial justice.

Mrs. Grimké's Poetry

The fourteen published poems by Mrs. Grimké show a decided maturing of poetic technique and sentiment from 1855 to the 1890's. In the *Journal* she disparages her earlier efforts. When compli-mented on her first poem, "To W. L. G. on Reading His 'Chosen Queen'" (which she had signed, "C. L. F."), Miss Forten replied, "If I ever write doggerel again I shall be careful not to sign my own initials." The verse is a warm and worshipful accolade to Garrison, who battles "With truer weapons than the blood-stained sword,/ And teachest us that greater is the might/ Of *moral* war-fare, noble thought and word." Similarly schoolgirlish is "A Part-ing Hymn," written "for examination" in 1856 at Salem Normal School. The "onward and upward" counsel of this sentimental fare-well are set in a pleasing, naturally flowing meter. Miss Forten read another poem of 1856, titled simply "Poem," at her normal school graduation. She was "heartily ashamed" of the "poor, miserable poem," and hoped it would not be published. "I think this will be the last of my attempts at poetizing," she wrote. The *Salem Reg-ister*, however, complimented the skillful writing and graceful de-livery of "Poem," which is but a slightly inferior sequel to Long-fellow's celebrated "Psalm of Life":

6. Quoted in Cooper, II, 42, with other letters and the Reverend Francis Grimké's obituary of his wife.

> No vain dreams of earthly glory
>   Urge us onward to explore
> Far-extending realms of knowledge,
>   With their rich and varied store;
> But, with hope of aiding others,
>   Gladly we perform our part;
> Nor forget, the mind, while storing,
>   We must educate the heart,—
>
> Teach it hatred of oppression,
>   Truest love of God and man;
> Thus our high and holy calling
>   May accomplish His great plan.

Among five poems of the years 1858–60, "Two Voices" (1858) offers a choice to a "homeless outcast": voice one counsels retributive "hate for hate and scorn for scorn" or the peace of the grave; voice two (which wins) exalts altruistic striving and suffering in a "holy cause" as far nobler. "The Wind among the Poplars" (1859) is a monologue on a lover lost at sea, and "A Slave Girl's Prayer," a diffuse supplication for death as the "only hope of peace." The best of this group is "The Angel's Visit" (1860?), which, said William Wells Brown, "for style and true poetical diction, is not surpassed by anything in the English language." [7] His compliment is perhaps extreme, but "The Angel's Visit" offers admirable variation in emotional range, a sustained narrative line, and adroit matching of sound and sense. In easy-flowing lines Miss Forten maintains a dreamlike mood edged with pathos for the musings of a sensitive motherless girl. Her despair is conveyed tersely:

> For bitter thoughts had filled my breast,
>   And sad, and sick at heart,
> I longed to lay me down and rest,
>   From all the world apart.

But after her angel mother's visit in a dream, the girl's soul knows harmony and peaceful courage, melodiously expressed in this final stanza:

> I woke, and still the silver moon
>   In quiet beauty shone;
> And still I heard amid the leaves
>   The night wind's murmuring tone;

7. *Rising Son*, p. 475.

> But from my heart the weary pain
> Forevermore had flown;
> I knew a mother's prayer for me
> Was breathed before the throne.

Among later poems "Charles Sumner" (1874) places this warrior among the "glorious band" of "Poet, and saint, and sage, painter and king" depicted in paintings which decorate his home, and the poet seeks guidance and courage from his departed spirit. "At Newport" (1888), a love poem in blank verse, sustains an artistic comparison of the sea's action to the heart's emotions. Another poem, "The Grand Army of the Republic," in ten four-line stanzas probably depicts Boston's Memorial Day celebration of 1890. The poet describes the proud march of the G.A.R., a society of Civil War Union veterans, and she draws a lesson from the past:

> The dead, the living,—All—a glorious host,
> A 'cloud of witnesses,'—around us press—
> Shall we, like them, stand faithful at our post,
> Or weakly yield, unequal to the stress?
>
> . . . .
>
> Lo, shall this day the joyous promise be
> Of golden day for our fair land in store;
> When Freedom's flag shall float above the free,
> And Love and Peace prevail from shore to shore.

Mrs. Grimké's last dated poem, "In Florida" (1893), recalls with yearning Florida's lush, fragrant flora and mild blue skies. The color, warmth, and indolence of the scene are communicated by personified Nature.

Two poems in blank verse of later years (undated) are Mrs. Grimké's best efforts. Richness is obtained through the use of run-on lines and shifting of caesuras and syllabic stress. "Charlotte Corday" (28 lines) has a tone of quiet simplicity and controlled tension which conveys this martyr's determined courage before her dramatic murder of Marat:

> She leans her head against her prison bars
> How wearily! The heavy, tear-dimmed eyes
> Gaze at us, from the pale pathetic face,
> In utter mournfulness. One slender hand
> Clasps the rough bars; the other holds the pen
> With which, in words with love and courage fraught,
> She bids farewell to kindred, home, and life.

The other poem, "Wordsworth" (20 lines), appreciatively greets the "Poet of the serene and thoughtful lay!" In youth, Mrs. Grimké writes, we cherish "The thrilling strains of more impassioned bards":

> But, in our riper years, when through the heat
> And burden of the day we struggle on,
> Breasting the stream upon whose shores we dreamed,
> Weary of all the turmoil and the din
> Which drowns the finer voices of the soul;
> We turn to thee, true priest of Nature's fane,
> And find the rest our fainting spirits need,—
> That calm, more ardent singers cannot give. . . .

The "mild and steadfast" quality of Wordsworth's tranquil song is nicely echoed in this tribute. Charlotte Forten Grimké was not a major poet; however, the quality of her mature verse and of her poetic prose indicates that she possessed sensitivity and creative skills beyond the ordinary.

SELECTED SOURCES

Brown, *BM*, 190–99.

Brown, William Wells. *The Rising Son*. Boston: A. G. Brown, 1874. Pp. 475–76.

*Cooper, Anna Julia. *Life and Writings of the Grimke Family*. 2 vols. in 1. "Personal Recollections of the Grimke Family," I; "The Life and Writings of Charlotte Forten Grimke," II. N.p.: Author, 1951. Copy: NNSch.

Dannett, Sylvia. *Profiles of Negro Womanhood*. Yonkers: Negro Heritage Library, 1964. I, 86–93.

*Forten, Charlotte L. *The Journal of Charlotte L. Forten*. Ed. Ray A. Billington. New York: Dryden, 1953.

Frazier, S. Elizabeth. "Some Afro-American Women of Mark." *AMECR*, 8 (April, 1892), 381–83.

JOHN WILLIS MENARD
1838–93

On July 30, 1968, the U.S. House of Representatives celebrated the hundredth anniversary of the election of the first black congressman, John Willis Menard.[1] The oratory in 1968 contrasted sharply with the acrimonious debates of the Fortieth Congress when Menard's election (November 3, 1868) from the second congressional district of Louisiana was contested by his white opponent, Caleb S. Hunt. The controversy, complicated by legalities of redistricting, contested elections, and the status of reconstructed Southern states, generated accusations of political chicanery, race prejudice, and fraud and coercion at the polls. Almost two months after Menard's certificate of election from Governor Henry C. Warmoth had been received, the House resolved that neither Menard nor Hunt was entitled to the seat and awarded compensation of $1,500 to each man.[2]

Although Menard never served, he was the first black man to speak in the House of Representatives. He argued the merits of his claim and insisted that the House show him no favor on account of his race but decide the case "on its own merits and nothing else." [3] Menard's fifteen-minute address drew widespread press comments

1. *Congressional Record* (House), 90 cong., 2 sess., pp. 24281–92.
2. *Congressional Globe*. All biographies of Menard state that he *won* the election and was excluded from Congress on account of his race. Constance M. Green, *The Secret City* (Princeton: Princeton University Press, 1967), repeats the often-quoted remark "attributed to James Garfield that it was 'too early to admit a Negro to Congress'" (p. 94). John Mason Brewer, *Negro Legislators of Texas and Their Descendants* (Dallas: Mathis, 1935), and others state that Menard was seated as a member of the Fortieth Congress in July, 1868 (p. 19). Detailed analysis of the *Globe* transcript, however, suggests that political opportunism and legal complexities of Reconstruction were at least as responsible for Menard's rejection as was racial prejudice.
3. Speech printed in full in *Globe*, p. 1683, and *Lays*, pp. 2–6. Engraving of Menard addressing Congress is in *A Pictorial History of the Negro in America*, eds. L. Hughes and M. Meltzer (New York, 1968), p. 209.

97

98 Invisible Poets

which he later reprinted in his book of poetry, *Lays in Summer Lands* (1879). These notices support Menard's election and lay his exclusion to racial bigotry and Democratic party villainy. They also offer the only descriptions of Menard that we have. The *Worcester Spy* said he was "a man of good stature and stout body, young and pleasant looking in the face, and features of which, though heavy, are mobile and vivacious, while the color is a dark brown." The *Cincinnati Commercial*, on the other hand, said that he had "of blood about half and half of two races," and, they added, "a nicely developed head phrenologically considered." Several papers agreed with the *New York Herald*'s praise of Menard's "cool readiness and clearness," his distinct delivery and commanding presence before the House.

John Willis was not the first Menard to enter public life. Pierre Menard (1766–1844), a "fur trader, merchant, and statesman" of French origin, migrated from Canada to Kaskaskia, Illinois, in 1791. He became the state's first lieutenant governor, and in 1839 an Illinois county was named in his honor. Pierre's nephew, Michael Branamour Menard (1805–56), was an Indian trader who founded Galveston, Texas, and Menard County in central Texas was named for him in 1858.[4] Although the precise relationship of these white pioneers to John Willis Menard remains unclear, they were probably his paternal forebears. John Willis was born in Kaskaskia, Illinois, on April 3, 1838. He worked on a farm for his first eighteen years; then he attended school in Sparta, Illinois, and in 1859 enrolled at Iberia College in Ohio.[5] Menard came to Washington, D.C., during the Civil War, probably early in 1862, to work as a hospital steward and then as a recruiting agent in Baltimore.[6] Appointed a clerk in the Bureau of Emigration in the spring of 1862, he thus became the first federal clerk of his race.

Menard strongly supported colonization efforts of the time. From

4. *DAB* (1933), pp. 528–29, 529–30. John Willis is not mentioned in either *DAB* entry, but the fact that both Pierre and Michael lived in Kaskaskia, John's birthplace, and that their ancestral relation to John is stated (without their names) by Barbadoes, suggests that John's father was from this family. Menard's death certificate gives Illinois as the birthplace of both his parents (their names are not given).
5. Biographical data are from Gibbs and Barbadoes unless otherwise noted. Iberia College (Presbyterian) was chartered in 1854, became Ohio Central College, and was discontinued in 1887. No record of Menard's schooling can be located. Information courtesy of John Mullane, Public Library of Cincinnati and Hamilton County, Cincinnati, Ohio.
6. *New Orleans Republican,* quoted in *Lays,* p. 10.

Washington on March 10, 1863, he wrote "A Reply to Frederick Douglass," denouncing Douglass's approval of black cooperation in the war and his belief that the races could live justly and peaceably together in a unified America. Rather, Menard favored black pacifism, separatism, and emigration. The war, he wrote, "is to consolidate the broken domain of the American Union," but clearly,

> this is a *white* nation; white men are the engineers over its varied machinery and destiny; every dollar spent, every drop of blood shed and every life lost, was a *willing* sacrifice for the furtherance and perpetuity of a white nationality. . . . Sir, the inherent principle of the *white majority* of this nation is to refuse FOREVER republican equality to the black minority.

Therefore, Menard continues, "the prosperity and happiness of our race and their posterity lay in a separation from the white race." Black people should "go to Africa or some other seaport," he concludes, and leave the whites to settle the war they began by themselves. Shortly afterward, perhaps in the summer of 1863, the emigration commissioner sent Menard to British Honduras to investigate it as a possible site for a black colony.[7] A report was published on his return to Washington late in 1864, but nothing ever came of it.

From 1865 until 1871 Menard lived in New Orleans and worked as a customs inspector and street commissioner. Here he also published a newspaper, the *Free South* (later the *Radical Standard*), and made his celebrated bid for Congress. Menard moved to Florida in 1871, residing in Jacksonville and Key West until 1888. As editor and publisher, he established the (Jacksonville) *Florida Sun* in 1872, and from 1881, with his son Willis T. Menard as publisher, he edited the *Key West News* (also called the *Florida News*) and the *Southern Leader* out of Jacksonville.[8]

Thomas Gibbs, in a biography of 1887, complimented Menard on his "peculiar qualifications" as an editor: "Fearless, independent and well trained; with an almost intuitive perception of a situation, a broad acquaintance with men and events, a skillful manager and a manhood of almost youthful vigor, he has yet before him a long life of usefulness" (432). During his seventeen years in Florida, Menard was also a clerk in the Jacksonville post office, a deputy col-

---

7. A poem in *Lays* is titled: "Estella, in Honduras, 1863."
8. The papers were weeklies with circulations of 400–500. Rowell's *American Newspaper Directory* (1873, 1885, 1886), pp. 46, 73, 84; Ayer's *American Newspaper Annual* (1883), pp. 135, 830.

lector of internal revenue, and a justice of the peace. He served a
term in the Florida legislature and in 1876 was elected a delegate
to the Republican national convention in Cincinnati.

Nothing is known about Menard's private life, but three poems
in his *Lays in Summer Lands* suggest that he married a Jamaican
woman and had two children, a boy and a girl.[9] Menard returned
to Washington for the five years before his death at age 55.[10] He
died of pulmonary emphysema on October 8, 1893, at which time
his occupation was given as "clerk." Menard was survived by his
widow and is buried in Washington's Graceland Cemetery.[11] In the
introductory biography to *Lays*, F. G. Barbadoes praised Menard
for his "capable and faithful" public service, which merited ap-
proval of his race and "of every true lover of justice and equality."
As if Barbadoes could envision the congressional celebration of
1968, he added, "I am sure that none will hesitate to award him the
merit he deserves, or deny him the place in history to which he is
justly entitled."

Menard's Poetry

Lays in Summer Lands, Menard's only published volume, con-
tains sixty-three verses. Its dedication to a lady "friend of past
years" is an appropriate beginning, for the major subject of Me-
nard's verse is women. Over twenty-five love poems are addressed
to women named Estella, Lucy, Mary, Martha, and Susie, to others
with mysterious initials, and to many who remain wholly anony-
mous. Although these pleas for love and musings over lost love vary
metrically, their cajoling language lacks passionate conviction or
fresh imagery. The anonymous lady in "Just over the Sea" is typi-
cal:

> She's a sweet, fairy one,
>   Whose soft, mellow voice,
>   Has made me rejoice
> In hours that are gone.

9. "To My Wife. (At Kingston, Jamaica, West Indies.)"; "My Talisman";
"Just over the Sea."

10. In Washington, Menard published and edited the *National Afro-American*
from 1890 to 1891. No extant issues of the monthly have been located. Penelope
L. Bullock, *The Negro Periodical Press in the United States, 1838–1909*, disser-
tation, University of Michigan, 1971 (facsimile rpt., Ann Arbor: University
Microfilms, 1972).

11. Death certificate, District of Columbia. Menard died at 1626 11th Street,
N.W. He was buried on October 11, 1893.

> Her footsteps so light—
> With tresses that curl,
> And fine teeth of pearl,
> With eyes quite as bright.[12]

Menard is fond of phrases like "locks of raven hair," "rosy lips," and "queenly charms" for his lady friends, and for Nature combinations such as "woodland bowers–pensive hours," and "verdant trees–fleetful breeze." Two love poems and a tribute, "To General Grant," are acrostics, but the interesting form does not improve the poetry. The acrostic to Mary Frances Kiger begins:

> Majestic one! with regal form and mien,
> A modern type thou art of Egypt's queen:
> Robust and tall, and crowned with raven hair,
> You are my ideal of a woman fair!

A long, unrhymed recollection of his Honduras visit, "Estella," is prose set into verse lines:

> Then my guide and myself started off, in a red canoe
>   for the landing,
> And like lost sheep we strolled along through the
>   grassy streets of the village.

Menard's love poems are clumsy in execution and repetitive in sentiment. Moreover, their heavily serious tone is unrelieved by the humor or teasing banter which give charm to the love musings of a Walden or a Horton. The closest Menard comes to playfulness is in "To Lucy":

> Lucy, push your veil aside,
>   When you pass my store;
> Let me see those eyes you hide,
>   Then I'll love you more!
>
> Dreamy eyes and chubby face,
>   Let me see you more;
> Full of love and life and grace!
>   When you pass my store.

Some of Menard's tributes to famous people and his poems on racial themes are more successful. The meter of "On Grant's First Election" is deftly sustained:

> All hail the Chief! the good, the great—
> The new-made King of Liberty!

12. This lady was probably his bethrothed: she resides "Just over the sea/ In a green sunny isle," and "I'll soon call her *my wife*."

> Let cannon, bell, and trumpet sound,
>   From mountain, valley, plain and sea!
>   And Dark and Light
>   No longer fight
> For wrong has yielded unto Right!

There are poems in praise of Lincoln, the singer Madame Selika, Phillis Wheatley, and the abolitionists Garrison, Douglass, and Sumner. Menard's race pride is strong, and his tone is at times indignant and bitter. Although "The Negro's Lament" ends optimistically, it vividly condemns the hypocrisy and discrimination of "Columbia":

> So fair and yet so false! thou art a lie
>   Against both natural and human laws,—
> A deformed dwarf, dropp'd from an angry sky
>   To serve a selfish, and unholy cause.

The most effective poem in the collection is "Good-Bye! Off for Kansas":

> Good-bye ye bloody scenes of long ago!—
>   Good-bye to cotton fields and hounds!
> From you, vile sources of my earthly woe,
>   My freed and leaping spirit bounds!
>
> Though free, my work to me no profit yields,
>   And for my politics, am mobb'd;
> No more thank God! upon these bloody fields
>   Shall I be of my labor robb'd!

The poet says he will "not come back" to the South, for "This land is cursed; we are in rags, half fed,/ Bull-dosed and killed by Yellow Jack!"

Lays in Summer Lands also includes a few compliments to Florida and a grisly tale, "The Murdered Bride," on the theme of reverse race prejudice. The aesthetic value of *Lays* is generally low, but the verses do reveal that John Willis Menard's private life was happily more complex than his biographers knew, and that his stance on racial issues was far less conciliatory than the famous address to Congress had shown.

SELECTED SOURCES

*Barbadoes, F. G. Preface to *Lays in Summer Lands*. Pp. v–vii.
*The Congressional Globe. 40 cong., 3 sess. (1869: January 5, February 17, 27, March 3). Pp. 182, 1318, 1683–96, 1875–76.

*Gibbs, Thomas V. "John Willis Menard, the First Colored Congressman Elect." *AMECR*, 3 (April, 1887), 426–32.

"Men of the Month." *Crisis*, 9 (January, 1915), 117 (date of birth incorrect).

Menard, Edith. "John Willis Menard." *NHB*, 28 (December, 1964), 53–54. All material is from *Lays*. Miss Menard is the poet's great-granddaughter.

———. "100th Anniversary of the Election of the First Negro: John Willis Menard." *NHB*, 31 (November, 1968), 10–11. Same as above.

Robinson, Wilhelmina S. *Historical Negro Biographies*. New York: Publishers Co., 1967. Pp. 99–100.

(ALFRED) ISLAY WALDEN
1847?–84

"As a Christian, I endeavor to do all I can for Christ; as a student, to compete with my class-mates; as a politician, to prove true to my country; as a citizen, to be law-abiding." [1] Walden wrote this credo only seven years after his emancipation. He had been a slave for eighteen years when in 1865, illiterate and half-blind, he set out to become an educated citizen and Christian minister. Walden was born into slavery in Randolph County, North Carolina, and sold twice as an infant.[2] The young boy, a skillful carpenter and hotel servant, was known as a "prodigy in figures" whose masters exploited his talent for reckoning by exhibiting him and betting on his ability to do difficult mental calculations. Walden was driving oxen in a North Carolina gold mine when informed that Lee had surrendered to Grant and that he was now free. He worked in other mines for a time; then, in the winter of 1867–68, he walked from western North Carolina to Washington, D.C., seeking medical help for his near-blindness and teachers to educate him for the ministry. In Washington, Walden supported himself by manual labor, wrote some political ballads and sold them on the streets, and organized several Sabbath schools for poor black children. His efforts were commended by J. L. H. Winfield, an official in the War Department, who had watched Walden's "steady growth in grace, his rapid mental development, his unceasing devotion to principle, and his earnest labors in behalf of the poor of his race" from the beginning of his stay in Washington.

1. Letter to Nancy Jane Smitherman, May 8, 1872, in *Miscellaneous Poems*, p. 21.
2. Walden's biography to 1877 is largely from introductions by J. L. H. Winfield and "C. C. H." and Walden's letters in *Miscellaneous Poems*, and from a "Sketch of His Life" by William R. Taylor in *Sacred Poems*.

Walden left the capital after about three years to work his way through Pennsylvania and New Jersey as a lecturer. He memorized several chapters of a textbook on anatomy and delivered these as a lecture on "Anatomy and Hygiene," afterward taking up a collection and selling his poetry to small-town audiences along the way. In this manner he came to New Brunswick, New Jersey, where on April 18, 1871, he was examined by the board of education of the Theological Seminary and recommended for "the usual certificate from Classis." [3] Shortly thereafter the Second Reformed Church of New Brunswick granted Walden a scholarship of $150 a year to study at Howard University, and he returned to Washington in the summer of 1872. Although by this time Walden had supposedly written many poems and could read well enough to master anatomy, he was tutored for three weeks by the daughter of a Howard professor until he could "write something which *resembled* his name, read pretty well in the Second Reader," and do long division (C.C.H.). Now he was ready to enter Howard's preparatory department, where he progressed rapidly in his studies. To raise money for living expenses Walden published *Miscellaneous Poems* in 1872 and an enlarged edition a year later.

In 1876 Walden graduated from Howard's normal school [4] and soon enrolled at New Brunswick Theological Seminary. In a letter of 1878 Walden describes his difficult life as a destitute seminary student. His defective vision compelled him to hire fellow students to copy lectures and to read to him. Unable to earn the usual fees for Sabbath preaching because there were no colored churches in the area, Walden begged the aid committee for loans to pay rent and gas bills, and in 1877 he published *Sacred Poems* to raise funds. While at the seminary Walden realized that his own sufferings were multiplied tenfold in the black community of New Brunswick. In October, 1877, he established a "Student's Mission" for sixty boys and girls he "gathered from the streets," two-thirds of whom, he writes, "were drunkards children," and some so destitute that he "had to buy soap that the peculiar scavengers might be removed." Walden ran his mission for two years, fighting the "overwhelming prejudice" of whites and the apathy of blacks. For the children he led a Sabbath school, organized a temperance society (the children

3. "Minutes of the Classis."
4. Walden's name appears in the *Catalogues of the Officers and Students of Howard University* (1872–76). His graduation is confirmed by W. A. Sojourner, Registrar, in a letter to me.

reformed their parents), a music class, a singing school, and a sewing circle; for the adults he set up a Benevolent Society. Walden labored without remuneration. Surely, he writes, New Brunswick students have "as much love for humanity" and are "equally responsible as to the welfare of our fellow beings" as Princeton and Yale seminarians who conducted Sabbath schools for their black communities.

After three years at the seminary Walden was examined, licensed, and ordained by the classis of New Brunswick on May 29, 1879.[5] He served the Presbyterian Church South that summer, and in the fall the American Missionary Association sent him as an evangelist to Lassister's Mills, North Carolina. The former slave returned to his birthplace, Randolph County, a certified teacher and minister. His field superintendent, Dr. Joseph Roy, described the joyful welcome home Walden received from his kinfolk, former fellow bondsmen, and the family of his old master. With Dr. Roy's assistance Walden organized a Congregational Church of twenty members; its sanctuary was a forest clearing. Within one year the congregation grew to sixty. They had a school and a frame church built through Walden's inspiration and direction which cost, by their minister's reckoning, four dollars in cash and 533 man and woman days of strenuous labor. In the autumn of 1880 they dedicated their "work of love," christening it "Promised Land Church." [6] Islay Walden spent the remaining four years of his life serving the Lassister's Mills congregation. He died there in 1884.

Walden's Poetry

In "Introductory Verses" to *Miscellaneous Poems* (1872), Walden acknowledges the smallness of his God-given poetic talent but hopes that each rhyme, like the biblical mustard seed, may be the "little thing/ From which the great and noble spring." He dedicates this volume "to the cause of Education and Humanity," and a year later, introducing a second edition, Walden rejoices that his verse has been found "useful." However, he again cautions the reader not to expect miracles:

5. "Minutes of the Classis."
6. References in the *American Missionary* indicate that in 1880 Walden also pastored the Salem Church of Troy and Hilltown, North Carolina. Courtesy of Dr. Clifton H. Johnson, Director, Amistad Research Center, in a letter to me.

> Remember, too, in Dixie
>   That I was born a slave.
> And all my early genius
>   Was locked within the grave.
>
> Remember my condition—
>   A mark within my eyes—
> And all my inspirations
>   Are showered from the skies.
>
> I cannot read of authors,
>   Nor those of noble fame,
> For I'm just a learning
>   The author, Milton's, name.
>
> I cannot borrow subjects,
>   Nor rob them of their style,
> My book amid their volumes,
>   Like me, is but a child.

Walden's verse resembles George Moses Horton's in its childlike and pious vision of life and its unsophisticated techniques. Walden's serious pieces which attempt to educate or exhort are poor poetry, as are some dozen letters and odes, tributes to his benefactors and teachers, on the order of his fifteen-stanza "Ode to Gen. O. O. Howard":

> O lead him o'er the Rocky Mounts!
> And let him drink from sparkling founts;
> And when he's where the water gleams,
> Then let him bathe in crystal streams.
>
>   .   .   .   .
>
> And when from scenes like these we go,
> To journey on with friend or foe,
> May happy thoughts around be showered,
> When we recall the name of Howard!

Equally unassuming are the dozen religious verses in this volume, although there are gleams of unintended humor—such as in "Temperance," where the poet exhorts Jesus, "Go save the drunkards of the land."

Walden seldom comments on his race and previous enslavement. In the few verses which mention freedom and justice, he expresses no recrimination or protest. "The Nation's Friend" is a tribute to Sumner, who pilots the ship Justice and equal rights towards a bright city of brotherhood. Walden dedicates "An Address to Dixie" to "the good will of all persons towards the prosperity of the South."

He pities Dixie's "wounded station," exults in the slaves' freedom, but forgives all:

> But Dixie, oh, the land of cotton,
> Let slavery die and be forgotten;
> And we will turn unto each nation
> With greater zeal for education.
>
> . . . .
>
> O like the mighty swelling ocean,
> Whose billows roll with great commotion,
> The races yet will come together,
> In ties of love that none can sever.

Walden reveals his love for Howard University in poems such as "Prayer for the School," "The Golden Rule," and "Philadelphia, Sept., 1872" in which he praises the faculty, requests a room reservation and "ten catalogues" to be sent by express. Like Horton, Walden is most original in verses which treat events and emotions of every-day life. His frankness, affectionate regard for people, and natural joy in living give these pieces on love and occasions a unique charm. Walden invites love from many young ladies, although he assures us in "One to Love" that, unlike a Mormon, he would "be satisfied with one." In "The Young Man's Comforter" he extolls a bachelor's life, and in "To Miss N. J." he confesses his love, urges the lady to join him at college, but qualifies the invitation:

> I might tell thee my heart is willing
>   That I should be thy guide through life,
> But while I am not worth a shilling,
>   Why should I seek thee for a wife?

Walden's affectionate proposals are playful, never passionate. He keeps a safe distance by adroitly changing the subject, as in the poem "Dedicated to a Young Lady Representing the Indian Race at Howard University." [7] His praise for Clara's pleasant ways, cheering looks, and grace leads into a description of their encounter in the dining hall where Clara asks what they are eating, and the poet replies:

> It's pork of course, or else it's beef;
>   Perchance it may be ham—

7. Walden wrote this verse as a tribute to the Indian race. A headnote states that his experience at Howard makes him certain that Indians can be civilized and Christianized; that as his race proved its loyalty and manhood "with the Sword and by the ballot," likewise the Indians will "in perhaps twenty years to come, if they are justly dealt with. They only ask our Government to give them good and true men, and they will do their part" (pp. 59–60).

> Except the baker cooked a goose,
> And passed it off for lamb.

After this romantic exchange he regrets that the bell ending dinner has rung and he can no longer look upon her "brilliant charms." Again in "Correspondent Solicited" Walden assures the lady that his letters will thrill her with pleasure,

> For thou canst see the stars are bright,
> And worlds around are swelling.
> Therefore it will be thy delight
> To overlook my spelling.

Any incident is a likely subject for Walden's occasional verses. "The Little Helper" pays tribute to a child who helped him cross the street; a poem, "Dedicated to the Junior Society," memorializes his expulsion from that group. Seeing a skating party fall through the ice inspires Walden to write "The Icy Poem" in thirty quatrains, and he tenders two eulogies to seamstresses who made him shirts.

In such love and all-occasion rhymes we catch glimpses of a sympathetic, naive, and dryly witty young man who yearns with equal ardor for a companion and an education. Perhaps his best poem, because it is the most personal one, is "Wish for an Overcoat," "dedicated to my own necessities and wants." With touching detail Walden conveys the pathos of poverty:

> Oh! had I now an overcoat,
> For I am nearly freezing;
> My head and lungs are stopped with cold,
> And often I am sneezing.

> And, too, while passing through the street,
> Where merchants all are greeting,
> They say, young man this is the coat
> That you should wear to meeting.

> Then, looking down upon my feet,
> For there my boots are bursting,
> With upturned heels and grinning toes,
> With tacks which long were rusting.

Tantalized by new clothes he cannot afford, the youth contemplates a wintry grave. But even in this poem, surely drawn from Walden's own painful experience, he does not remain serious—or perhaps it is the reader who cannot take seriously the poem's ironic ending, the ragged student's wish for some Horatio to "tell the story,/ That I have lived a noble life" and that death came "Not by a cold alone,/ But partly bread and butter."

Walden's usual lighthearted response to things of this world is sadly missed in *Sacred Poems* (1877). These thirteen brief hymns extol the powers of God and Jesus and summon sinners to Christian faith and prayer with assurance of heavenly reward. Twelve of the verses are dated April 20 to May 6, 1877, and their hasty composition is evident in the uninspired repetition of sentiments, hymn-book language, and verse form. Stanzas are so alike that they may be readily interchanged among the hymns. A random combination of stanzas from three different hymns produces this "poem" which is no worse than one of Walden's originals:

> Great God, I love thy holy name,
>   And all thy blessings too;
> I will take heed to all my ways
>   And what I speak or do.
>
> O righteous Father, Holy One,
>   Behold my wearied soul,
> And help me while I try to reach
>   The final, Heavenly goal.
>
> Salvation Lord, belongs to thee,
>   The earth and sea are thine
> Nor blessed can the people be,
>   But through thy kingly line.

Only one hymn, "The Transition," is freshened by metaphor: man's life is compared to an ocean wave which struggles to reach the shore but is scattered by strong billows so that its identity is lost, part merging with the waters of the deep, part rising as vapors to the skies. But, Walden concludes, man is really not like the wave "whose parts can never meet,"

> Ah! no, for I'll arise
>   Upon the last great day;
> My spirit from its God shall come,
>   My body from the clay.
>
> United we shall stand
>   Eternally in one,
> Yes, in the likeness of my God
>   The image of His son.

Islay Walden's poetic skills were very limited, as he realized. However, it is remarkable that he so quickly rose from slavery by his own efforts and left a record in verse of his native intelligence, sensitivity, and courage. Although his didactic verse is commonplace, it illuminates his struggles, while the homespun pieces remain a precious legacy of Walden's ingenuous talent.

SELECTED SOURCES

"Minutes of the Classis of New Brunswick, April 19, 1853–October, 1882." Vol. V.

Raven, John H., comp. *Biographical Record Theological Seminary, New Brunswick, New Jersey, 1784–1934.* New Brunswick: Rev. A. Laidlie, 1934. P. 144.

Roy, Joseph E. "An Open Letter from Dr. Roy." *The Christian Intelligencer,* November 11, 1880, p. 9.

Walden, Islay. MS letter to Dr. Demarest, September 21, 1878.

Above materials and a graduation photograph of Walden are in the Gardner A. Sage Library, New Brunswick Theological Seminary.

ALBERY ALLSON WHITMAN
1851–1901

The Negro still invincible,
Bearing the tests of honor well,
Will leave with those who lead the van,
A proud, inevitable man . . .[1]

Honor, pride, and inevitable manhood—these words summarize the creed of Albery Whitman, who lived in bondage for twelve years but could later write, *"I never was a slave"*; rather, a boy who enjoyed the "blessings of cabin life and hard work," one who lost all his "substance" to slavery's laws but never his manhood. For Whitman, adversity was "the school of heroism, endurance the majesty of man and hope the torch of high aspirations" (NM; RF).[2]

The poet was born to slave parents in Hart County, Kentucky, on May 30, 1851.[3] His mother died in the spring of 1862, and his father just after emancipation.[4] Orphaned at the age of twelve, Whitman worked on the farm of his birth near Mumfordville, Kentucky, before moving on to Louisville. He lived there and in Cincinnati for a time. In Troy, Ohio, Whitman worked in the "plough shop" of A. T. Beedle & Company and attended common school for five months. Now about eighteen, he spent five months as a railroad construction worker, secured another two months of schooling in Troy, and became a schoolteacher in Carysville, Ohio, and in Kentucky near his old home. After teaching for about a year

1. "The Freedman's Triumphant Song" (1893), p. 5.
2. Unless otherwise noted, biography and quotations are Whitman's, from his prefaces to *Leelah Misled* (LM), *Not a Man, and Yet a Man* (NM), *Rape of Florida* (RF), *Twasinta's Seminoles* (TS, 1885).
3. Death certificate, Fulton County, Ga.
4. Whitman is known to have had at least one sibling, identified in 1934 as Kate Bright of Pratt, Kansas. John E. Green, letter to Mr. Valentine, NNSch.

(around 1870), Whitman enrolled at Wilberforce University, where he studied under Bishop Daniel A. Payne for six months and began his poetic career. *Essays on the Ten Plagues and Miscellaneous Poems* (1871?) sold about 1,000 copies (LM), but none of these has survived. Whitman's second work, *Leelah Misled* (1873), was an 1,180-line tale of seduction in white society.

Albery Whitman did not graduate from Wilberforce, nor does he record his ordination as an A.M.E. minister. However, in 1877 he was general financial agent of Wilberforce University, an elder in the church, and pastor of an African Methodist Episcopal congregation in Springfield, Ohio (NM). In 1877 he published *Not a Man, and Yet a Man*, a metrical extravaganza of over 5,000 lines on the loves and adventures of Rodney, an octoroon fugitive slave. The object of *Not a Man* was twofold: to publicize the high aims and accomplishments of Wilberforce, beneficiary of the book's profits, and to introduce the poet (who would welcome donations) to his public (NM). This extraordinary poem, dedicated to "The Abolition Fathers," did establish Whitman as the leading Afro-American poet of his day.[5] Nevertheless, he yearned to attain the poetic skills and national prominence of his idol, Henry Wadsworth Longfellow, whose influence on *Not a Man* is marked. On November 10, 1877, Whitman sent Longfellow a copy of *Not a Man* "as a tribute of respect," accompanied by a letter which salutes him as "Chief of American poets and friend of my poor race." In a second letter of January 27, 1878, Whitman thanks Longfellow for "the few lines" which "have already done great good" and asks him to further remember "that the one who was once a slave, and is now a young and poor man, is endeavoring to know something." Longfellow probably ignored this note, for on March 5, 1878, Whitman wrote again, humbly, apologetically, and devotedly, sending regards and a request for help from Whitman's "best friend," J. H. Hilton, who had known " 'the prince of modern bards' " and his father, Stephen, in Portland, Maine. This touching appeal, and Whitman's correspondence with Longfellow, concludes:

5. The dedication of *Not a Man*, in "free verse," is a moving declaration of Whitman's faith: "To those who loved the negro in mankind,/and pitied him,/and stooped to help him in his low estate,/assailed by fierce opinions,/and told his grievances in the ear of God,/until He heard them,/and shook proud slavery on His lap of storm,/and shook the fetters from the bondman's arms,/and safe now in the citadel of right,/their conquests hearing on the tongue of time,/their triumphs reading in young freedom's eyes,/and looking forward,/the full fruition of their bright hopes see,/the nations of all earth forever free."

And now while I again beg pardon for intruding, I *assure* you, Sir, that in *all of your life,* you never did an act of kindness to a poor young man who feels more indebted than I.

You have controlled my life. Had you not have said a kind word to me, I would have been discouraged, and ere this, had ceased to "try." You are my literary Salvation.

I pray each day that God may prolong your days. My greatest ambition is to see your face. And, I *intend* to see it. I go once a week to the Library here, to look on your picture.

Sincerely
A.A. Whitman[6]

Because of the favorable reception of *Not a Man,* Whitman wrote Longfellow, his wealthy friends were arranging to send him on a tour of Europe (January, 1878); therefore, he resigned his post at Wilberforce. The poet never got to Europe. Rather, for the next fourteen years he established churches and led congregations in Ohio, Kansas, Texas, and finally Georgia, at St. Philip's in Savannah and Allen Temple in Atlanta. Meanwhile, his renown as "Poet Laureate of the Negro Race" grew with *The Rape of Florida* (1884), reissued as *Twasinta's Seminoles* (1885, 1890), a romance of the Seminole Indian Wars; a collection of lyric poems, *Drifted Leaves* (1890); a pamphlet, *World's Fair Poem* (1893); and *An Idyl of the South* (1901), largely a tragic epic of a beautiful octoroon and her Southern aristocratic lover.

All of Whitman's protagonists in his long poems are octoroons, whites, or Indians of superior intelligence, moral and physical courage, and sensitivity. His ideal heroes are not black men, but Whitman was proud of his race and its potential. In 1884 he wrote:

> I am a negro, and as such, I accept the situation, and enter the lists with poised lance. I disdain to whine over my "previous condition." I despise the doctrine of the *slave's allowance.* Petition and complaint are the language of imbecility and cowardice—the evidences of that puerile fear which extinguishes the soul (RF).

Born in the year of *Uncle Tom's Cabin,* Whitman repudiated Mrs. Stowe's stereotypes. "The time has come when all 'Uncle Toms' and 'Topsies' ought to die. *Goody goodness* is a sort of man worship: ignorance is its inspiration, fear its ministering spirit, and beggary its inheritance" (RF). To counteract the goody-goods and clown-child-beast caricatures of a burgeoning minstrel tradition, Whit-

6. Whitman's letters are in the Houghton Library, Harvard University; I am indebted to Deborah B. Kelley for her research and the photocopies. Letters quoted by permission of the Harvard College Library.

man created larger than life virile men and passionate but chaste women, always self-sufficient, self-respecting, great-souled lovers of freedom and of others like themselves. Each was a paradigm of "America's *coming* colored man," as Whitman saw himself, "Genius, in a right good soul" whose creations "of real merit *only* will correct the world's judgement and force its respect." "To this end," he wrote, "I have laid out my life" (TS, 1885).

It is fitting that Whitman's heroes—his self-portraits—were not black men, for the poet's own complexion and features made him indistinguishable from white, according to his contemporary, the poet James Corrothers.[7] Whitman married a handsome woman, Caddie, who appears from her portrait to be entirely Caucasian. Their daughters were mistaken for white by theatrical agents who discovered them singing jubilee songs at a church concert. After the turn of the century the girls, Essie, Mable, and Alberta, became an acclaimed vaudeville team, the Whitman Sisters. From 1910 to 1930, joined in the later years by a stepsister, Alice, the sisters sang and danced in "every vaudeville house in the U.S.A.," played "command performances for European royalty," and ran a major theatrical booking agency. After 1930 Essie, Mable, and Alice (all now deceased) lived in Chicago, and Alberta moved to Arizona, where she was still living in 1969.[8] Undoubtedly Whitman would have enjoyed seeing the Whitman Sisters as "the toast of the Pantages Circuit" in the roaring twenties, but he did not live to share their triumph.

However, Whitman did enjoy recognition in his lifetime from critics and fellow poets, including William Simmons, Corrothers, George M. McClellan, and Bishop Payne.[9] McClellan lavished praise on *The Rape of Florida,* but he denounced "the man himself" for his lack of learning, his "expressible egotism," and for "styling

7. *In Spite of the Handicap* (New York: George H. Doran Co., 1916), p. 64.
8. "Beautiful Whitman Sisters Won International Acclaim on Stage," *Ebony* (March, 1954), p. 57; *Hue* (June 30, 1954), pp. 43–44; *Variety,* May 15, 1963; *Jet* (January 20, 1969), p. 44. In photos accompanying these articles, Essie appears to be the oldest sister, followed by Mable, Alberta, and Alice. Mable was deceased by 1954; Essie, an evangelist, died at 81 on May 7, 1963, in Chicago; Alice died at age 61 in January, 1969. If Alice's age at death is accurate, she was born in 1908, seven years after Whitman's death. In the photos Alice and Alberta strongly resemble each other (and their mother, Caddie), but not the older girls, while Essie and Mable are much alike and resemble Albery Whitman. Both younger girls, therefore, were probably only Caddie Whitman's daughters.
9. McClellan, "The Negro as Writer," in Culp, pp. 279–80; Payne, *Recollections of Seventy Years* (1888; rpt. New York: Arno, 1968), pp. 238–39.

himself as the William Cullen Bryant of the Negro race." For Payne, Whitman's *Not a Man* was "the greatest of all that can be called poetry," but he found a grievous flaw in his former pupil: "O Whitman, Whitman! canst thou not break the chains that bind thee to the chariot-wheels of intemperance? Why boast of thy freedom from the white man, and yet be the slave of alcohol?" Intemperance may indeed have hastened Whitman's death. He contracted pneumonia in Anniston, Alabama, and within a week (on June 29, 1901) had succumbed to the infection, with debility the contributory cause of death. At the age of fifty Whitman died at his Atlanta, Georgia, home and was buried in that city's South View Cemetery.[10] The poet was survived by his widow and their daughters.

Whitman's Poetry

"Poetry," Whitman wrote, "is the language of universal sentiment. . . . Her voice is the voice of Eternity dwelling in all great souls. Her aims are the inducements of Heaven, and her triumphs the survival of the Beautiful, the True, and the Good" (RF). His critical theory echoes Poe, and much of his poetry steps to the measures of Longfellow, Byron, Tennyson, Whittier, and Scott. But Albery A. Whitman had no less the ear for music, the eye for beauty, and the soul of these poets. He wished to emulate them but lacked their disciplined craftsmanship developed through long, secure years of apprenticeship and education he never knew. Twelve years a slave, Whitman transformed himself by manual labor and force of mind and will from a pauper farmboy into a respected minister and the poet hero of his race. Despite only a year of formal schooling, he became thoroughly conversant with the celebrated English and American poets he naturally adopted as models of "The Beautiful, The True, and The Good." Much of Whitman's poetry is technically weak and diffuse, marred by careless versification, burdened with overblown rhetoric and didactic digressions. However, he did supremely well with what he had: a sure dramatic sense, a talent for suspenseful narration, romantic description, communication of pathos, irony, and lovers' emotions, and the courage to attempt difficult meters and epic-length poems. Above all, he had a sense of honor, race pride, and a code of manliness which his poetry urged on all who struggled for racial progress. In the twenty-eight years from *Leelah Misled* to "The Octoroon,"

10. Death certificate.

Whitman's talent matured, his intellectual and emotional responses deepened, and his technical skills improved.

In *Leelah Misled* (1873), the heroine is a "sweet young blonde, of form and feature neat," a rosy-cheeked, blue-eyed, innocent and cheerful maiden, to the manor born. The poem's slim plot is the seduction and abandonment of Leelah by a wealthy philanderer, McLambert, a tale that requires at most fifteen of Whitman's 118 stanzas. *Leelah Misled* is largely a vehicle for the poet's thoughts and feelings on innumerable subjects, and his poetic models beckon from Parnassus:

> The battling gods of Milton's epic page;
> The loftiness of Byron's well wrought rhyme;
> The pictured thought of Shakespeare's peopled stage;
> The lay of Scott, and Spenser's verse sublime,
> Proud Europe have immortalized in song. (IV)
>
> . . . .
>
> Yet, since Columbia's fettered sons are free,
> May not one from the scenes which gave him birth
> Draw forth a lay, the theme of which may be
> No mean purport—nor tale of trifles' worth? (V)

Whitman's lay dwells on man's distortion of Nature's laws and beauties, the transience of human joy, national traits of Europeans, virtue and sin, the state of Georgia, excellence in women, time, and pagan and Christian religions:

> The Hindoo dies at Bramah's chariot wheels,
> The Mexican his human victims burn,
> The African before a serpent kneels,
> And learned Rome adores her sacred urns;
> Mahomet's votary for his prophet dies,
> And many tribes bow down to wood and stone,
> And think it right; but lauded to the skies,
> The precepts of the blessed Christ alone
> Are a religion, and these precepts are—
> Oppress no one, but for the injured care. (CXII)

A reader must pick his way through these "quagmires," as Whitman names his theological digressions, to find the story of Leelah and the moral of it all: To err is human, to forgive divine.

The versification of the 197-page *Not a Man, and Yet a Man* (1877) is as varied and fascinating as the escapades of its hero Rodney. Whitman mimics the music of other poets, but he adroitly employs each style to enforce the mood and meaning of a particular narrative sequence. The double plot of *Not a Man* is unified by its single action: the quest for freedom. Each trial proves Rodney's manhood, and each setback triggers a recovery on a level nearer his ultimate goal, Canada. Of Whitman's five long poems, *Not a Man* is least disturbed by preceptive asides, and its major characters are most competently developed. The brief summary and excerpts below can suggest Whitman's technical and narrative virtuosity, but only the whole poem can reveal its dramatic construction, a designed contrast of good and evil elements—men, events, places —which remains integral to the action, yet rises above it to give the poem an added ethical dimension.

The village of Saville, Illinois, and its luminaries are portrayed in musical rhymed couplets by a first-person narrator. He imaginatively reconstructs an Arcadia of sincere law-givers and simple villagers enjoying rude tasks and hunting. Parson David Deems is their soul-saver:

> And ever in his careful placid face
> The sweet light shone of vital inward grace,
> Like dawnings of a better world—no glare
> Of hot ambitions e'er ascending there,
> Nor earth's polluting fires. His was no mien
> Of sanctity affected, while between
> His precepts and his practice, regions lay
> Untraversed in his life; but as the day,
> The cloudless lustre of his zealous soul
> Beamed solid forth, and held in mute control,
> Or stirred with song-cheer all within his reach.
> He practiced how to live as well as preach.

Above all in virtue and physique towers Rodney. He is a fearless hunter, skilled woodsman, great lover, with all the traditional nineteenth-century virtues. The twenty-year-old, six-foot three-inch Rodney is only eighty-five per cent Saxon, however; therefore he is "held in chains."

Saville's heroes, culture, and metrical style are juxtaposed to those of the Sac Village, introducing the poem's Indian subplot in the verse of Longfellow's "Hiawatha":

> Ye who pore for weary hours,
> In the deep wild nooks of legend,
> In the forest-nooks of legend,
> Gath'ring up these strange old relics,
> For your idle thoughts to play with;
> Such as wigwams rude, and war posts,

> Belts of wampum, bows and arrows,
> Scalping knives, and rough stone hatchets,
>
> . . . .
>
> And inconstancy and cunning,
> In the savage world of promise;
> Ye who pore for weary hours
> In these pathless nooks of legend,
> Wake, and hear of Nanawawa.

Deep in the "woody depths of romance" Nanawawa, daughter of chief Pashepaho—"powerful and warlike stabber"—receives her suitors, falls in love with a captive slave, White Loon, and seduces him on the shores of her "lakelet": "In the right hand of Kaskaskia/ And the left hand of Cahokia,/ And the regions of the Wabash." Whitman readily sustains Nanawawa's trochaics for some twenty-six pages. At times they become hypnotically singsong:

> Nanawawa sang a camp song,
> And the Stabber joined the singing,
> Till asleep they sat and sang yet,
> Till they went to sleep a singing. . . .

Whitman returns to the heroic couplets of Saville to introduce its other citizens, villainous Sir Maxey and his white hunters. They plunder the Indian village and murder Nanawawa with sadistic ruthlessness that seems gratuitous in context. However, Rodney scores several dramatic points by standing fast as Sir Maxey flees when the Sacs retaliate.

The poem's basic contrast has been established. On one hand are the brave, innocent, and natural Indians of Sac Village, joined by a few estimable rustics of Saville and the heroic Rodney; on the other hand, the treacherous, "civilized" white men. More than half of the poem remains for Rodney's further adventures in love and war, as a slave and a freeman. In the honored tradition of American literary heroes, Rodney travels from village to city, from Northern forest to Southern plantation, over wastelands and across rivers. He fights an entire Indian tribe to rescue Sir Maxey's lovely daughter Dora; later he confronts Dora's suitors, who gaze in awe at Rodney on horseback, discount him as a rival, but then arrange to have him sold down South. The rich irony of Whitman's Elizabethan couplets exposes the swains' pretentious condescension:

> "A servant dog, a stalwart negro clown,
> Unhorse a knight, the queen of love to crown?
> Nay, thanks to Jove, the negro's proper sphere,

Is by him wilfully abandoned ne'er.
His longings suited to his station are;
For faithfulness he craves a master's care,
And craves no more; he stoops a bashful face
From azure looks, and love's white-arm'd embrace.
Born to be ruled, kind nature seals his breast
'Gainst Cupid's darts and Hymen's visions blest.
In him ambition's merest insolence,
And chivalry is brazen impudence."

"In the House of the Aylors" in Florida, several scenes (and meters) later, Rodney falls in love with a Creole, Leeona. The narrative moves briskly through Aylor's discovery of their love, Rodney's capture and escape, Aylor's rape of Leeona, and her desperate flight:

Behold yon mother fleeing from her home!
A master's child upon her frantic breast,
And by a master's savage bloodhounds prest;
And this, too, where in every steepled town,
The crucifix on human wrong looks down!
Think then no more of heathen lands to rave,
While in America there breathes a slave!

Rodney kills the dogs and men pursuing Leeona, and the runaways seek refuge in Kentucky. Whitman pauses here to compliment the land of his birth although "she merits scorn" for sharing "the pollutions of a slavish bed." [11] After many months and weary miles Rodney and Leeona find happiness in Sussex Vale, Canada, where by chance beloved Dora also lives as a pious sister of mercy:

She is happiest always among those that her hands have
    made happy.
Her heart is a fountain of kind words, and like Aquila
    of old,
She delights in the church of God, in Christ and his
    holy Apostles.

In "The End of the Whole Matter," Rodney and his two sons are soldiers in the Union Army. This section celebrates peace and free-

---

11. Whitman here reiterates his faith in the inevitable recognition of his genius:

I love Kentucky; tho' she merit scorn
I can't despise the land where I was born.
Her name I cherish, and expect to see
The day when all her sons will cherish me.

. . . .

Then let my countrymen, when I am dead,
Where I was born, make my eternal bed.

dom in solemn and stately measures (the hexameters of Longfel-
low's *Evangeline*), anticipating a classless society where all enjoy
"Free Schools, free press, free speech, and equal laws":

> Let lawlessness no longer stagger forth
> With his destructive torch, nor South nor North;
> And let the humblest tenant of the fields,
> Secured of what his honest labor yields
> Pursue his calling, ply his daily care,
> His home adorn and helpless children rear,
> Assured that while our flag above him flies,
> No lawless hand can dare molest his joys.

In *The Rape of Florida* (1884), reissued as *Twasinta's Seminoles*
(1885, 1890), Whitman became the first black poet to use Spenser-
ian stanza in a poem of epic length. He attempted the " 'stately
verse,' *mastered only* by Spenser, Byron, and a very few other great
poets," he said, because "some negro is sure to do everything that
any one else has ever done, and as none of that race have ever exe-
cuted a poem in the 'stately verse,' I simply *venture in*" (RP). Tech-
nically, Whitman's venture is successful. Through 251 stanzas he
handles the demanding rhyme scheme with ease, but his Alexan-
drines often drag along like Pope's "wounded snake." In the "Invo-
cation," Whitman praises Bryant and quotes the bard's compliment
to him:

> "The stuff's in him of robust manliness,
> He is a poet, singing more by ear
> Than note." His great heart filled with tenderness,
> Thus spoke the patriarch bard of Cedarmere
> Of me, who dwelt in a most obscure sphere;
> For I was in the tents of bondage when
> The muse inspired, and ere my song grew clear,
> The graceful Bryant called his fellow-men
> To mark what in my lay seemed pleasing to him then.

The Rape of Florida rehearses events of the Seminole Wars, waged
sporadically from 1816 to 1842 by the U.S. Army against the Semi-
noles and their black Maroon allies (and slaves) in an effort to evict
them from Florida. In Whitman's account Osceola "sat gloomily
and nursed a bitter hate" as dragoons attack Chief Palmecho's
Seminoles. The army is routed with the aid of "hero-born" Atlassa,
a noble, handsome warrior who loves Palmecho's daughter Ewald,
a beauty of Spanish, Indian, and black lineage. Under a flag of
truce the Seminoles are brought to the conference table in San Au-

gustine, where "Palmecho spoke of wars, and rights, and lands," but
"the hardened pirates" "gave him chains instead." Made captive by
"perfidy and guile," the Seminoles are shipped to exile in Santa
Rosa, Mexico.

Action and characterization receive minimal attention from the
poet, for this treacherous rape of Florida is parabolic. To Whitman
it exemplifies the superiority of primeval Nature (Eden) over the
world of Mammon, of fierce-spirited red and black braves over
white men, and of "love in the forest"—love of God and among
natives—over the hatreds and hypocrisies in San Augustine, "a
church and prison joined." For the Seminoles and Maroons, exiled
from a corrupted land by "Priestcraft and Tyranny," Mexico arises
from the waves as a pristine paradise for the dark-skinned races to
ennoble in freedom. Amid the symbolic landscapes Palmecho, At-
lassa, Ewald, and Abraham (an old Maroon)[12] enact a morality
poem, and are all but effaced by homilies on honor, freedom, race
pride, love, and themes of *memento mori* and *ubi sunt*. The poetry,
both narrative and homiletic, is diffuse, abstract, redundant, and
frequently marred by awkward shifts from high to low diction;
however, occasional stanzas show strength of style and feeling.
Whitman scorns the black man's "quiescence in disgrace" and would
see him "*Pressing* and fighting in, for place and power!":

> Ah! I abhor his protest and complaint!
> His pious looks and patience I despise!
> He can't evade the test, disguised as saint,
> The manly voice of freedom bids him rise,
> And shake himself before Philistine eyes!
> And, like a lion roused, no sooner than
> A foe dare come, play all his energies
> And court the fray with fury if he can;
> For hell itself respects a fearless manly man!

As in all his poems, Whitman sings best on "Who has not truly
loved, has never truly lived." A handful of lyrics like his boat song
beautify *The Rape of Florida*:

> "Come now, my love, the moon is on the lake;
> Upon the waters is my light canoe;
> Come with me, love, and gladsome oars shall make

12. Whitman may have modeled his Abraham on the famous full-blooded
Negro slave from Pensacola who fled to the Seminoles after the War of 1812
and acted as their interpreter, counselor, war leader, and negotiator during the
Seminole Wars. See Kenneth W. Porter, *The Negro on the American Frontier*
(New York, 1971), pp. 295–337.

> A music on the parting wave for you,—
> Come o'er the waters deep and dark and blue;
> Come where the lilies in the marge have sprung,
> Come with me, love, for Oh, my love is true!"
> This is the song that on the lake was sung,
> The boatman sang it over when his heart was young.

Whitman's final volume, *An Idyl of the South* (1901), consists of two long poems: "The Southland's Charms and Freedom's Magnitude" in 74 stanzas, and "The Octoroon" in 161 stanzas, all ottava rima. "The Southland's Charms" is a potpourri of ideas and feelings erratically arranged. As the poet's imagination travels from his Southern boyhood to a perfect future society, he muses on the home joys, unspoiled nature, chivalry, and slavery of olden days. He describes the Civil War with its valorous black and white soldiers, and he urges industrialization, "Broad civilization: wealth, expansion, progress" for the South. There are occasional worthy stanzas, but the poem is primarily valuable as a record of the poet's mind in the year of his death.

"The Octoroon," on the other hand, is an artistic testament to Love, "the only Redeemer of intelligent beings," to Woman, "Earth's noblest creature," and to the Mind's Immortality. Sheldon Maury, a youth as handsome and patrician as a Norse God, falls deeply in love with his octoroon slave Lena.

> Just in the dawn of blushing womanhood;
>   Her swan-neck glimpsed through shocks of wavy hair;
> A hint of olives in her gentle blood,
>   Suggesting passion in a rosy lair;
> This shapely Venus of the cabins stood,
>   In all but birth a princess, tall and fair;
> And is it any wonder that this brave
> And proud young master came to love his slave?

Their lives "flowed together like a melody." Whitman exalts their honorable love with lyrical hymns to the interracial unions of Pocahontas and Captain Smith, Solomon and Sheba, Moses and "the Oreb Shepherdess," and Boaz with his "flower of Moab." His finest poetry glorifies young love:

> When genial Spring first hears the mating thrush,
>   Where waters gossip and the wild flowers throng,
> Love rears her altar in the leafy bush,
>   And Nature chants the sweetest bridal-song.
> When love is free, with madness in its rush,
>   Its very strength defends the heart from wrong.

> Love, when untutored, walks a harmless way,
> With feet, though bare, that never go astray.

Through imagery and sound Whitman constructs a sanctified "green world" for Sheldon and Lena. Later, when Lena is sold by Sheldon's father to preserve the Maury honor, the poetry's spasmodic lines and harsh alliteration convey cosmic discord as the frenzied lover rides to Lena's rescue through infernal darkness:

> And night came on. Earth-jarring thunders roared
>   And rolled afar. Behind the inky banks
> The sun had sunk in terror. Up, up soared
>   The scurrying clouds and spread like serried ranks
> With murky banners flying,—swirled and poured
>   Through lurid arches,—while demoniac pranks
> The vivid lightnings cut and onward came,
> Stabbing the darkness with their spears of flame.

Sheldon finds Lena has escaped unsullied from her brutish new master, but she lies dying in a woodsman's cottage. The pathos of reunion and of Lena's peaceful death and simple funeral escapes effusive sentimentality, for broad nature imagery and abstract theologizing distance the emotion. The poet's thoughts on faith and immortality in the final eleven stanzas are not overly didactic, and their solemn tone of glad acceptance blends with the tragic love story, as in this fine stanza:

> The wild moose shivers in the north land's breath,
>   Where Huron's wave upbraids the fretful shore;
> The marsh fowl far to southward wandereth
>   And calls her tribes to milder climes explore;
> All Nature seems to sigh: "Remember death,
>   For all the living soon shall be no more."
> But mark how Faith sweeps on with tireless wing,
> To find for e'en the fowl an endless spring.

Whitman planned a sequel to "The Octoroon," dealing with "complications in the social order" in the antebellum South, but the *Idyl* of Sheldon and Lena remained his last word on the subject. For its tight construction, consistent tone, and lyrical beauty, "The Octoroon" is his most artistic endeavor.

Whitman's lyric poems appear in three collections.[13] Appended to *Not a Man* (1877) are eighteen "Miscellaneous Poems" which vary widely in style and subject. They include the sentimental "To

---

13. Two uncollected lyrics are "Woods and Rocks—A Reverie" and "A Contrast," *AMECR*, 2 (1886), 190–92, and 15 (July, 1898), 547.

Baby's Canary, Accidentally Killed"; a eulogy to the poet Joshua
McCarter Simpson; a sonnet, "The Montenegrin"; a humorous bal-
lad, "Solon Stiles," with verse in German dialect; some undistin-
guished nature pieces, and an uncommon labor poem, "The Great
Strike":

> Whenever Communism's snaky head
> Is raised against the heel of Capital,
> I want it crushed neath Law's majestic tread,
> And yet would heed poor honest labor's call.

"Ye Bards of England," in heroic couplets, pays homage to "Chau-
cer singing with the Nightingales," "gentle Thompson," the inimi-
table Shakespeare, and "Missolonghi's chief of singers," Byron: "A
wounded spirit, mournful and yet mad,/ A genius proud, defiant,
gentle, sad." Another group of twenty-three lyrics in as many differ-
ent patterns of meter, rhyme, and stanza length make up *Drifted
Leaves* (1890). Whitman's feat of versification does not produce
individual poems of merit, although it creates a unique collection.
The poet eulogizes Stonewall Jackson, Custer, and Grant; he muses
over the beauties of autumn, of starry skies, and of an eagle's flight;
and he gazes optimistically into America's bright future. "Where
the Yellow Sumacs Grow" tenderly memorializes the poet's mother,
and the quatrains of "Genius" reiterate Whitman's faith in genius's
ability to transcend adversity:

> Though Superstition place
>   Her thorns upon his brow,
> Amid a jeering populace,
>   And crucify him now:
>
> Genius at last will rise,
>   Triumphant from the dust;
> The cynosure of wondering eyes,
>   The inevitable must.

Drifted Leaves includes the only two dialect poems in Whitman's
canon. His "Tobe's Poem. Home Time—Sundown" (in three stan-
zas) is an engaging song to a Southern evening:

> De lightnin' bugs er flying wid er zig-zag flame,
> De beetle bugs er goin' wid er droan;
> De 'backer flys er huntin' fur de Jimpson weeds,
> An' de toad fraug's er hoppin' mighty lone;
> An' its home time, sundown,
> Time fur ter drive up de cows;
> Hometime, sundown,
> An' de darkies am er comin' to de house.

World's Fair Poem (1893) contains two poems: "The Veteran,"
a tribute to Civil War heroes which is a trite, flag-waving hurrah
in nine six-line stanzas, and "The Freedman's Triumphant Song" of
over 250 lines. The latter recounts the efforts in peace and war by
which Afro-Americans have demonstrated their loyalty and love for
America. Whitman militantly defends full citizenship for his race,
which was increasingly threatened in this period of growing legal
segregation and foreign immigration. The black man will never
leave his native land:

> And hold we will, 'gainst all who boast
> *Our* flag, just hailed from foreign coast:
> To *such*—who never tilled a field,
> To such, we cannot, *will not* yield.
> Our rights are not *conferred* but, WON
> Through sweat and blood—in storm and sun,
> And here contending to the end
> We'll fight it out with foe or friend.

Whitman's finest lyrics are not in these separate collections but in
his longer poems as single stanzas or, more often, as self-contained
sequences on love, nature, a person or brief event.

It is uncertain whether Albery Whitman or Frances E. W. Harper
was the more prolific black poet of their century, considering the
lady's twenty-three-year head start. Quantity aside, Mrs. Harper
won acclaim as a prophet in her own country and enjoyed all spir-
itual and financial rewards of popularity. She had no need to plead
for recognition, as Whitman does in "A Question":

> Shall my hand lie cold on the strings of my lyre,
> And the heart that is warm lose its pathos and fire,
>   Ere my countrymen hear my song?
> Shall the bard who sings in the tents of the slave,
> And now wakes his harp for the free and the brave,
>   Unheeded wander along?   (DL, 1890)

For Mrs. Harper poetry was consciously a tool: she wrote "songs
for the people" to uplift them, save their souls, and reform their
habits. For Albery Whitman, on the other hand, poetry was "sur-
vival of the Beautiful": he wrote poems because he loved poetry
and cherished an ideal of art for art's sake and for the sake of prov-
ing the race's creative talent. Preaching, however, came naturally
to him—it was his vocation. Thus the beautiful suffers adulteration
whenever Whitman cannot restrain his justifiable pride in "a little

learning" and a large intelligence. But unlike Mrs. Harper and their contemporaries, he does not burden the poetry with many "Thou shalts" and "shalt nots." His atypical Christianity disdains ritual and dogma to sing God in Nature, love between man and woman, and the free mind's eternal power. Like another Whitman (although with greater inhibitions and far less talent), this good black poet celebrates himself, hymns the bard as seer and the oneness of all body and soul.[14]

Albery Whitman's poetry is not utilitarian, which sets him apart from all his fellow poets with a cause. Although he exalts manliness and insists on race loyalty, he generally avoids accusatory polemic as well as sentimental and self-pitying rhetoric. Whitman escapes the influence of Booker T. Washington's ideology, and he avoids utopianizing life on the old plantation in dialect verse. His work is rather an attempt at full-blown Romantic poetry, looking back to legendary pastoral worlds—clearly marred by race prejudice, seeing the present as a sphere of unlimited human potentiality, and looking forward to an ideal earth perfected by human love and poetic genius. Whitman's egoism and his tendency to express any and every fluttering of his heart in verse bind him even closer to the effusive Romantic poets, while the allegorical dimensions of his work separate him further from black poets of his era. Whatever a line count may reveal, by aesthetic standards of any age Whitman was a better poet than Mrs. Harper. Moreover, his poetry offers more profound perceptions and a more catholic range of subjects and versification than the laureate Dunbar's lyrics. Albery Whitman dared to be an innovator and a "fearless manly man" in his poetry. All obstacles considered, his was a splendid ambition and a considerable achievement.

SELECTED SOURCES

Brawley, Benjamin. *The Negro Genius.* 1937; rpt. New York: Biblo & Tanner, 1966. Pp. 110–16.
———. "Three Negro Poets: Horton, Mrs. Harper, Whitman." *JNH*, 2 (October, 1917), 384–92.
Brown, Sterling A. "Albery Allson Whitman." *DAB* (1936).

14. There is no evidence at this time that Albery Whitman had read or known of Walt Whitman's poetry.

"An Idyll of the South—The Octoroon." *AMECR*, 18 (July, 1901), 88–
   91.
Loggins, 336–41.
Simmons, 1122–26.

HENRIETTA CORDELIA RAY
1852?–1916

"Her curious air of detachment from things ordinary, her entire absence from affectation, her genuine self-forgetfulness, made her charming. A classmate once said of her that she appeared as one unspotted by the world. Always affable she dispensed only kindness and looked for nothing but goodwill." Thus described in Hallie Brown's *Homespun Heroines,* Miss Ray was a paragon of maidenly virtue, and we have no reason to doubt the portrait. She was born in New York City,[1] probably in the early 1850's, a daughter of Charles Bennett Ray and his second wife, Charlotte Augusta Burrough of Savannah, Georgia. Charles Ray, a former blacksmith, was a Congregational minister, a pioneer abolitionist and operator of an Underground Railroad station in his New York home, editor of the *Colored American,* and a distinguished leader of educational, missionary, suffrage, and temperance organizations. H. Cordelia Ray, as she preferred to be called, was one of seven children, two boys and five girls, of whom only three girls lived to adulthood. One sister, Charlotte E. Ray, graduated from the Howard University law school in 1872 and was admitted to the bar of the Supreme Court of the District of Columbia, becoming the first black woman lawyer in Washington.[2] Henrietta and her elder sister Florence, neither of whom married, were lifetime companions; they, too, received excellent educations. Henrietta was reputedly a graduate of the Sauveneur School of Languages and proficient in

1. Elizabeth Frazier, "Some Afro-American Women of Mark," *AMECR,* 8 (April, 1892), 384.
2. Many sources note Charlotte Ray's law career. The earliest reference is by Frances E. W. Harper in her speech to the Women's Congress, 1877, quoted in "Coloured Women of America," *The Englishwoman's Review,* NS 57 (January 15, 1878), 14. Miss Ray's degree and its date confirmed by W. A. Sojourner, Registrar, Howard University, in a letter to me.

Greek, Latin, French, and German.[3] She and Florence earned the master of pedagogy degree in 1891 from the University of the City of New York.[4]

Miss Ray made her public debut as a poet in Washington, D.C., on April 14, 1876. To commemorate the Emancipation Proclamation and honor the Emancipator, Afro-Americans donated $17,000 for a Freedmen's Monument, sculpted in bronze by Thomas Ball. Thousands of jubilant citizens and the highest government dignitaries attended its unveiling by President Grant at ceremonies presided over by John M. Langston and keynoted by Frederick Douglass's oration. Miss Ray's eighty-line ode, "Lincoln," to the "Emancipator, hero, martyr, friend!," read by William E. Matthews, was a highlight of the program.[5] Another of her memorial poems introduced a biographical sketch of her father which she and Florence published in 1887. Their collection of testimonials won acclaim for its "high judgement, good taste, literary tact and excellence." [6] Miss Ray published many poems in periodicals during the last twenty years of the century as well as two collections, *Sonnets* (1893) and *Poems* (1910), the latter dedicated to Florence and their "loved ones who have entered the life immortal."

For about thirty years H. Cordelia Ray was a teacher in New York.[7] After her public school career she tutored pupils in music, mathematics, and languages and taught English literature to classes of teachers. A review of *Poems* from 1913 finds Miss Ray and her sister living in Woodside, Long Island, both of them "retired on

3. William H. Robinson, *Early Black American Poets* (Dubuque: William C. Brown, 1969), p. 138. The Sauveneur School could not be located, nor could Miss Ray's linguistic skills be confirmed.

4. Helen Cleverdon, Archivist, New York University Libraries, in a letter to me. I am also indebted to Charles F. Gosnell, Director of Libraries, and G. B. Reynolds, Alumni Federation Secretary, both of N.Y.U., for their assistance in locating this record.

5. Accounts of the event and Miss Ray's ode are in *Oration by Frederick Douglass Delivered on the Occasion of the Unveiling of the Freedmen's Monument* . . . (Washington: Gibson, 1876); and Joseph T. Wilson, *Emancipation, Its Course and Progress* . . . (Hampton, Va.: Normal School, 1882). For a human interest account, see Mrs. Grimké's "From Washington," in Anna J. Cooper, *The Life and Writings of Charlotte Forten Grimké* (N.p.: Author, 1951), II, 30–33. Freedmen's Monument photograph is in *Ebony*, 18 (September, 1963), 107.

6. *AMECR*, 4 (1888), 468–69.

7. Miss Ray taught in the girl's department of Colored Grammar School No. 1 (135 Mulberry Street) in 1868, and in No. 80 (in the 1890's), where Charles L. Reason was principal. References courtesy of John E. Ramsay, New York City Board of Education.

pension through length of service" from the New York school
system.[8] Miss Ray's quiet, productive life as a poet and teacher
is neatly memorialized by these comments from Hallie Brown:
"Her gifts were exceptional. . . . Her modesty was excessive."

Miss Ray's Poetry

Seen as an enchanted playground populated by fairies or, more
often, as the consecrated handiwork of God, a benignly beautiful
earth and heaven are the subject of some five dozen poems by
Miss Ray and the backdrop for many more. Her fanciful nature
invariably lacks vitality, for neither emotion, thought, nor the mirror
of verisimilitude quickens it; no living people bathe in her "lisping
streams" or sport through "embowered glens," thrilling to "rare
pellucid hues of dawning" or "sheeny stars." Miss Ray's fondness
for archaic diction and syntax, for personification, mythological
allusions, and copious adjectives, further stiffens the wax flowers,
stuffed birds, and canvas sunsets in her verse museums:

> The lucent lake was lit with sheen,
> Shining the crested waves between,
> And through the purpling air
>   The young birds trilled their lightsome lays,
>   To join the hymn of Nature's praise,
> And earth was passing fair.
>   ("A Thought on Lake Ontario")

> With her buskins tipped with dew,
> Came a fair, enchanting fay,
> Tiptoeing the forest through;
> Who was it but smiling May?
>   ("May's Invocation")

> Sunshine and shadow play amid the trees
> In bosky groves, while from the vivid sky
> The sun's gold arrows fleck the fields at noon,
>   Where weary cattle to their slumber hie.
> How sweet the music of the purling rill,
> Trickling adown the grassy hill!
> While dreamy fancies come to give repose
> When the first star of evening glows.
>   ("July")

8. "Two Books of Real Merit," *AMECR*, 29 (January, 1913), 296–97. No
data on Miss Ray's life after 1913 have been located. The Library of Congress
Catalogue gives her date of death as 1916.

Miss Ray's philosophical poems—uniformly serious, deeply pious, and idealistic—counsel serene resignation and optimism. These include sonnets like "Aspiration," "Self-mastery," "The Quest of the Ideal," and verses such as "God's Ways, Not Our Ways," "Reverie" (His will be done), "Questioning" (every cloud has a silver lining), "Compensation" (harmony arises from discord), and "Repose" (love of mankind and duty brings repose).

In a very few poems, however, Miss Ray is moved by the vicissitudes of art and love to remove her rose-colored glasses. In "Invocation to the Muse" she begs for return of poetic inspiration. "Broken Heart" and "Shadow and Sunshine" are anguished cries of an "unfulfilled heart" which ultimately finds solace in Jesus. Several pieces in the "Chansons D'Amour" section of *Poems* betray disappointment in love which is expressed in two poems with rare warmth and candor. "Love's Vista" begins:

> Love oped a vista rare with stars
> That overshone a dewy height;
> Glad-Heart enwrapt in dreams, saw naught
> Save radiance and bloom and light.

Glad-Heart, lured by a cooing dove, strays "reckless down the glades." But the dove wails, stars go out, and Glad-Heart is urged to go back.

> Yet sweet, sweet dove, when life is drear,
> Come chant again that dreamy lay;
> O tender love, send shining stars
> To light her soul, once more, some day.

Such yearning is felt again in "My Spirit's Complement," with its finely developed conceit, which follows Glad-Heart's lament:

> Thy life hath touched the edges of my life,
> All glistening and moist with sunlit dew,
> They touched, they paused,—then drifted wide apart,
> Each gleaming with a rare prismatic hue.
>
> . . . .
>
> God grant our souls may meet in Paradise,
> After the mystery of life's sweet pain;
> And find the strange prismatic hues of earth
> Transmuted to the spotless light again.

A third, less artistic poem, but one simpler and more touching than Miss Ray's 145 others, is "Verses to My Heart's Sister," a confession of the pain of loss—from deaths of her four brothers and sisters and both parents—and of love for her sister Florence:

> So nearer clung we, sister,
>   And loved each other more;
> The tendrils of our natures
>   Twined closer than before.
> We could speak to no other
>   Of those sweet, holy things,
> So tender yet so nameless
>   Which sorrow often brings.
>
>   . . . .
> And shall not those sweet loved ones
>   Missed here so long! so long!
> Join with us in the music
>   Of an all-perfect song?
> We feel a gladder cadence
>   Will thrill their rapt'rous strain,
> When we are with them, sister,
>   All, ne'er to part again?

Except for a few such personal poems, Miss Ray's verse labors under the blessing of a fine education. She shows familiarity with classical and contemporary culture in sonnets to Milton, Shakespeare, Raphael, and Beethoven, and in the trilogy titled "The Seer, The Singer, and The Sage" (Dante, Longfellow, and Thoreau). "Shakespeare" illustrates her traditional approach:

> We wonder what the horoscope did show
> When Shakespeare came to earth. Were planets there,
> Grouped in unique arrangement? . . .
>   . . . The air
> Is thick with beauteous elves, a dainty row,
> Anon, with droning witches, and e'en now
> Stalks gloomy Hamlet, bent on vengeance dread.
> One after one they come, smiling or scarred,
> Wrought by that mind prismatic to which bow
> All lesser minds. They by thee would be fed,
> Poet incomparable! Avon's Bard!

Although Miss Ray's language, thought, and sentiments are impoverished, her technical skills are unusually rich. She successfully employs diverse stanzaic forms, many, it seems, of her own devising. The poems are generally rhythmic without being sing-song, and many benefit from irregularities in line length and metrical pattern. Miss Ray's ear for end rhyme seldom fails, and the rhymes, although trite, occasionally fall into original schemes. This freedom from conventional versification gives at least technical interest to some otherwise forgettable poems such as the lengthy, ornate "Ode on the Twentieth Century." Similarly departing from tradition, Miss

Ray sets several ballads into rhymed couplets or triplets. But the innovative forms do not redeem her hackneyed story lines and defective diction. The forty-eight stanza "Rhyme of the Antique Forest," for example, begins: "In the antique forest lonely,/ Dwelt a pensive maiden only." Following six stanzas of forest description, Countess Una gazes on Luna; her page announces Sir Hubert's death in battle; their daughter, Bianca, grows up (slowly), and longs for love; a knight finds her sleeping in the woods:

> Rose-encolored, oval-moulded
> Was her profile; eyelids folded
> O'er her eyes hid deepest meaning
> From the knight above her leaning.

But the knight is already married, etc.

Nature, Christian idealism and morality, love, and literature are Miss Ray's major poetic concerns. Racial issues, historical or contemporary, are not versified; however, the struggle for freedom and equality inspires ten poems, all of them tributes to champions of freedom like Garrison, Phillips, Sumner, Lincoln, L'Ouverture, and Robert Gould Shaw, and to the writers Mrs. Stowe and Dunbar. Her "In Memoriam, Frederick Douglass" is perhaps the best of these tributes:

> Shall the race falter in its courage now
> That the great chief is fallen? Shall it bow
> Tamely to aught of injury? Ah, nay!
> For daring souls are needed e'en today.
> Let his example be a shining light,
> Leading through duty's paths to some far height
> Of undreamed victory. All honored be
> The silv'ry head of him we no more see!
> Children unborn will venerate his name,
> And History keep spotless his fair fame.

Like so many nineteenth-century poets, H. Cordelia Ray versified only socially acceptable sentiments and a picture-book world. She suppressed natural feelings and thoughtful scrutiny of human relationships, actions, and ideas to serve a Muse for whom poetry was more a skill than an art, more a penmanship exercise than a new, complex creation of heart and mind. Miss Ray's technical virtuosity makes her fidelity to artificiality and respectability the more regrettable, for when she shed the inhibiting Muse, her potential talent could be glimpsed.

SELECTED SOURCES

Brown, Hallie Q., comp. *Homespun Heroines and Other Women of Distinction.* Xenia, Ohio: Aldine, 1926. Pp. 171–75.
Ray, F. T. and H. C. *Sketch of the Life of Rev. Charles B. Ray.* New York: J. J. Little, 1887.

GEORGE CLINTON ROWE
1853–1903

George Clinton Rowe made his mark as a minister, editor, and author in the Deep South during the last three decades of the nineteenth century. He was born in Litchfield, Connecticut, on May 1, 1853, the son of Solomon D. and Adeline S. (Johnson) Rowe.[1] Until he was twenty-three Rowe lived in Litchfield, attended its schools, and served an apprenticeship on the *Litchfield Enquirer* (1870–73), where he earned the first certificate of trade granted to a black man by that paper. Rowe developed a youthful interest in natural history and donated his collections of minerals, birds' eggs, and reptiles to Litchfield schools. From 1876 until about 1880 Rowe worked at the Normal School Printing Office in Hampton, Virginia, on the *American Missionary, Southern Workman, Alumni Journal,* and *African Repository.* His life's service as a missionary began here with his establishment of the Ocean Cottage Mission in Little England and the building of Hampton Institute's chapel.

Rowe had studied theology privately in Litchfield and had been examined by the board of examiners of Yale College. However, his active Congregational work began in 1881 with ordination by the Georgia Association at Cypress Slash. From 1881 to 1885 Rowe was pastor of Cypress Slash Congregational Church at McIntosh, Georgia; from 1885 until 1897 he led the church, mission, and school activities of Plymouth Congregational Church in Charleston, South Carolina. During his term as a missionary in Charleston, Rowe published the 113-page *Thoughts in Verse* (1887), followed by *Our*

1. Biography is from *Congregational Year-Book*, Haley, and Rowe's letters to Furman. I am indebted to Dwight L. Cart, Librarian, Congregational Library of the American Congregational Association, Boston, and to E. L. Inabinett, Librarian, South Caroliniana Library of the University of South Carolina, for photocopies of the *Year-Book* and letters, respectively.

Heroes: Patriotic Poems (1890); a poem, *Decoration* (1891); several *Memorial Souvenir* verse tributes (1890, 1894, 1903); and an address, *The Aim of Life* (1892).[2]

Rowe was not only a respected missionary and prolific author but also an editor and a busy organization man. For three years he edited and published the *Charleston Enquirer* (1893–96). He stated the *Enquirer's* goal in a letter to Professor Charles J. McDonald Furman, a subscriber who became a helpful critic of Rowe's poetry: "We are trying to make the paper one that is helpful to our people; one that throws light on our race development, that our friends and enemies may see that we are not retrograding nor standing still" (1895). Rowe sent copies of his books to Furman, and in later letters told of literary honors he had received: he won a gold medal for the best poem on the A.M.E. Zion Church at its 1896 centennial in New York (1897); his publications were exhibited at the Paris Exposition and brought a "pleasant recognition" from President McKinley (1900); and he delivered his poem, "Race Development," at the dedication of "the Negro Building" of an interstate exposition (1901).

Rowe worked for race advancement with many organizations from the 1880's until his death. For eight years he was statistical secretary and treasurer of the Georgia Congregational Association (about 1888–96); president of the Preacher's Union, a Charleston interdenominational body (about 1891–96); a delegate and moderator at National Councils; member of an anti-lynching convention; trustee and treasurer of the Frederick Deming, Jr., Industrial School, Maryville, South Carolina; and member of the Literary Congress for the Atlanta Exposition.

Rowe's vocation remained missionary work, and in 1897 he left Plymouth Church for Charleston Battery Mission, where he organized the Battery Church and led it for the six years until his death. At the age of fifty George Clinton Rowe died of heart disease on October 3, 1903, in Charleston.[3] He was survived by his wife Miranda (Jackson), whom he had married in Litchfield on July 8, 1874, and by seven of his nine children. In his portraits Rowe appears an unimposing man. His dark oval face with heavy-lidded eyes, high forehead, close-cropped hair, and generous handlebar

2. A pamphlet of poems, *Sunbeams,* was supposedly published in Hampton, Va., in 1880, but no copy of it has been found.

3. Death certificate, Charleston County, S.C. Age at death incorrectly entered as 48.

moustache suggests a mild and bookish nature. But in a relatively short lifetime Rowe wrote, preached, and worked vigorously to promote Christianity and Afro-American progress. A fitting epitaph for Rowe might be taken from *A Noble Life,* his memorial to the Reverend Joseph Price, president of Livingstone College in Salisbury, North Carolina:

> The tongue of fire is silent now,
>   The loving heart is still,
> The mind, surcharged with burning thought,
>   Yet loyal to God's will—
> Has ceased to plan for mortals here,
> Is active in another sphere.

Rowe's Poetry

All but a handful of the seventy-one selections in *Thoughts in Verse* (1887) are versified sermons. The Reverend George Rowe preaches virtuous living, labor, and love of God as the road to racial progress. He gives assurance that God's inscrutable ways and power behind all "natural causes" will be revealed when our delusive life, "fleeting as the noontide hour" and "full of unrest and mystery," is happily left behind for the immutable glories of Heaven. Verses may be chosen at random to illustrate Rowe's creed: "The Life Boat," "The Christian Life," "Faith," "Go Work," "The Hour of Death," "It Is Not All of Life to Live," and "Power of a Song" all counsel patience and piety in passionless verse. It is impossible to refute the critic who found Rowe's volume "destitute of the imagination that fires and the grace of rhythm that charms," having at most "some fairly happy rhyming" here and there.[4] Stanzas such as these are typical:

> Noble band of earnest teachers,
>   From this scene a lesson take:
> Be not only able preachers,
>   But in practice progress make.
> Teach by precept and example,
>   In the day and in the night,
> Follow e'er the Great Exemplar!
>   And thy evening shall be light.
>   ("True Nobility")

> It is not the way of this strange world of ours,
> To honor its heroes with garland of flowers,
> For those who do much for poor suffering mankind

4. Anonymous review, *AMECR,* 4 (1888), 457–58.

> Are the ones who may suffer and be left far behind.
>> ("A Record Above")

> Let us all sail bravely onward,
>> To our Father's house above,
> Where the billows are forgotten,
>> In a life of peace and love.
>> ("The Sailboat")

In the same style Rowe versifies five psalms and writes several poems to his sister Irene, his mother Adeline, daughter Agnes, and his wife, here addressed as "Wilhelmina":

> I know a maid of gentle grace,
>> With eyes like stars of night,
> With such a lovely beaming face—
>> Where'er she is 'tis light!
> She has a large place in my heart,
>> 'Tis hers where 'er I go,
> May we as lovers never part—
>> Sweet Wilhelmina Rowe.

Other poems like "Plymouth Choir" and "Cypress Slash" recall the Reverend Mr. Rowe's ministries, and "Retrospect" offers the sights and sounds of a country boyhood:

> I think of the slow-footed turtle
>> That lived by the brook in the vale,
> Where delicate violets and myrtle,
>> And arbutus their fragrance exhale.
> How he clumsily fell in the water,
>> As the feet of the school-boy approach,
> Fright'ning the *chub* and the *sucker*,
>> And startling the shy little *roach*.

Thoughts in Verse also includes six almost identical "In Memoriam" verses which in turn resemble Rowe's *Memorial Souvenir* pamphlets. All are traditional eulogies to Christian warriors now gone to their well-deserved eternal blessedness with God.

Only three poems in *Thoughts in Verse* touch on racial themes. Two, of the "Excelsior" type, are addressed to the teachers of Georgia; and "The Reason Why" commends a black soldier's heroism in the Civil War. All fifteen poems in *Our Heroes* (1890), however, are directed toward "the elevation of the Race." In the preface Rowe states the book's object: "To inform our people that there is much unwritten history, of noble deeds, inspiring sayings, and of true manhood and womanhood, undiscovered; and to create that race pride which is necessary to the growth, progress, and prosperity of any people." The title poem, "Our Heroes," is this statement of purpose in verse, followed by tributes to fighting heroes like Toussaint L'Ouverture, Robert Smalls, and Crispus Attucks; to religious leaders and educators, Bishop Daniel A. Payne and Lucy C. Laney; and to the poet Frances E. W. Harper. "Crispus Attucks," in eleven stanzas, is representative:

> (5) But who was Attucks? Afric's son;
> Who toiled for years, but never won
> A freeman's just reward.
> A man of stature, strong and brave,
> Yet held in bondage as a slave,
> By men who worshipped God.

> (8) While men of wisdom gathered round,
> Seeking to know where might be found
> Deliverance from the foe—
> How to throw off the British yoke,
> A swarthy negro fearless spoke—
> And struck the primal blow.

The final poem in the book, "Historic Truth," describes the rich architectural and scientific achievements of the Egyptians, descendants of Ham.

Although the verses of *Our Heroes* are technically smoother and more varied than Rowe's earlier efforts, they remain pedestrian. Aesthetic merit aside, the historical significance of *Our Heroes* is suggested in its introduction by the Reverend J. H. M. Pollard and echoed by a review in the *Orangeburg* (South Carolina) *Plain Speaker*: "The glow he has cast over the originals in 'Our Heroes' permeates his reader and throws out all prejudice formed on preconceived poetical models. . . . We learn to look beyond the worldly envelope of a man to the integrity of his conscience. . . . It should especially be placed in the hands of the young." [5]

SELECTED SOURCES

The Congregational Year-Book, 1904. Vol. 26. Portland, Maine: National Council of Congregational Churches, 1904. P. 41.

* Haley, James T., comp. *Afro-American Encyclopaedia.* Nashville, Tenn.: Haley & Florida, 1896. Pp. 108–9, 589–90 *et passim.*

*Rowe, George Clinton. MS letters to Professor Furman (1895, 1897, 1900, 1901). Charles James McDonald Furman Papers, South Caroliniana Library, ScU.

5. Quoted in advertisement, *AMECR,* 7 (October, 1890), back page; other advertisements of Rowe's work are in this volume, p. 238, and 7 (January, 1891), last page.

TIMOTHY THOMAS FORTUNE
1856–1928

As an influential, versatile newspaperman and a relentless agitator
for the rights of Afro-Americans (a term he forced into popular
acceptance), T. Thomas Fortune reigned for over a quarter-century
as the "Dean of Negro Editors" and the "Prince of Negro Jour-
nalists" in the United States.[1] He was born in Marianna, Florida,
on October 3, 1856.[2] Both his parents, Emanuel and Sarah Jane
(Bush), were slaves who gave to their two sons and three daughters
the mixed racial heritage of their Seminole Indian, Irish, Jewish,
and African forebears. In 1868 a Ku Klux Klan reign of terror drove
the family from Marianna, where Emanuel had been a successful
shoemaker and tanner, to Jacksonville. Here the elder Fortune pros-
pered in business, engaged in Republican politics, and held several
elective municipal offices. Young Timothy received less than three
years of formal schooling, but he gained a practical education in
politics and journalism during his teens as a four-term page in the

1. Fortune, "Who Are We? Afro-Americans, Colored People or Negroes,"
VN, 3 (March, 1906), 194–98; New York Age, June 9, 1928. Fortune's titles
appear frequently, e.g., Penn, p. 138.
2. Date of birth from death certificate, Pennsylvania. Scattered and largely
repetitive biographies of Fortune differ mainly in the dating of his early ac-
tivities (1868–87) and in evaluation of his work and personality in later years.
I have adopted dates given by Fortune in his articles or by A. Terry Slocum,
whose dates are from Fortune's reminiscences, "After War Times—A Boy's Life
in Reconstruction," Norfolk Journal and Guide (Summer, 1927). A recent full-
length biography, Emma Thornbrough, T. Thomas Fortune: Militant Journalist
(Chicago, 1972), appeared after the completion of this chapter. Thornbrough
is also vague about Fortune's early dates, but her work, based on a thorough
analysis of Fortune's correspondence in the Booker T. Washington Papers (Li-
brary of Congress) and a private collection of Fortune family papers, is a good,
balanced account of his life and thought.

Florida Senate and a printer's devil and typesetter on four Florida newspapers.[3]

In 1872 Fortune clerked in the Jacksonville post office and worked as private secretary to General Josiah T. Walls, a Florida congressman. Subsequently, through two federal appointments, he became a mail route agent of the Railway Postal Service in Florida and an inspector of customs in Delaware (1873–75?). At the age of nineteen Fortune enrolled at Howard University and studied in the preparatory and normal departments. Soon, however, he lost his savings in a bank failure and went to work setting type and writing a column for the [Washington] *People's Advocate* while he read law at Howard in the evenings. On February 22, 1877, Fortune married Caroline Charlotte Smiley of Jacksonville and returned to that city about a year later to teach school and work again on the *Daily Union*. He began writing poetry at this time, and during the next twenty-five years he composed the fifty poems that would be published in 1905 as *Dreams of Life* as well as many other poems, some published in periodicals and some which he discarded as not good enough "to instruct or amuse the reader." [4]

Fortune's fifty-year career in journalism began in earnest in 1879 in New York City. He was a compositor on the *Weekly Witness*, when, with two partners, he took charge of a failing paper, *Rumor,* and in 1880 changed its name to the *New York Globe.* The *Globe* failed financially on November 8, 1884, but two weeks later Fortune alone established *The Freeman.* As publisher, editor, and printer, he ran his *Freeman* until October, 1887, when debts and political pressures forced him to turn over the paper to his brother Emanuel junior and Jerome B. Peterson; they changed its name to the *New York Age.*[5] For the next two years Fortune wrote articles and editorials principally for Charles Dana's *New York Sun* and *Evening Sun,* where he rose to assistant editor under Amos J. Cummings. When his brother Emanuel became fatally ill in 1889, Fortune returned to the *Age* and remained its celebrated, controversial editor until 1907.

3. The *Marianna Courier* (before 1868), *Tallahassee Sentinel* (1869–71?), *Jacksonville Courier* and *Jacksonville Daily Union* (1872–74?).
4. *Dreams of Life,* p. 9. According to Thornbrough, Fortune often tried to have his poetry published but could not find a publisher or raise money for a private printing before 1905 (pp. 211–12, 293).
5. Rowell's *American Newspaper Directory* (New York, 1885, 1886, 1901), pp. 375, 414, 767; Ayer's *American Newspaper Annual* (Philadelphia, 1906), p. 597; Penn, pp. 134–37.

"I began active work as an agitator, as a journalist, in 1879," he wrote, "and ceased from my work as an agitator in 1907." [6] During these twenty-eight years, in thousands of incisive articles and editorials, in speeches, monographs, and books, Fortune agitated for Afro-American independence and power in every area of life. At the same time, he castigated the establishment, blamed white society for the race problem, and demanded immediate restitution and retribution for crimes against blacks.[7] Fortune posed this question:

> When murder, usurpation, intimidation, and systematic wrong are practiced in open violation of law; when the Negro who steals from society what society steals from him under the specious cover of invidious law is hung upon the nearest oak tree, and the white villain who shoots a Negro without provocation is not so much as arrested —when society tolerates such an abnormal state of things, what will the harvest be? (*Globe*, January 13, 1883).

WAR is Fortune's answer, WAR against mobocracy, terrorism, slaughter, arson, and robbery, using the white man's weapons: brute force and cruelty. The black man can expect no protection from state and national governments, courts, or the Constitution; no support from the white press; and neither mercy nor justice from his white neighbors. Therefore "let him use the dagger, the torch, and the shotgun. There is no other appeal; no other argument will avail" (*Globe*, January 5, 1884). Fortune justified violence, defensive and offensive, on the grounds of simple justice: "What is fair for the one is fair for the other, and if the scamps lynch and shoot you, you have a right to do the same" (*Freeman*, July 18, 1885). Throughout the age of accommodation Fortune eloquently urged a brand of black activism unmatched until recent years. His "revolutionary talk" to an enthusiastic Brooklyn crowd in 1900 is ancestor to today's militant rhetoric:

> You must organize and keep your powder dry and be ready to demand an eye for an eye, a tooth for a tooth, for there is coming a

6. "The Breath of Agitation Is Life," *AMECR*, 31 (July, 1914), 6.
7. No complete bibliography of Fortune's writings (1879–1928) exists. His major ideas are articulated in the books and articles in my bibliography, in these notes, in the Slocum and Thornbrough bibliographies, and especially in Fortune's editorials for the *Globe, Freeman, Age,* and a dozen other papers, many available on microfilm. Accessible samples of Fortune's journalism are in *The Black Press, 1827–1890,* ed. Martin E. Dann (New York, 1971); see also Donald E. Drake, "Militancy in Fortune's New York *Age*," *JNH*, 55 (October, 1970), 307–22.

great crisis for the negro in this country in which much blood may
be shed. . . . If the law can afford us no protection then we should
protect ourselves, and if need be die in the defense of our rights as
citizens. . . . There can be no compromise in a life and death strug-
gle.[8]

For protection and civil rights agitation, in 1887 Fortune organ-
ized an Afro-American League. His statement of purpose, published
in the *Freeman* on June 2, 1887, begins with a solemn declaration
of black independence: "There come periods in the history of every
people when the necessity of their affairs makes it imperative that
they take such steps as shall show to the world that they are worthy
to be free, and therefore entitled to the sympathy of all mankind
and to the co-operation of all lovers of justice and fair play." The
Afro-American League, he continues, would combat suppression of
the ballot, the "reign of lynch and mob law," inequality in distri-
bution of school funds, the South's penitentiary system with its chain
gangs and convict leases, and discrimination on common carriers
and in places of public accommodation and recreation. "These mat-
ters reach down in the very life of a people," he writes, and when
such fundamental "principles are disregarded and outraged, it be-
comes the imperative duty of the aggrieved" to preserve their hu-
man rights, through the ballot and the courts if possible; if not,
by answering violence with violence. Fortune's summons drew
eager support, and by 1889 branches of the League flourished in
forty cities. However, in 1893, through internal dissension and
public indifference, it foundered. Five years later Fortune, with
A.M.E. Bishop Alexander Walters and other race leaders, reorgan-
ized the League as the Afro-American Council. Thereafter, until
its demise in 1908 (although Fortune retained the presidency
through bitter controversies until 1903), the Council was infiltrated
and then wholly dominated by Booker T. Washington and his
conservative ideology.[9]

Fortune's radicalism extended from the political-social sphere
through the economic and cultural life of the race. He gave early

8. "Crisis for the Negro Race," *New York Times*, June 4, 1900, 6:7.
9. Fortune, "The Afro-American League," *AMECR*, 8 (July, 1890), 2–6;
Herbert G. Renfro, "Is the Afro-American League a Failure?" *AMECR*, 9
(July, 1892), 9–18; Mrs. N. F. Mossell, "The National Afro-American Council,"
CAm, 3 (August, 1901), 291–305; Cyrus F. Adams, *The National Afro-Ameri-
can Council* (Washington, 1902); Emma L. Thornbrough, "The National Afro-
American League, 1887–1908," *Journal of Southern History*, 27 (November,
1961), 494–512; Meier, pp. 128–30, 172–74 *et passim*.

support to the Knights of Labor and the Colored Farmers' Alliance, and in his book, *Black and White* (1884), he denounced the monopolistic control of land, capital, and the means of production by an educated, wealthy minority in America.[10] In this era of industrial slavery which replaced chattel slavery, he wrote, the laboring poor of both races, North and South, must recognize "that they have a *common cause,* a *common humanity* and a *common enemy*" (242); they must unite and sieze their share of national land and wealth. While such redistribution of wealth proceeded, Afro-Americans must prosper within the capitalist system. Fortune urged the race to establish black businesses, banks, and labor unions, to hire black workers and buy from black merchants. If they were to rise financially, blacks must be educated. For the South, Fortune supported technical-industrial training;[11] where schools were segregated, he demanded black teachers for black children and equal funding of black schools from tax monies. In the North there must be equal educational opportunity on all levels. Fortune's *New York Age* led a successful fight for school integration and a civil rights bill in New York under Governors Grover Cleveland and Theodore Roosevelt.

Race advancement in all areas, he felt, required unified action and a strong sense of cultural identity. Afro-Americans must have their own newspapers, and these should publicize black actors, singers, writers, artists, and celebrate events in black history as Fortune's *Age* did.[12] From 1884 through the 1890's he led the Afro-American Press Association. To further implement racial solidarity, Fortune espoused a national Afro-American Church and a black National Guard unit; he encouraged formation of an African Historical Society in 1890; he organized the Citizens' Protective League (1900) and, with Washington, the National Negro Business League (1900).

Fortune's *Globe, Freeman,* and *Age* represented what he later called "the old journalism": "a fighting machine which feared no man or combination of men." He was a man "who cleaved close

10. *Black and White* was one of the very few publications by an Afro-American to be reviewed in white magazines of the century. See *The Nation,* November 27, 1884; *Dial,* December, 1884; *The Critic,* February 14, 1884; and see T. McCants Stewart, "Black and White Reviewed," *AMECR,* 1 (January, 1885), 189–99.

11. *The Kind of Education the Afro-American Most Needs* (Tuskegee, Ala.: Tuskegee Institute, 1898), 10 pp.

12. Fortune, "On Syndicating News," *AMECR,* 8 (October, 1891), 231–42.

to the line of race rights and loyalty, and could not be swerved from his purpose by bribes or intimidation." [13] His uncompromising and often vitriolic journalism made Fortune a man who was worshipped, feared, or hated, but never ignored. Theodore Roosevelt, as police commissioner of New York, is quoted as saying, "Tom Fortune, for God's sake keep that dirty pen of yours off me." But in later years Fortune attacked Roosevelt's racial policies, appointments, and handling of the Brownsville affair; thus Fortune was denied several federal positions he coveted. In 1902, however, he received a six-month appointment as special immigrant agent of the Treasury Department and proceeded on a fact-finding mission to the Philippines.[14] Among his admirers Fortune claimed Frederick Douglass, Emmett J. Scott, T. McCants Stewart, John E. Bruce "Grit," Joseph Pulitzer, Charles A. Dana, and President William McKinley—but he earned the enmity of many influential men like Alexander Crummell, W. Monroe Trotter, and W. E. B. Du Bois.[15] Fortune's unique relationship with Booker T. Washington ran an erratic course from about 1881 to 1915. During the 1890's Fortune frequently visited Tuskegee. He became Washington's confidant and backstage political advisor, the unacknowledged writer, compiler, and editor of Washington's books and speeches, and his chief publicist through the *New York Age*. Their warm friendship endured despite frequent acrimonious quarrels, for Fortune claimed in 1899 that they shared "basic views in the race question":

> He [Washington] speaks always from the point of view of a leader who lives and labors in the South, and who believes that in order to gain one point in manhood development something can well be yielded upon another, and that we are to depend mostly upon education, property and character to pave our way to success; while I speak from the standpoint of a man who lives and labors in the North, and who does not believe in sacrificing anything that justly belongs to the race of manhood or constitutional rights.[16]

13. "Old Afro-American and New Negro Journalism," *Favorite Magazine*, 9 (Autumn, 1920), 477.

14. Quoted by the New York *Amsterdam News*, June 6, 1928. See Fortune's three-part article, "The Filipino," *VN*, 1 (March, May, June, 1904), 93–99, 199–208, 240–46.

15. Encomiums from Dana, McKinley, Douglass, Amos Cummings, John Swinton, and others are quoted at length by Jessie M. Holland, "T. Thomas Fortune," *AMECR*, 19 (January, 1903), 670–74. Accuracy of these quotations is uncertain. Fortune's friendship with Bruce and quarrel with Crummell are detailed in MSS letters, Bruce Collection, NNSch; W. E. B. Du Bois. "The Lash," *Horizon*, 1 (May, 1907), 6.

16. Interview in *Boston Globe*, quoted in Emma L. Thornbrough, ed., *Booker T. Washington* (Englewood Cliffs: Prentice-Hall, 1969), pp. 112–13.

Fortune moderated his protest in the early 1900's and supported what he called the "money, property, and other material-getting movement" of Washington, with its stress on self-help, morality, and business-building. His shift from a "period of agitation" to a "period of acceptance of the situation," Fortune wrote, was necessary at the time, for the race needed to achieve a position of power from which "we should again take up the agitation for the civil and political rights denied us." [17]

The Dean moved temporarily from militancy to acceptance, perhaps partly to rescue his faltering hold on the *New York Age*. From the late 1880's Washington had made personal loans to Fortune and had invested regularly in the *Age*, which was always on the verge of bankruptcy. After 1900 Washington pressed with ever-increasing vigor for control of the *Age's* editorial policies and, in fact, its entire operation.[18] In 1907, when the *Age* was incorporated with Washington a principal (secret) stockholder, Fortune succumbed to the frustrations and burdens he had borne for years. Always deeply in debt, harassed by political and personal attacks, habituated to heavy drinking since the 1890's, and depressed by separation from his wife and by his failure to achieve the race's elevation which he had fought for during forty years, Fortune suffered a physical and mental breakdown. In September, 1907, he sold his interest in the *Age* to Fred R. Moore, who secretly had Washington's financial backing. He resigned from almost all organizations, and with this loss of power found himself deserted by his former supporters.

Sick and destitute, for the next three years Fortune begged in vain for work and money to support his family and keep himself alive. His health and influence were irreparably damaged, but in 1910–14 Fortune returned to the battlefield, sporadically working as associate editor of the *Philadelphia Tribune* and the *Age*, as a writer for the New York *Amsterdam News*, an editor of the *Colored American Review*, publisher and editor of the *Washington Sun*, and an occasional lecturer; but none of these endeavors brought him a living wage. Still as brilliant and bravely independent as before his breakdown, Fortune persevered, explaining in 1914, "I have not ceased to be a journalist, and do not expect to cease

17. "The Breath of Agitation Is Life," p. 9.
18. For Washington's takeover of the *Age*, see Emma L. Thornbrough, "More Light on Booker T. Washington and the *New York Age*," *JNH*, 43 (January, 1958), 34–49; and August Meier, "Booker T. Washington and the Negro Press," *JNH*, 38 (January, 1953), 67–90.

to be one; an annalist, a recorder, a thinker, sobered by experience and matured by adversity." [19]

During these bleak years Fortune lived alone in Newark, Trenton, and rural Monmouth County, New Jersey. In 1917 he obtained the post of assistant director of the New Jersey Negro Welfare Bureau, a state agency newly formed to aid Southern migrants.[20] In the early 1920's Fortune became editor of Marcus Garvey's papers, *The Negro Times* and *The Negro World* (1923–28), organs of the United Negro Improvement Association. Fortune's work for Garvey's black separatist movement gave his enemies further proof of his instability and inconstancy. However, the shift to Garvey can be seen as a logical and timely alliance in the interests of black power.

From the beginning of his career Fortune had confidently preached "the ultimate absorption of the Afro-American into the warp and woof of American life." He fought for repeal of miscegenation laws and supported mixed marriages like Frederick Douglass's in 1884 (Fortune himself was very light-skinned with Caucasian features). Moreover, he firmly opposed emigration-colonization schemes, believing that "the African here is an American by birth, education, and religious belief. He takes only an American's interest in Africa and what goes on there." [21] Although he celebrated Africa as a source of race pride, Fortune never wavered in his faith that America was the Afro-Americans' homeland. In *Black and White* he wrote:

> The white men of the South had better make up their minds that the black men will remain in the South just as long as corn will tassel and cotton will bloom into whiteness. . . . Africa will have to be evangelized *from within,* not *from without.* . . . The black people of this country are Americans, not Africans; and any wholesale expatriation of them is altogether out of the question (143).

During his editorship of Garvey's publications, Fortune did not express support for the U.N.I.A.'s well-publicized tenets of race purity and "back to Africa" for all blacks. He realized that these were but secondary and long-range objectives of the movement which he readily ignored while wholeheartedly agreeing with their major immediate aims, continually emphasized by Garvey: "We

19. "The Breath of Agitation Is Life," p. 6.
20. *Trenton Daily State Gazette,* October 31, 1917.
21. "Race Absorption," *AMECR,* 18 (July, 1901), 54–66; "Will the Afro-American Return to Africa?" *AMECR,* 8 (April, 1892), 387–91.

are organized for the absolute purpose of bettering our condition, industrially, commercially, socially, religiously, and politically . . . to lift ourselves and to demand respect of all humanity." Garvey's appeals for "self-help and self-reliance," racial solidarity, self-defense, a free Negro press, and justice and equality in all areas of life echoed Fortune's philosophy and won his allegiance.[22]

Thus Fortune seized upon both Garvey's and Washington's well-organized popular movements as promising vehicles for race advancement, while (in the case of Garvey) playing down the extremes of black nationalism and (in the case of Washington) vigorously opposing political conservatism and social accommodation. Because he supported a variety of programs and individuals at different times during his career, Fortune was charged with irresponsibility, unprincipled expediency, or at least inconsistency.[23] He was aware of his reputation and with Emersonian wisdom replied that consistency for its own sake was stupidity, stagnation was death to the race, and flexible activism only would insure race progress. Fortune's shifts drew wide criticism, but less noticed was his life-long adherence to such basic principles as political independence for Afro-Americans, technical-industrial training for Southern blacks, solidarity of effort and race pride, and attainment of civil-economic advances through both agitation for reform and self-help.

Whatever his cause of the moment, Fortune's trenchant prose proved equal to it, and he remained a fighting journalist until the last. In the decade before his death, in addition to editing Garvey's publications, he was a correspondent and contributing editor for many papers, including the *Washington Eagle, Negro Outlook* (Memphis), New York *Amsterdam News, Norfolk Journal and Guide, Birmingham Reporter, Hotel Tattler,* and *Baltimore Afro-American.* In May, 1928, after a month's illness, Fortune came to the Philadelphia home of his son, Dr. Frederick White Fortune. Here he died of heart disease on June 2, 1928, and was buried in Philadelphia's Eden Cemetery on June 6.[24] He was survived by his wife, two of his five children (Dr. Fortune and Mrs. Jessie Bowser), and several grandchildren.

22. *Philosophy and Opinions of Marcus Garvey,* comp. Amy Jacques Garvey, 2nd ed., 2 vols. in 1 (London, 1967), I:54, 37; II:15, 22–26, 135–42 *et passim.*
23. For Fortune's political alliances, see Seth M. Scheiner, "Early Career of T. Thomas Fortune, 1879–1890," *NHB,* 27 (April, 1964), 170–72, and his bibliography. Meier's is a modern view that Fortune was "notoriously inconsistent" (p. 36 *et passim*); for contrast see Slocum, pp. 69ff., 104ff.
24. Death certificate.

Fortune's death at age 72 brought a flood of eulogies in belated tribute to his half-century of struggle for Afro-American rights.[25] Today, when many of his radical proposals have become realities, Fortune is better appreciated as a father of the black power movement who lived by the motto he coined: "The negro wants to have engraved on his heart, 'I will not retreat, I will not yield, I will be heard.' "[26]

Fortune's Poetry

T. Thomas Fortune wrote the fifty poems in *Dreams of Life* (1905) during the last quarter of the nineteenth century when he was the most outstanding Afro-American in journalism.[27] His poetry offers fascinating glimpses of Fortune's ideals and aspirations, of his self-image and his sentimental nature that are nowhere revealed in his fine prose writings. Recurring in all the poems are several themes: all is vanity, and the paths of glory lead but to the grave; "love is life and life is love," but true love is usually found too late or is defeated by a cruel world or a vain woman; liberty and love should be fought for and cherished; the Promethean-Byronic hero is the most admirable of men.

In short lyrics, Fortune's technique is seldom equal to the task of expressing his sentiments effectively. The lyrics are generally weakened by archaic and hackneyed diction, forced end rhymes, and choppy meters, as in these stanzas:

> A few rashly seek to forget in red wine
> Th' affection they strove with their love to entwine,
> But they are far wiser who pine not, but choose
> To seek and secure them an easier won rose.
> ("The Heart That Is Pining")
>
> Oh, take me again to the clime of my birth,
> The dearest, the fairest, to me on the earth,
> The clime where the roses are sweetest that bloom,
> And nature is bathed in the rarest perfume!
> ("The Clime of My Birth")

25. See obituaries: *Negro World*, June 16, 1928; *New York Age*, June 9, 1928; New York *Amsterdam News*, June 6, 1928; *Philadelphia Tribune*, June 7, 1928; *Pittsburgh Courier*, June 9, 1928. Copies in Vertical File, NNSch.
26. "Crisis for the Negro Race," 1900.
27. Reviews of *Dreams* in black periodicals were unusually harsh, perhaps reflecting Fortune's unpopularity in 1905. See *Alexander's Magazine*, 1 (September 15, 1905), 11–12; VN, 2 (October, 1905), 721–22.

On the other hand, a blend of simple diction and formal pattern gives strength of feeling to the melancholy "Edgar Allan Poe":

> I know not why, but it is true—it may
> In some way, be because he was a child
> Of the fierce sun where I first wept and smiled—
> I love the dark-browed Poe. His feverish day
> Was spent in dreams inspired, that him beguiled,
> When not along his path shone forth one ray
> Of light, of hope, to guide him on the way,
> That to earth's cares he might be reconciled.
> Not one of all Columbia's tuneful choir
> Has pitched his notes to such a matchless key
> As Poe—the wizard of the Orphic lyre!
> Not one has dreamed, has sung, such songs as he,
>   Who, like an echo came, an echo went,
>   Singing, back to his mother element.

Fortune's "Emanuel," modeled on "Adonais," is a tender elegy in twenty-eight Spenserian stanzas for Fortune's elder brother, who died at the age of twenty-seven. The poem is technically correct with skillful use of enjambment, the rhyme is not overpowering, and allusions are handled well. However, the language remains prosaic and, as in all of Fortune's longer poems, reiteration of sentiments is chronic. The title poem, "Dreams of Life," is also prolix but not without interest as, in a logically structured scheme, the poet traces careers of monarchs, conquerors, and their fabled monuments to ultimate destruction by man's greed, vanity, and lust for power. Some cogent stanzas in sections VI–IX urge universal liberty, justice, and equality:

> (VIII)   There were no kings of men till men
>   Made kings of men, and of the earth;
>   There were no privileged classes when
>   First Nature, man and beasts, had birth.
>   . . . . .
> (IX)   The giant warrior clothed in steel,
>   The high-walled city, ravaged plain,
>   The angry millions as they reel
>   To battle, death, or woe and pain—
>
>   The world in thrall to him whose might
>   And cunning triumph o'er his kind—
>   Did God make Might the test of Right,
>   Or man,—blind leader of the blind!

Fortune's narrative poems, "Mary Conroy," "Sadie Fontaine," "Mirama," "Fah-Fah," "Dukalon," and "The Bride of Ellerslee,"

vary in length and quality. Moralistic digressions frequently slow
the action, and exigencies of rhyme and meter obscure thought.
However, the language of "Fah-Fah," a Seminole Indian romance,
is precise, and without frills this legend of rival lovers moves at a
pleasingly steady pace. Most characters and plots of the narratives
are indebted to the plantation tradition. Sadie Fontaine, the beau-
tiful fateful octoroon, marries an arrogant Southern plantation lord,
Maurice Lefair. When her parentage is revealed, Lefair commits
suicide and Sadie marries a Frenchman. Two of Fortune's protago-
nists, Guy Dukalon and Ralph Bondly, are fully drawn Byronic
wanderers, fated "to love the world and reap its hate." Bondly in
particular is the melancholy, mysterious, world-weary solipsist, a
good and generous drop-out from life who loves nature and a beau-
tiful woman with all the passion of his superior poetic soul.
Bondly's sixty-six-page quest for love, "The Bride of Ellerslee," is
faithful in form and tone to Byron's *Tales*. Fortune's characters are
vividly developed and brought to life: the hero, Bondly; his love
Nada, a Southern beauty of royal Spanish blood; her gouty, selfish
father Garcia, who despises the Saxon race; and Aunt Sara, the
black mammy and "Voudoo Queen" of the plantation. Although
unnecessarily long, this tale of love's triumph over race prejudice
is generally successful.

Fortune's stand on race is the same in his poetry as in his prose.
He decries prejudice, favors amalgamation, and urges militant re-
sistance to oppression. The hero of "Bartow Black" was personally
known by Fortune in Florida, where he was murdered by the
Ku Klux Klan in 1870. When warned by the Klan that it would be
death to exercise his franchise, Black replied:

> This is my home, and here I die,
>   Contending for my right!
> Then let them come! My colors fly!
>   *I'm ready now to fight!*

It is not surprising that one of Fortune's best poems, "Byron's Oak
at Newstead Abbey," should be a tribute to the "outlaw" poet:

> I love him well, this wayward child of song,
>   Whose life in all was passing strange;
> With mind so bitter sweet, so weak, so strong—
>   With power to soothe, to charm, estrange;—
> Within his grasp the harp was made to flow
> The sweetest, saddest notes the heart can know!
>   . . . .

> And he will live when Newstead and its tree
>   Have crumbled back to mother dust;
> His name is linked with song and liberty,
>   And time such fame can never rust!
> E'er Albion's glorious name must pale and wane,
> While Byron's fame through endless time will reign!

Over a dozen poems in *Dreams* lament unfulfilled love and the death of loved ones, conveying Fortune's loneliness and pain as, over the years, he lost his parents, brother and sisters, three children, and finally, through his own choice, the love of his wife. Most of the other fifty poems reflect on varieties of heroism. Sadness pervades Fortune's convictions that power is a burden, public acclaim a transient privilege, and the man who dares to challenge society inevitably suffers. Although the world often judged him as a tiresome egoist intemperately seeking personal glory, Fortune, like his hero Byron, was a sensitive Romantic and a courageous, race-proud man who grappled with a hostile world for the good of others in the certain knowledge of his painful defeat.

SELECTED SOURCES

Bruce Collection and Fortune (Vertical) File, NNSch: letters and articles.
Meier, August. *Negro Thought in America: 1880–1915.* Ann Arbor: University of Michigan Press, 1963.
Penn, I. Garland. *The Afro-American Press and Its Editors.* 1891; rpt. New York: Arno, 1969.
Simmons, 785–91.
*Slocum, A. Terry. "Timothy Thomas Fortune: A Negro in American Society." B.A. senior dissertation. Princeton, 1967. Copy: NNSch.

GEORGE MARION McCLELLAN
1860–1934

A Goddess bestows on a poet at birth acute sensitivity to beauty and capacity to love, and she takes him into "the service of human sorrows." She forecasts that the child shall have "learning and the cultivation of aesthetic tastes" but win no recognition for his talents; that he will feel brotherhood with all who are oppressed but will stand helpless to alleviate their misery. Finally the goddess promises, "Of all the disgrace and degradation of thy race thou must be a part" and learn wisdom through bitterness. "The Goddess of the Penitentials," a sketch appended to *Poems* (1895), is McClellan's self-portrait at age thirty-five and an uncanny presentiment of the frustrations and tragedy that darken his later years.

The poet was born in Belfast, Tennessee, on September 29, 1860, the son of George Fielding and Eliza (Leonard) McClellan. His life history until age twenty-one is unknown. About 1881 McClellan enrolled at Fisk University, where he earned the B.A. degree in 1885. From 1885 to 1887 he studied at Hartford (Connecticut) Theological Seminary, and in 1887–90 he served as a Congregational minister in Louisville, Kentucky.[1] During this ministry, on October 3, 1888, McClellan married Mariah Augusta Rabb of Columbus, Mississippi, in that city;[2] however, from about 1890 the couple was frequently separated. Mrs. McClellan graduated from Fisk's normal department in 1891, served on the Fisk faculty (1891–92), and earned her B.A. in 1895.[3] Meanwhile, McClellan continued his studies at Fisk to earn the M.A. in 1890; simultaneously he commuted to Hartford, which granted him the bachelor of divinity degree in 1891. The following year McClellan was a minister in

1. Chronology of 1885–96 in *Catalogues of Fisk University.*
2. Marriage certificate, Lowndes County, Miss.
3. Sylvester Dunn, Registrar, Fisk University, in a letter to me.

154

Nashville, and from 1892 until 1894 he traveled extensively through New England as financial agent for Fisk University. The Fisk *Catalogues* record his next position as chaplain of the state normal school in Normal, Alabama, from 1894 to 1896.[4]

In 1895 McClellan published *Poems,* a collection of fifty-seven verses and five sketches, and a year later he reprinted twelve of the verses as *Songs of a Southerner.* McClellan had composed these poems at odd places and times: when he was a student teacher on vacation in the swamps of Mississippi during college days, at train stations while traveling for Fisk, and about his native hills of the Highland Rim of middle Tennessee. The scenes and activities of his youth and young manhood became the substance of his art; his objective as a writer, stated in his essay "Race Literature" in *Poems,* was to counteract charges that the Negro is incapable of high development since he "had contributed essentially nothing to literature." A race literature, he writes, "is a plant of slow growth, the cultivated gift of many generations" which expresses "a national life." The black writer, only thirty years away from slavery, suffers the great disadvantages of lack of education, time, security, and an "inspiring history" necessary to produce a race literature. McClellan confesses in *Poems* that his own work lacks "special merit" because he never had "leisure and freedom from the constant struggle for daily bread." His poverty is painfully evident in an application for scholarship aid he submitted to Hartford Seminary in his senior year, 1890. He had received $72 in 1889, now has on hand "$.0000," and is $35 in debt. He requests funds for seminary expenses to supplement what he may earn from "chance preaching," which must go to support two sisters in school and his wife.[5] Within a few years McClellan had gained two more dependents, his sons Lochiel (born about 1892) and Theodore (1895).

From the turn of the century, fulfilling the prophecies of his goddess, McClellan enjoyed a successful teaching career in Louisville but was beset by financial and personal woes. From 1899 until 1911

4. Levi Watkins, President, Alabama State University, in a letter to me, could find no record of McClellan's association with the school. However, McClellan's tales, "Old Greenbottom Inn" and "For Annison's Sake," take place on the campus of an "Industrial and Normal School of 400 Negro students" in northern Alabama where the narrator is chaplain.

5. Photocopy courtesy of Nafi Donat, Archivist, Case Memorial Library, Hartford Seminary Foundation. I am greatly indebted to Mr. Donat for his helpful letters to me and for photocopies of McClellan's correspondence, "Especial Book Announcements," and other papers held by the seminary.

he taught geography and Latin at Central Colored High School, and from 1911 to 1919 he succeeded his friend, Joseph Seamon Cotter, Sr., as principal of the Paul Dunbar School.[6] During the first decade, in 1906, McClellan paid $500 to publish and advertise *Old Greenbottom Inn,* a novella and four stories. The publisher held back all but 250 of the 1,000 copies because McClellan owed him $100. To raise this sum and get his books for a Christmas sale, he resorted to a "prize offer," sending out 100 circulars, but he received only $8 in reply.[7]

Such publication problems seemed minor beside the greater misfortune which befell the poet ten years later. His younger son, Theodore, was stricken with tuberculosis, and for money to save Theodore's life, McClellan privately published *Path of Dreams* (1916). It contains a tender tribute, "To Theodore": "The erstwhile rushing feet, with halting steps,/ For health's return in Denver watch and wait," while "Love and memories of noiseless tread,/ . . . Kneel nightly now in agony of prayer." A recipient of McClellan's prospectus for *Path of Dreams* with his letter appealing for funds mentions the "heroic struggle of an intelligent and loving father, on behalf of his sick and despised son, despised because of his race." [8] McClellan took Theodore to Los Angeles for treatment, probably in July, 1916. Although details of the boy's battle for life are uncertain, it is clear that he was refused admission to a sanitarium on account of his race, and he died of tuberculosis in Los Angeles on January 5, 1917, at the age of twenty-one.[9] Offering a second edition of *Path of Dreams* in 1929, McClellan wrote: "When I lost the fight, I was so utterly broken in soul and body over the death of the boy, all further effort to sell the book was dropped." The ten new poems of 1916 as well as many in the earlier *Poems* reveal that his son's death was not McClellan's first encounter with sorrow. It is likely that he

6. Charles E. Patterson, Administrative Assistant, Louisville Public Schools, in a letter to me.

7. McClellan, letter to an anonymous recipient of his "prize offer," from Hartford, November 24, 1906. Reviews of *Old Greenbottom Inn* appear in *Alexander's Magazine,* 3 (February 15, 1902), 210, and 6 (June 15, 1908), 87–88. The date of the first review (1902) suggests that an edition earlier than 1906 was published, but I have not located it.

8. James H. Roberts, letter to Professor Jacobus, Hartford Seminary, March 30, 1916.

9. Death certificate of Theodore R. McClellan, Los Angeles County. Certificate, filled out by McClellan, states that Theodore had been a resident of the county for six months. He was buried in Rosedale Cemetery, Los Angeles, on January 8, 1917.

was estranged from his wife, perhaps as early as 1895, and almost surely in the 1920's, when he resided in California.

McClellan had returned to Louisville for a few years after his son's death, but from 1921 through 1925 he lived in Los Angeles. He attended the University of California extension division as a special student in 1921, worked as a probation officer for the county and as a teacher.[10] His whereabouts in 1926–28 are unknown. In 1929, from his "home" in the YMCA of Nashville, Kentucky, Mc-Clellan wrote to Hartford Seminary, requesting a list of alumni to whom he mailed his "Especial Book Announcements." [11] This twelve-page prospectus offered a package of three books for $1.50: a second edition of *Path of Dreams*; *Gabe Yowl* (a murder story, included in the 1916 *Path*); and a new work, *The History of American Literature*. From his long experience as "a teacher of secondary and college English and of English and American Literature," Mc-Clellan recognized the need for an integrated textbook of black and white literature. He hoped to publish the *History* in the spring of 1930, but either the Depression or personal problems intervened, and none of the volumes appeared.

In the four years from his "Announcements" until his death, Mc-Clellan may have taught school in Nashville or in Louisville, where he lived in 1933. In April, 1933, he again requested an alumni list from Hartford and the date of the seminary's May commencement. He planned to leave Louisville shortly, he wrote, travel East, and arrive in Hartford for commencement, the first since his own in 1891. There was no further word from George Marion McClellan. The seminary records his death date as May 17, 1934, place unknown.

McClellan's life spanned four decades of the nineteenth century and three of the twentieth. As a transitional figure, his life and art reflect the plight of Afro-Americans who in their leap from slavery to citizenship felt compelled to forswear their race and its culture to win a place in white society. McClellan continually struggled to raise himself to a position of respect and influence in order to bring credit to the race. To this end he earned three college degrees in ten years while working as a minister, and he taught school for

10. "Especial Book Announcements," p. 1; Los Angeles *City Directory* (1922–30), references courtesy of Marian Marquardt. McClellan's address in 1922–25 was 1669 East 50 Place.

11. "Announcements" includes commendations of *Path of Dreams* from Reuben Post Halleck, Bliss Carman, Joseph S. Cotter, Alice Hegan Rice, J. E. Spingarn, and others.

thirty years. As a black artist McClellan was torn between two cultures, and because he was so gifted a man, highly intelligent, sensitive, ambitious, and race-proud, he suffered keenly from what Du Bois called "double consciousness": the sense of "measuring one's soul by the tape of a world that looks on in amused contempt and pity" while longing to express the "soul-beauty" of the race.[12] McClellan's sense of twoness and of estrangement from both races is the major theme of his poetry.

Like the persecuted hero of his story, "Gabe Yowl," McClellan was an "educated nigger" who felt an unreconcilable contradiction between these terms. He was a man of deep faith and great personal courage whose double consciousness of himself as an American and a Negro inspired and crippled his endeavors.

McClellan's Poetry

McClellan's sixty-seven lyrics treat traditional white subjects—nature, love, and religion—in graceful, classical meters, with restrained diction, sober thought, and refined sensibilities. They appear to offer little originality of subject, sentiment, or detail, yet these poems are spiritual autobiographies whose speaker is the poet (as he admits in the introduction to *Poems*), and they communicate McClellan's struggle to merge two selves, the natural black one and the alien white one.

The speaker usually lies "in indolent repose," daydreaming. He longs to recapture the innocence, peace, freedom, and ecstatic harmony with nature his soul enjoyed before it was corrupted and splintered by experience in the white world; or he envisions a transcendental integration of all souls with the Spirit of his landscapes that will lead mankind to full Christian fellowship. "Lines to Mount Glen" (a poem of eighty-two lines) expresses all elements of McClellan's separation-estrangement-regeneration theme. The poet lies at the base of Mount Glen, his "early childhood friend" which he has come home to worship:

> And so
> It was Old Glen we came at first to love
> In this soft scented air now long ago,
> When first I brought my youthful heart to thee,
> All pure with pulsing blood still hot

12. *The Souls of Black Folk* (1903; rpt. New York: Fawcett, 1961), pp. 16–18.

In its descent of years in tropic suns
And sands of Africa, to be caressed
By thee. And to your lofty heights you bore
Me up to see the boundless world beyond,
Which nothing then to my young innocence
Had aught of evil or deceptive paths.
With maddening haste I quit thy friendly side
To mix with men. And then as some young bison
Of the plain, which breathes the morning air
And restless snorts with mad excess of life,
And rushes heedless on in hot pursuit
Of what it does not know: so I, Old Glen,
As heedlessly went out from thee to meet
With buffeting, with hates, and selfishness,
And scorn. . . . And in the fret
And fever of the endless strife for gain
I often sigh for thee, my native peaks,
And for that early life for me now past
Forevermore.

The stranger luxuriates in the "gentle grace so indefinable" flowing from the mountain's heart to his, but he knows such bliss is temporary. He cannot regain childhood's "all-believing innocence" and must return to the fretful life of men. The poem concludes with his vision of a new Eden:

And here in this perfume of May, and bloom
Luxuriant, and friendly rioting
Of green in all this blooming waste, is seen
A glimpse of that which He, the Lord of all,
Intended there should be with things and men
In all this earth, a thing which yet will be,
A universal brotherhood.

Contemplation of a beloved landscape gives rise to similar sentiments in many poems, including "To Hollyhocks," "In Summer," "The Path of Dreams," "Heart Yearnings," "The Harvest Moon," and "May." The poet has lost a part of himself, the original black soul, invariably exemplified in these poems by the Southland and boyhood with their typical image cluster: light, heat, luxuriant vegetation, pulsating life, heights, and dreams. "A September Night" describes a bayou surrounded by great cotton plantations; it links sensual odors, lush foliage, and rhythmic sounds of alligators, katydids, and insects' wings to the black man's joyous shouts, songs, and laughter, all of which the poet can observe but not share. In "The June" (106 lines), the Southern countryside vibrates with sound and blazes with light and heat. It is described as brilliant, gleaming, golden, shimmering, "teeming everywhere with life and hope." A dreamer recalls his idyllic childhood in these hills, "Bare feet, and careless roving bands of boys/ That haunted lake and stream in halcyon joys." He feels the unseen sublime spirit of the wood, summons all to wear once more the "boyish spirit," and contrasts the lost world with present reality:

> In these no hot contentions, endless strife,
> Nor aching hearts, consuming greed of life,
> No soul-corrupting lusts, debasing sin,
> Nor blighted lives where innocence has been
> Are ever brought by June. But to assuage
> The sorrows of mankind from age to age
> A subtle charm, a bliss, a merry tune
> Abideth in the country lap of June.

McClellan's tributes to his native state, such as "The Hills of Sewanee," "A Song of Nashville," "May Along the Cumberland," and "After Commencement at Fisk University," also express nostalgia for familiar haunts, unfulfilled dreams, and the self now lost.

This black self, for McClellan, is the natural soul, spontaneous, warm, singing in harmony with the land and its guiding Spirit. The black man who pursues whiteness repudiates the law of nature which, to the poet, is the law of God. He points out the hazards of leaving one's native place in another group of poems in which the natural qualities of rivers, insects, birds, and flowers lend themselves to direct analogy with man. In "Youthful Delusions" a young man is reproached for yearning to roam abroad too soon; he will encounter the "lurking woe" of the world and be poisoned for his ambition. Flowers blighted by winter are like this man. In "The Bridal Wreath's Lament," the haughty flower opens its tender leaves and buds to the "soft, deceitful, sighing winds" of spring, only to be frozen by a stealthy storm. Likewise in "A January Dandelion," the thoughtless weed is misled by premature warm days to leave its natural bed:

> And yet, thou blasted, yellow-coated gem!
> Full many hearts have but a common boon
> With thee, now freezing on thy slender stem.
> When once the heart-blooms by love's fervid breath
> Is left, and chilling snow is sifted in,
> It still may beat, but there is blast and death
> To all that blooming life that might have been.

In "A Belated Oriole," the poet claims kinship with the shivering bird, caught in a December storm up North when all his kind and

ALBERY ALLSON WHITMAN. *Not a Man, and Yet a Man* (1877).

JOHN WILLIS MENARD. *African Methodist Episcopal Church Review*, 3 (April 1887), 427.

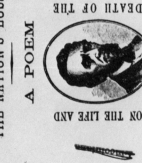

The Emancipation Car by Joshua McCarter Simpson.

The Nation's Loss by Jacob Rhodes.

The Freedmen's Monument. Joseph T. Wilson, *Emancipation* (1882).

LINCOLN

WRITTEN FOR THE OCCASION OF THE

UNVEILING OF THE FREEDMEN'S MONUMENT
IN MEMORY OF ABRAHAM LINCOLN
APRIL 14, 1876

BY

H. CORDELIA RAY

NEW YORK
1893

Lincoln by Henrietta Cordelia Ray.

GEORGE MARION MCCLELLAN.
"Especial Book Announcements"
(1929), Case Memorial Library,
Hartford Seminary Foundation.

TIMOTHY THOMAS FORTUNE.
Dreams of Life (1905).

JOSEPHINE D. HEARD.
Morning Glories (1890).

JAMES D. CORROTHERS.
Robert Kerlin, *Negro Poets and
Their Poems* (1923).

WALTER H. BROOKS. D. W. Culp,
Twentieth-Century Negro Literature
(1902).

JAMES EPHRIAM McGIRT.
Avenging the Maine (1899).

JOSEPH SEAMON COTTER, SR.
Links of Friendship (1898).

CHARLES DOUGLAS CLEM. MISS IRENE CLEM.

DANIEL WEBSTER DAVIS. MRS. LOTTIE DAVIS HARRISON.

Benjamin T. Tanner. William
Simmons, *Men of Mark* (1887).

Frank Barbour Coffin.
Coffin's Poems (1897).

Alice R. M. Dunbar Nelson.
D. W. Culp, *Twentieth-Century
Negro Literature* (1902).

Paul Laurence Dunbar.
Lyrics of Lowly Life (1896).

his mate have fled home to southern skies. The North, dull winter skies, treacherous icy winds and snow, and adulthood symbolize the alien world which McClellan longed to be part of but found uncongenial, often hostile and destructive.

The destruction of youthful love through death of passion or lovers' separation is the theme of McClellan's love poems. A tone of bittersweet pain and yearning sighs through a dozen poems like "Resentment," "The Message of a Dead Rose," "Estrangement," and "A Faithless Love." As in the nature poems, happiness belongs to the past, linked to images of spring and summer in the Southland and to youthful dreams. Other poems such as "My Madonna" and "Thanksgiving Day in New England" poignantly express the loneliness and homesickness of a man in the North estranged from his Southern home.

No humor and little joy brighten McClellan's verse. His most hopeful mood combines selfless stoicism and faith in God, as in "Hydromel and Rue," "Service," "Prayer," and "As Sifted Wheat." His devotion to Gospel idealism prompts him to Christianize a pagan myth in "The Legend of Tannhauser and Elizabeth" (some 460 lines of blank verse). He handles the meter with ease and in unadorned language, without moralistic digressions, swiftly narrates Tannhauser's enchantment by Venus and year-long stay in the Venusburg, his singing in praise of Venus before the Thuringian court, and his fruitless pilgrimage to Rome, where the Pope denies his plea for mercy: "'you may hope/ For God's forgiveness when my staff puts forth green leaves.'" When Tannhauser fails to return with the pilgrims from Rome, fair Elizabeth dies of a broken heart. Later Tannhauser dies of grief just as messengers from the Pope come singing

> Of a great marvel wrought by God, for now
> The staff put forth green leaves in token of
> Tannhauser's full redemption from his sins.

McClellan's faith in God's healing power finds strongest expression in his best-known poem, "The Feet of Judas." Traveling to Fisk in August, 1884, McClellan was forcibly evicted from a train in Alabama. The humiliation left him with "a burning hatred which was consuming" him. "I prayed to have the hatred taken out of my soul," he writes, and "followed the prayer by writing 'The Feet of Judas,' and all feeling of hatred for any human being left me forever." [13]

13. "Especial Book Announcements," pp. 10–12.

The poem's simple diction and repetition of the theme line through
five stanzas give strength to his earnest testament:

> Christ washed the feet of Judas!
>   The dark and evil passions of his soul,
> His secret plot, and sordidness complete
>   His hate, his purposing, Christ knew the whole,
> And yet in love, He stooped and washed his feet.
>
>   .   .   .
>
> Christ washed the feet of Judas!
>   And thus a girded servant, self abased,
> Taught that no wrong this side the gate of Heaven
>   Was ever too great to wholly be effaced,
> And though unasked, in spirit be forgiven.
>
> And so, if we have ever felt the wrong
>   Of trampled rights, of caste, it matters not,
> What ere the soul has felt or suffered long,
>   Oh, heart! this one thing should not be forgot;
> Christ washed the feet of Judas!

McClellan's humble pacifism in this poem and his moderate posture
on race relations in others like "Daybreak" are belied by the mili-
tancy of his fiction. In many stories his contemptuous anger at the
abuses of slavery and at racial discrimination breaks forth undis-
guised. These contradictory attitudes, expressive of McClellan's
double consciousness, are clarified by his account of the genesis of
"The Feet of Judas." Most black men, he writes, quietly accepted
Jim Crow segregation on trains; "But there were a few Negroes who
would fight and I was one of them from boyhood up. I made it a
rule never to carry a pistol. I had many 'rows' and I knew if the
whites ever put hand on me as they did many Negroes I would use
a pistol if I had it on me." Twice McClellan was told to leave the
train; twice he refused. At a station "noted for its mob spirit," a
group of white men approached the car. "I could have gone out of
the car in time to save myself from being dragged out but I had
never run in my life. I think that will be true when I die." [14]

McClellan chose passive resistance, concealing the bitter anger
and violence he naturally felt. His poetry became the outlet for
such emotions, but here again they were artfully disguised. Mc-
Clellan's poetry is distinctly his, readily distinguishable from other
poetry on similar subjects. No other black poet offers his metrical
and stanzaic variety and faultless rhyming so smoothly executed as
to appear effortless, nor does anyone achieve such complexity of

14. *Ibid.*, p. 11.

texture which puzzles and haunts the reader. It is as if the poems were white outside and black inside, for the poet combines description of generic panoramas, overt analogical statements, and graceful diction to generate a cool, detached tone, while from beneath the surface surge deeply personal hungers, bright memories, and painful regrets. McClellan's poems, like the poet himself, lack organic unity—which is indeed their message.

SELECTED SOURCES

Catalogues of Fisk University. 11 vols. 1885–96. NN.
*McClellan, George M. "Especial Book Announcements." N.p., 1929. 12 pp. Case Memorial Library, Hartford Seminary Foundation.
*———. Letters to Hartford Seminary, 1906–33 (MSS). Case Memorial Library, Hartford Seminary Foundation.
White, Newman I., and Jackson, W. C., eds. *An Anthology of Verse by American Negroes.* Durham, N.C.: Trinity College, 1924. P. 92.
WWCR, I, 187.

JOSEPH SEAMON COTTER, SR.
1861–1949

Bardstown, Kentucky, where Stephen Foster wrote "My Old Kentucky Home," was the birthplace of Joseph Cotter, a poet and storyteller described by Robert Kerlin as "an Uncle Remus with culture and conscious art." [1] He was born on February 2, 1861, to Martha Vaughn, a freeborn woman of half African, half Indian-and-English blood, and her common law husband Michael J. Cotter, a Scotch-Irishman who was her employer in Louisville.[2] Joseph Cotter's light-complexioned, broad, square face with its high cheekbones and Caucasian features reveals this racial mixture. Cotter's mother was a literate, fervently religious woman with strong dramatic instincts, and her songs and stories formed Cotter's early education. In *Links of Friendship* (1898) Cotter says he could read at the age of four but had no formal schooling until he was twenty-two. From the age of eight he worked in a brickyard, a distillery, and as a teamster.

In 1883 Cotter enrolled in a Louisville night school and after only ten months began teaching while he continued his evening education. Louisville public school records show Cotter's steady practice of the self-help ethic he preached in his poetry. He attended Louisville night normal schools from 1887 until 1892, earning the life grammar certificate and the life principal certificate. Appointed to teach in the Louisville schools in 1889, he taught at Western Colored School (1889–93?), was principal of Ormsby Avenue Colored School (1895) and Eighth Street School (1903–6?). He served as principal of Paul L. Dunbar School until 1911, when his friend the poet George M. McClellan succeeded him, and Cotter became principal of Samuel Coleridge-Taylor School, a post he held until June, 1942. Cotter's drive for self-improvement was so strong that he began college at age seventy-two. In 1933–35 he studied at Indiana

1. *Negro Poets*, p. 75.
2. Death certificate, Kentucky; Kerlin, *Negro Poets*, pp. 70–71.

University, Kentucky State Industrial College, and Louisville Municipal College.[3]

During his fifty-three-year career as an educator Cotter also worked for race advancement with many local and national organizations, including the Louisville Colored Orphans Home Society, Kentucky Educational Association, Author's League, Association for the Study of Negro Life and History, and NAACP.[4] In addition, he published nine volumes of poetry, stories, plays, sketches, and songs and frequently contributed to periodicals such as the *Louisville Courier-Journal* (from 1884), *National Baptist Magazine* (1894–1908), *Voice of the Negro* (1904–7), *Southern Teachers Advocate* (Kentucky; 1905–6), and *Alexander's Magazine* (1905–9). Beginning in 1895 with *A Rhyming,* a thirty-two-page pamphlet that sold for twenty cents, Cotter's poetry collections were: *Links of Friendship* (1898), *A White Song and a Black One* (1909), *Collected Poems* (1938), and *Sequel to the "Pied Piper of Hamelin"* (1939). He published *Negro Tales* (1912), a volume of seventeen stories; *Negroes and Others at Work and Play* (1947), which included plays, poetry, stories, and songs; and a commemorative history of Louisville's "Little Africa" (1934). His play in blank verse, *Caleb, the Degenerate* (1903), dramatized Booker T. Washington's gospel of work and industrial education which Cotter supported all his life. From the earliest poems to "The Negro's Ten Commandments" (1947), he consistently advocated this gospel:

(5) Read not thyself out of toiling with the hands, and toil not thyself out of reading; for reading creates dreams, and toiling makes one akin to the ox. Therefore he who simply dreams is dying, and he who dreams not is already dead.

(7) Learn thou the worth of a dollar and how to keep it from damning thee.

(9) Socially thou shalt go no nearer thy brother than he comes to thee. Aversion in him should slay the thought of advance in thee.

(10) If thou hast a mind to live by being honest, industrious, frugal and self-sacrificing, remain in the South where thou shalt surely reap thy character's worth; but if thou hast a mind to die through sloth, ignorance and folly, get thee far from it, for the burden of burying such is becoming intolerable.

In his thirtieth year, on July 22, 1891, Cotter married Martha Cox

3. Charles E. Patterson, Administrative Assistant, Louisville Public Schools, in a letter to me.
4. *Who's Who in Colored America,* p. 108.

of Louisville. Their eldest son, Joseph S. Cotter, Jr., was a promising poet, author of *The Band of Gideon,* when he died at twenty-three. Cotter's other two children and his wife also predeceased him. On March 14, 1949, at age eighty-eight, Cotter died in his Louisville home. A memorial service at the Church of Our Merciful Saviour (Episcopalian) on March 17 was followed by burial in Greenwood Cemetery. Cotter was survived by a sister, Mrs. Gertrude Marshall, a foster son, Charles Carter, and an adopted son, William Fields.[5] Surviving him also were three generations of Louisville students he lovingly educated, the many volumes he wrote, and his remarkable example of success achieved through self-help and selfless hard work.

Cotter's Poetry

During five decades of poetry-writing, Cotter's interests range from industrial education in the 1890's to the "zoot suit" and atom bomb in 1947. In both dialect and standard English verse he urges social and moral reform, sectional reconciliation, and brotherhood. He satirizes the foibles and frailties of blacks but also praises their strengths and accomplishments; he philosophically examines God's ways and mysteries of human nature; he comments on historical events and pays homage to notables like Frederick Douglass, William Lloyd Garrison, Cassius M. Clay, Presidents McKinley, Taft, and Roosevelt, Booker T. Washington, and W. E. B. Du Bois; he extols good literature and his literary idols: Shakespeare, Milton, Tennyson, Riley, Holmes, Swinburne, Poe, and his close friend Dunbar. Finally, Cotter writes story ballads and light verse enlivened by wit and striking imagery.

Cotter's major concern is race advancement, to be gained by a mixture of race pride, humility, hard work, education, and a positive, optimistic outlook. He chides lazy, aggressive, extravagant, and parasitical blacks who will never succeed in "The Loafing Negro," "The Don't-Care Negro," "The Vicious Negro," "I'se Jes' er Little Nigger," and "Negro Love Song" (WS).[6] He praises those who are moving upward in "Ned's Psalm of Life for the Negro" (CP); in "The Negro Woman" (CP), which charges the female "To give the

5. Obituary in funeral program. I am indebted to Charles E. Patterson for a copy of the memorial service program.
6. Volume in which a poem first appears: (L) *Links of Friendship,* (WS) *A White Song and a Black One,* (CP) *Collected Poems,* (S) *Sequel to the "Pied Piper of Hamelin,"* (N&O) *Negroes and Others.*

plan, to set the pace,/ Then lead him in the onward race"; and in "The True Negro" (N&O):

> Though black or brown or white his skin,
> He boldly holds it is no sin,
> So long as he is true within,
>   To be a Negro.
>
>   . . . .
>
> He loves his place, however humbling,
> He moves by walking, not by stumbling,
> He lives by toiling, not by grumbling
>   At being a Negro.

Devoted to the ideology of Washington, Cotter advocates self-help, money-getting, and accommodation in verses like "Tuskegee," "The Negro's Educational Creed," and "Dr. Booker T. Washington to the National Negro Business League" (WS):

> Let's spur the Negro up to work,
>   And lead him up to giving.
> Let's chide him when he fain would shirk,
>   And show him when he's living.
>
>   . . . .
>
> What deeds have sprung from plow and pick!
>   What bank rolls from tomatoes;
> No dainty crop of rhetoric
>   Can match one of potatoes.
>
>   . . . .
>
> A little gold won't mar our grace,
>   A little ease our glory.
> This world's a better biding place
>   When money clinks its story.

Caleb, the Degenerate (1903), a four-act play in blank verse subtitled, "A Study of the Types, Customs, and Needs of the American Negro," dramatizes the credo of Cotter's preface: "The Negro needs very little politics, much industrial training, and a dogged settledness as far as going to Africa is concerned. To this should be added clean, intelligent fireside leadership."

Cotter introduces the characters as archetypal Negroes: Caleb, a money-hungry atheist, murders his father, philosophizes in pun-ridden Elizabethan diction, goes mad, and dies; Rahab, an amoral politician and emigrationist, corrupts everyone. Caleb and Rahab typify "unwise, depraved leadership." In contrast, the "highest types" are a magniloquent Bishop and his daughter Olivia, who teaches in the industrial school and unwisely loves Caleb. The

Bishop sprinkles abstruse theological arguments with homilies: "Industrial training is the thing at last," "God's love and handicraft must save the world," "Work is the basis of life's heritage." Olivia, who has written a book, *The Negro and His Hands*, idealizes "hewers of wood and drawers of water" and the true religion:

> Hope is the star that lights self unto self.
> Faith is the hand that clutches self's decree.
> Mercy is oil self keeps for its own ills.
> Justice is hell made present by a blow.

Although *Caleb* is poor drama and mediocre poetry, it is probably the most original tract supporting Washington's policies and as such has considerable sociohistorical interest.

In later years Cotter recognized the value of Du Bois's "Talented Tenth" doctrine in "The Race Welcomes Dr. W. E. B. Du Bois as Its Leader" (S):

> To work with the hands
>   Is to feed your own mouth
> And maybe your neighbor's;
>   To work with the mind
> Is to unleash the feet of millions
>   And cause them to trip
> To the music of progress;
>   We welcome you, prophet,
> You who have taught us this lesson of lessons.

"We welcome you," the poem continues, "Race-called leader of Race . . . Christ-called saver of souls . . . God-sealed brother and prophet." In his subsequent work Cotter supports the combined doctrines of Washington and Du Bois.

Cotter's didactic verse, which appears in every volume, is usually trite in sentiment and style. An exception is the philosophical "The Wayside Well" (CP), with its pleasing design and imagery:

> A fancy halts my feet at the way-side well.
> It is not to drink, for they say the water is brackish.
> It is not to tryst, for a heart at the mile's end beckons
>   me on.
> It is not to rest, for what feet could be weary when a
>   heart at the mile's end keeps time with their tread?
> It is not to muse, for the heart at the mile's end is food
>   for my being.
> I will question the well for my secret by dropping a
>   pebble into it.
> Ah, it is dry.

Strike lightning to the road, my feet, for hearts are like
    wells.
You may not know they are dry 'til you question their depths.
Fancies clog the way to Heaven, and saints miss their crowns.

Using a variety of verse forms which complement their subjects,
Cotter's tributes to those he admires are often successful. "William
Lloyd Garrison" (WS) communicates the militancy, courage, and
altruism of the "God-like" abolitionist; a tender eulogy, "To the
Memory of Joseph S. Cotter, Jr.: Which" (S), asks with simplicity
whether the poet and his son will meet in eternity; and in "Algernon
Charles Swinburne," Cotter parodies Swinburne's themes and ver-
sification to show his admiration:

> Thy gift was a yearning
> That paradised learning,
> And ended in turning
>   All seasons to Junes
> Through death that caresses,
> Through hatred that blesses,
> And love that distresses,
>   And words that are tunes.
>
> A Milton may ghoul us,
> A Shakespeare may rule us,
> A Wordsworth may school us,
>   A Tennyson cheer;
> But thine is the glory,
> Star-sprung from the hoary,
> Flame-decadent story
>   Of the munificent ear.

Such facile rhyming, musicality, and unorthodox word coinage and
word usage distinguish some of Cotter's tales in verse like "The
Tragedy of Pete" (S) and "Sequel to the 'Pied Piper of Hamelin'"
(L). The latter, a lively narrative in thirty stanzas of from four to
twenty-one lines, recounts the search of the people of Hamelin for
their children, lured away by Robert Browning's "Piper." After
many years the childless adults of Hamelin die, and "a race of rats"
occupies the town:

> They swarmed into the highest towers,
> And loitered in the fairest bowers,
> And sat down where the mayor sat,
> And also in his Sunday hat;
> And gnawed revengefully thereat.
> With rats for mayor and rats for people,
> With rats in the cellar and rats in the steeple,

> With rats without and rats within,
> Stood poor, deserted Hamelin.

Cotter's nursery-rhyme tone and rhythms in this "Sequel" are especially effective. A poem of later years, perhaps his most original effort, is reminiscent of Lewis Carroll's lyrical nonsense verse. The tweny-four-stanza "Love's Tangle" (CP) fascinates as it perplexes, and the tangle escapes definition. The poem begins:

> As Simile to myth and myrrh
> She led gruff care to slaughter,
> And saw the moonlight vow to her
> In dimples on the water.

"This maiden on the rillet's brink,/ Hemming the garb of Day," sends birds to woo her lover with song and a sonnet. This seems to be the maiden's song:

> "O rillet, O rillet,
> I see in your face
> A maid with a skillet
> A fish with a grace.

> "And maidens and skillets
> And fishes and graces
> Are all out of place
> In out-of-way places.
>   .   .   .   .
> "O maidens with skillets
> And rillets with fishes,
> I pray that you strangle
> His bliss with my wishes.

After an answering song to the breeze by her lover, the poem ends:

> He begged her for a pardoning kiss,
> He read her song and sonnet;
> Then pressed her throbbing head and found
> A wig pressed to her bonnet.

Added to this great variety of poems are several unpretentious observations of human nature from a personal point of view, like Cotter's casual appreciation, "On Hearing James W. Riley Read (From a Kentucky Standpoint)" (L) and his colloquial greeting, "Answer to Dunbar's 'After a Visit'" (L). Although the aesthetic quality of Cotter's verse is extremely uneven, his catholic tastes and techniques, and his consistent race-consciousness combined with sympathetic regard for the needs, joys, and aspirations of all people, give him well-deserved celebrity among the black poets.

SELECTED SOURCES

Jones, Paul W. L. "Two Kentucky Poets." *VN*, 3 (August, 1906), 586–88.

Kerlin, Robert. "A Poet from Bardstown." *South Atlantic Quarterly*, 20 (July, 1921), 213–21.

———. *Negro Poets and Their Poems*. Washington, D.C.: Associated Publishers, 1923. Pp. 70–81 *et passim*.

Thompson, R. W. "Negroes Who Are 'Doing Things': Joseph Seamon Cotter." *Alexander's Magazine*, 1 (August 15, 1905), 25–26.

Townsend, John Wilson. "Kentucky's Dunbar. Joseph S. Cotter." *Lore of the Meadowland*. Lexington, Ky.: J. L. Richardson, 1911. Pp. 23–27.

Who's Who in Colored America. Ed. Thomas Yenser. 3rd ed. New York: T. Yenser, 1933. P. 108.

DANIEL WEBSTER DAVIS
1862–1913

Three schools in Virginia (at Richmond, Staunton, and Petersburg) bear the name of D. Webster Davis, an educator and Baptist minister, popular orator, versatile writer, and outstanding leader of Richmond's Afro-American community for twenty years. Davis was born on March 25, 1862, in Caroline County, Virginia, where his parents, John and Charlotte Ann (Christian) Davis, had been born and were slaves until emancipation.[1] Webster (the name he preferred) and his sister moved to Richmond with their widowed mother shortly after the Civil War. There he attended local schools and at age sixteen graduated from Richmond High and Normal School. For two years Davis worked at odd jobs until he was of age to teach, and in 1880 he began a thirty-three-year career as seventh grade teacher at Baker Street School in Richmond. During these years Davis also conducted summer normal schools throughout Virginia and taught summer school in West Virginia and the Carolinas.

A co-worker at the Baker Street School, Elizabeth Eloise Smith, became Mrs. Davis on September 8, 1893, about the time that Davis was attending the Lynchburg Baptist Seminary (Virginia Theological Seminary and College) to train for the ministry.[2] After ordina-

1. Biography is largely from letters, newspaper clippings, and a manuscript article sent to me by Davis's daughter, Lottie Davis Harrison, and from Davis's death certificate (copy in my possession). I am indebted to Annie R. Goode of Virginia Union University for an introduction to Mrs. Harrison and for copies of Davis's work; also to Mrs. H. E. McGahey of the Virginia Baptist Historical Society, Virginius C. Hall, Jr., and William M. E. Rachal of the Virginia Historical Society for their assistance.

2. There is some uncertainty about Davis's formal education. According to Mrs. Harrison, he received an A.M. from Guadalupe College and a D.D. from Lynchburg Seminary (dates unknown). Hartshorn assigns both degrees to Guadalupe; Culp notes an honorary A.M. only from Guadalupe in 1898. Guadalupe was founded by Baptists in Seguin, Texas, in 1884, and a record of it after

tion in 1895 he became pastor of the Second Baptist Church in South Richmond from July, 1896, until his death. Under the Reverend Mr. Davis's leadership this congregation increased from 32 to 500 members and erected a modern brick building, dedicated in 1905, which bears a commemorative window to Davis. The pastor's showmanship in the pulpit gained him wide popularity and engagements as a commencement speaker and lecturer to church, college, and civic groups in the United States and Canada.

Under the auspices of the Central Lyceum Bureau, for example, he made a notable tour of Ohio, New York, and New England in the winter of 1900; in July, 1902, he delivered a series of seventeen lectures on "Negro Ideals" at the Hampton (Virginia) Summer Normal Institute.[3] Davis's erudite, artistically structured lectures combined homespun anecdotes, historical facts, contemporary statistics, and quotations from the Bible, Shakespeare, and Greek mythology. His flamboyant platform style is described in this typical press comment on his lecture to a Toronto convention, "The Sunday-School and Church as a Solution of the Negro Problem." He sat on the platform, "a very quiet and a very black Negro, short, chunky, and square-jawed." Then he rose to speak:

> In another moment Niagara's current was dwarfed. There was a torrent of impassioned African eloquence, vibrant, sonorous, ringing, the syllables and words at times tumbling over each other in their impatience to be uttered, again slow, deliberate and deep-toned. . . . The words were perfectly chosen, at times uttered with genius. . . . One moment he had his audience in roars of laughter, the next the tears would start. . . . The audience broke loose in a tumult of applause, and the last few words of the oration were drowned. . . .[4]

In his speeches Davis sometimes flattered the Anglo-Saxon race and asked their help for his people, earning rebuke from modern critics like J. Saunders Redding for his "apparent conviction that the way

---

1925 cannot be located. William L. Spearman of the United Negro College Fund in a letter to me verifies that "Guadaloupe" is no longer in existence.

3. Davis was the first black man to give a series of lectures at the Chautauqua Assembly at Laurel Park, near Northampton, Mass. (July, 1900). Some of his commencement speeches were delivered at Waters Normal Institute, Winston, S.C.; St. Paul Normal and Industrial School, Lawrenceville, Va.; Georgia State Industrial College, Savannah, Ga.

4. Delivered to the International, Interdenominational Sunday School Convention, Massey Hall, Toronto, Canada, June 27, 1905; lecture printed in full in *Masterpieces of Negro Eloquence*, ed. Alice M. Dunbar Nelson (New York: Bookery, 1914), pp. 291–304; press comment quoted by Mrs. Harrison, MS article, p. 5.

for the Negro was the way of cheerful, prideless humility" and de-
pendence (Redding, 53). Davis did say to the Toronto convention,
"I come with no bitterness to North or South. For slavery I acknowl-
edge all the possible good that came to us from it; the contact with
superior civilization, the knowledge of the true God, the crude
preparation for citizenship; yet, slavery had its side of suffering and
degradation." Such conciliatory statements echo Booker T. Wash-
ington, whose ideology is manifest in Davis's notes for the Hampton
series and in his lectures, "Gumps" (or "Some Fools I Have
Known"), "Jim Crow's Search for the Promised Land," "The Race
Problem—Its Ins and Outs," and "Paying the Fiddler." [5]

> Negro must work out his destiny largely in the South. The Negro
> must seek heartiest co-operation of all his friends both North and
> South.
>
> Negro must learn to help himself, to rely more and more on himself,
> start in all lines of business for himself, be aided by those of his own
> race. This is what "Self Help" movement in Va. really means.
>
> He must not hope to be a governor, before he has learned to govern
> himself. . . . He should strive not so much for political office as for
> political influence as affords protection for his property and his life.
> We need more carpenters, blacksmiths, farmers, cooks, laborers, than
> doctors, lawyers and preachers. . . . Labor, all labor is noble and
> holy.

Like Washington, Davis criticized the faults and foibles of his
race. On the other hand, Davis emphatically blamed white society
for the race problem:

> For every unjust act, for every lynching, for every burning, for every
> unfair conviction, for every crime against truth and right America
> must pay the Fiddler. She is paying the Fiddler now for human
> slavery, and the Negro problem, at which the whole country North
> and South stands appalled, is simply the stupendous debt with com-
> pound interest we owe the stern Fiddler Justice for 250 years of
> human slavery.

Moreover, unlike the Sage of Tuskegee, Davis demanded equal op-
portunities and privileges for blacks in education, occupations, po-
litical and social life. He continually preached, "Inculcate race love
and race pride. . . . *Put Negroes pictures on our walls.* . . . Give
a Negro message to the world." Davis thus undercut the accommo-

5. Davis's notes and lectures are in two unpublished notebooks. I am greatly
indebted to Mrs. Harrison for lending me the notebooks and copies of Davis's
unpublished poetry. Unless otherwise noted, all prose quotations are from the
notebooks.

dationist doctrine at every turn. He recognized what modern historians have only recently acknowledged: that Washington was not in fact a carbon copy of the old-time foot-scraping house slave, "Uncle Ned." Uncle Ned, Davis writes, "died at Appomattox in '65 and is never coming back again. Many thought Booker Washington was Uncle Ned come back again, they found it was his son."

> Uncle Ned was a chairbacker, his son is a preacher. Uncle Ned was a conjurer, his son is a doctor. . . . Uncle Ned was passive, his son must be active. . . . We must now contend for place with the greatest race. Survival of the fittest—Struggle in the animal world. Uncle Ned's son must prepare for the struggle. He must stand by his guns, unafraid.

The new black man, Davis writes, is as willing to fight for the flag in '95 as Uncle Ned in '65, but he demands his own officers. In support of black leadership and in keeping with his mixed moderate-militant ideology, Davis welcomed T. Thomas Fortune's radical Afro-American League (1887), Washington's National Negro Business League (1900), and Du Bois's Niagara Movement (1905). All, he wrote, are necessary.

Davis captivated both Anglo-Saxon and Afro-American audiences by enlivening his stern messages with poignant tales of black heroism, dozens of ethnic jokes, and dialect verses. To the exhortations and entertainment he added the appeal of Christian idealism, his faith that the white nation's conscience would make racial justice prevail, and, above all, his faith that the race's unquestioned acceptance of the Gospel's spiritual and ethical dogmas would alone bring "the Negro's ultimate elevation to the heights of civilization and culture." "We are to rise," he said, "by the virtue, character and honesty of our men and women." [6]

Although Davis emphasized the primacy of piety and moral living, he did not deny the value of education and wealth for race advancement.[7] To inspire black youth with pride in their heritage and to encourage their progress in commerce and the professions, Davis labored for four years (with Giles B. Jackson) to prepare *The Industrial History of the Negro Race* (1908, rev. 1911). This

6. "The Sunday School and Church." Davis's priorities never varied: "The road is straight before us—*Justice, honesty, truth, virtue, wealth* and above all *religion*" ("Jim Crow's Search").

7. See Davis's essay, "Did the American Negro Make, in the Nineteenth Century, Achievements Along the Lines of Wealth, Morality, Education, etc., Commensurate with His Opportunities? If So, What Achievements Did He Make?" in Culp, 38–41.

400-page volume chronicles Afro-American accomplishments in religion, education, business, farming, banking, literature, and art.[8] In addition to the *History*, which was used as a textbook in the Richmond public schools for many years, Davis wrote a biography of the Reverend William W. Browne (1910) to publicize the highly successful financial and benevolent ventures of the United Order of True Reformers.

Like "True Reformer Browne," Davis won respectful admiration from both races during a lifetime of service to the black community of Richmond. In addition to his contributions as a minister, teacher, lecturer, and prose writer, he published two collections of poetry, *Idle Moments* (1895) and *'Weh Down Souf* (1897), and edited a weekly newspaper, *Social Drifts*. Davis aided black economic development as vice-president of the Virginia Building, Loan and Trust Company and the Negro Development and Exposition Company, and he represented his race on the governing board of the Society for Better Housing and Living in Richmond. Davis served as secretary of the Richmond YMCA and president of Jonesboro A. & I. Academy; he was an active member of the Dunbar Literary and Historical Society, the St. Luke Circle, the True Reformers, and held the rank of thirty-third-degree Mason.

The Reverend D. Webster Davis's community and colleagues demonstrated their esteem for him during his last years and at his death. Early in 1910 when his health failed, friends raised money to send the family to Hot Springs, Arkansas. Here Davis found relief but not recovery; returning to Richmond, he died of nephritis on October 25, 1913, at age fifty-one.[9] His elaborate funeral at the First Baptist Church drew the largest crowd in the church's history "to witness the last rites over one of the most prominent and influential colored men the South had ever produced." The *Richmond Planet* further reported that a "solid wall of humanity" blocked streets and adjoining yards through which police cleared a path for

8. A chapter, "The Negro in Literature" (recorded in its entirety in Davis's notebook) is an unusually comprehensive and astute bibliographical survey. Davis discusses the major black prose writers, including Frederick Douglass, George Williams, E. H. Crogman, I. Garland Penn, Joseph T. Wilson, William Wells Brown, John M. Langston, William Simmons, William Still, Bishops Daniel A. Payne and H. M. Turner, Anna J. Cooper, John E. Bruce, Kelly Miller, R. C. O. Benjamin, Sutton Griggs, Charles Chesnutt, Washington, and Du Bois; he also comments on the neglected early black poets (Horton, Harper, Whitman) and his contemporaries, Corrothers and Dunbar.

9. Death certificate. At his death Davis resided at 908 North 7th Street, Richmond.

the coffin.[10] By order of Richmond's superintendent of schools, J. A. C. Chandler, all colored schools adjourned for the day.[11] Teachers, students, and leading ministers from many cities, like the Reverend Walter H. Brooks of Washington, joined in tribute with prominent citizens of both races, including members of the Richmond school board, president of the Virginia Baptist state convention, and representatives of Virginia Union University. Nine organizations participated, including those in which Davis had been most active as well as the Knights Templars and Knights of Pythias.

The death of D. Webster Davis was mourned as a loss to the entire city of Richmond. An editorial in the white *Richmond Times-Dispatch* eulogized the man who had brought "many diverse minds together for common labor in a common cause":

> Richmond is poorer today by the passing from its community life of a man who served the splendid duty of being an interpreter for the negro. Webster Davis, educator, minister and author, had earned the respect and admiration of his own race and of his white friends by his simplicity, sincerity, and unselfishness. . . . His understanding of negro problems made him of great service to the people of Richmond who worked for better life among the other race.[12]

On October 28 Davis was buried in Greenwood Cemetery. Mrs. Davis, who lived until 1960, raised and gave a college education to their three children: Daniel W. Davis, Jr., who died in 1966, Coleridge Dunbar Davis, and Mrs. Lottie Davis Harrison.

In 1898 Davis had written to John Edward Bruce, the New York journalist, thanking him for a "magnificent" review of *'Weh Down Souf* and asking for further publicity "in some of 'de whi folks papuz." [13] The dialect phrase in Davis's evenly flowing florid handwriting recalls the showmanship that won him renown as an orator, but it also reveals his keen understanding of contemporary black-white relations. Moreover, it emphasizes the ironic protest conveyed by Davis's choice of " 'weh down souf"—the most feared phrase in slavery days—for a poem extolling the Southland and for the title of his poetry collection. By assuming the roles of moderate "interpreter for the negro," of naive "darky" poet and clownish orator,

---

10. "Rev. Dr. Davis Passes Away," *Richmond Planet*, XXX, no. 49, n.d. (October 30, 1913?). Photocopy courtesy of Mrs. Harrison.
11. Mimeographed notice dated Richmond, October 27, 1913.
12. "The Loss of an Interpreter," October 28, 1913, p. 4. The *Times-Dispatch* also reported Davis's death (October 26, 1913, p. 2) and funeral (October 29, 1913, p. 9). Copies courtesy of William M. E. Rachal.
13. MS 1283, Bruce Collection, NNSch.

D. Webster Davis worked successfully within the Southern estab-
lishment with one thought in mind: "Let each of us dedicate our-
selves to the glory of our race and each become immortal." Like
Washington, Davis was an unsentimental pragmatist and far less
accommodating than he seemed. Davis's legacy to his race is a rich
store of imaginative poetry and forceful prose, and the image of a
dedicated, race-proud man who rose "up from slavery" to lead the
Afro-American community of Richmond and the South.

Davis's Poetry

In his poetry, as in his prose, Davis amplifies the race's achieve-
ments and teaches Gospel idealism and self-help. To these he adds
the humorous nostalgic view of antebellum plantation life in his
dialect verse. Davis stated his literary goals succinctly: "People want
to be instructed and entertained. The writer who can do this is the
one in demand."

Davis's poetry in standard English, about one-third of his output,
is generally sentimental or moralistic in tone and written in com-
monplace or stiffly classical language. Nevertheless, its catholic
range of subjects and variety of metrical forms are notable. "Child-
hood's Happy Days" (in eight stanzas) recalls the pains and medi-
cines, torments of school, wintertime chores, and hand-me-down
clothes young Webster endured. But the poet anticipates better
days ahead:

> Still I find that life's a "hustle" from the cradle to the tomb,
> With little beams of sunshine to lighten up the gloom.
> If we can help a brother, and mix our cares with joys,
> Old age will be as happy as the days when we were boys,
> Till at last we sing in rapture heav'nly songs of love and praise,
> When our bark is safely anchored—there to spend our happiest days.

Davis's sixteen-stanza "Emancipation" celebrates the event, de-
scribes the sorrows of slavery with full Christian forgiveness, and
praises Negro heroism and the blessed freedom now come. Another
celebratory piece, "Exposition Ode," read at the opening of the
Negro Building at Atlanta (1895), echoes Washington's famous
address at the Exposition: "Too long we've looked outside ourselves
to seek some guiding star;/ We'll cease and 'let our buckets down
in places where we are.'" In this ode Davis envisions "a new sun
dawning" with "disfranchisment, injustice and prejudice gone," as

black and white rejoice and live together in their beloved " 'Dixie Land.' "

Among other nondialect pieces in his two collections are "A Rose," a simple, neatly turned love poem; "Old Normal," a tribute to Richmond High and Normal School; and "I Can Trust," a devotional poem in an interesting, deftly sustained meter:

> I can not see why trials come,
>   And sorrows follow thick and fast;
> I cannot fathom His designs,
>   Nor why my pleasures cannot last,
> Nor why my hopes so soon are dust;
>   But I can trust.

Davis summarizes his ideals in "The Negro Meets to Pray," written for the Negro Young People's Christian and Educational Congress in Atlanta (1902) and published in his *Industrial History*.[14] An inspirational poem in twenty stanzas of regular iambic pentameter, it is impressively strong in Christian faith and hope for race progress:

> We seek the truth, nor wish one fault to hide;
>   The truth alone is that can make men free,
> Expose the sores, the remedies applied
>   Will soothe and heal, and give true liberty.
>
> Not to complain of burdens hard to bear;
>   To fret and whine, resolve and go away;
> We meet to plan how we can do our share
>   To lift the load—the Negro meets to pray.
>   . . . .
> No flaming swords, no curses loud and deep,
>   We bring to-day, though we have suffered long.
> Oh, rouse, ye race, from calm indifferent sleep,
>   And face life's work—then only are we strong.
>
> God hear us now, and guide our thoughts aright,
>   Give inspiration from above today;
> Plan for us well, and help us see the light;
>   By Thy command, Thy children meet to pray.

On the rare occasions when Davis's work appears in black literary anthologies, it is his dialect verse that is selected. In 1896 William Dean Howells praised Dunbar's dialect pieces in *Lyrics of Lowly Life* as expressions of the hearts and minds of the race "whose poetry had hitherto been inarticulately expressed in music, but now

14. "The Negro Meets to Pray" also appeared in *AMECR*, 19 (October, 1902), 573–74, with a photograph of Davis.

finds, for the first time in our tongue, literary interpretation of a very artistic completeness." More than a year before Dunbar's lionization began, however, Daniel Webster Davis had versified the traditions, idiosyncrasies, and moods of the Southern black in *Idle Moments,* enlarged in 1897 as *'Weh Down Souf.*[15] The quantity and sustained charm of Dunbar's poetry, which brought him worldwide celebrity, eclipsed Davis's contributions. But Davis in many poems conveys with equal humor, warm affection, touching realism, and irony the lives of black folk in his native Virginia. The introduction to *Idle Moments* says, "Much that is best in the American Negro is traditional; all that is worst is historical, and not of his writing." Davis versifies the traditional: church-going, holiday celebrations, superstitions and trickery, recreations, and good eating of plantation days.

With gentle mockery this modern clergyman-poet re-creates old-time sermons with their vivid metaphors and biblical allusions in "Skeetin' on de Ice," "De Chana Cup," and "Payin' fur de Hydin'." He sympathizes with folks who mourn that "De ol'-time groans an' shouts an' moans am passin' out ub sight" to be replaced with "stylish" religion, where old-timers accustomed to "de linin' ub de hymns" must now "foller 'long behin'." In Davis's poetry plantation religion is the black community's major source of pleasure, of proud fellowship and supportive identity, whether enhanced by "banjer music," shouts, dancing, and finery, or expressed as simply as:

> "I'm Baptis' bred,
>   An' Baptis' born,
> An' when I'm ded
>   Dar's a Baptis' gone."

Food of the poet's boyhood is a favorite source of mouthwatering reminiscence in such poems as "Bakin' an' Greens," "Cookin' by de Ol'-Time Fire-Place," "Is Dar Wadermilluns on High," and "Hog Meat." Davis celebrates the best-loved dishes: "Virginny pun'kin pie," "ash-cake between de collud leaves," roast possum, "ginger snaps and cider" at Christmastime, and a dozen delicacies from the generous porker. His affection for "good ol' fashion ways" extends to the Southland as a whole:

15. A majority of the poems in *Idle Moments* had previously appeared in the *Richmond Planet* and *Educator, Social Drifts,* the *Virginia Baptist, Young Man's Friend, Southern News,* and *New York Age.* A four-page prospectus for *'Weh Down Souf,* issued by the Helman-Taylor Company, is held by NNSch and ViHi.

O, de birds ar' sweetly singin',
   'Weh down Souf,
An' de banjer is a-ringin',
   'Weh down Souf;
An' my heart it is a-sighin',
Whil' de moments am a-flyin'
Fur my hom' I am a-cryin',
   'Weh down Souf.

Like Dunbar, Davis is a musical poet whose lilting melodies create an idealized paradise of leisurely summer days when "de pickaninnies 's playin'," "wadermilluns" ripen, and cares vanish:

When de sun is shinin' brightly, jes' erbout de time
   ub noon,
An' de flies ar' lazy buzzin' wid a sweet an' lubly
   chune,
I'se a settin' dar a-noddin', like a scholar wid his
   book,
While de fishes is a-bitin' all de bait frum off my
   hook.
                 ("Fishin' Hook an' Worms")

Very often (as in the title poem, "'Weh Down Souf," and "When de Sun Shines Hot") the title becomes the poem's refrain, intensifying the image of a circumscribed, harmonious world in a long-ago and far-away fairy tale setting.

Poems like these are denounced by modern Afro-Americans for reinforcing the stereotypes of shiftless, rhythmical, and gluttonous blacks popularized by the minstrel tradition. Davis's *'Weh Down Souf* is cited as proof of his Pollyanna reasoning, his Uncle Tomism, and a childlike nostalgia for an unreal past. Such criticism of Davis is soundly refuted by his unpublished prose, which reveals that he used the dialect poems in his lectures as exempla of evil habits bequeathed to the race by slavery, a crippling debt which modern blacks had to liquidate. Although there are "Negroes and Negroes," he wrote, the race is judged by members of its lower class. These he described as the shiftless, extravagant and showy, untidy, dishonest, unreliable, imitative, superstitious, and immoral blacks who pull down the entire race and must be regenerated by their teachers and ministers. Thus Davis's poems become teaching aids. In the lecture "Gumps," for example, the "old gump" complains that everything is worse than it used to be. Davis recites "Cookin' by de Ol'-Time Fire-Place" (celebrating plantation feasts); then he says that things and cooks are in fact much better than they were, that the race must not look back but live and work in the present to construct a better future. Three poems illustrate the lecture "Uncle Ned and His Son," a comparison of old and new Afro-Americans. Davis begins with "Fishin' Hook an' Worms" (portraying the shiftless, carefree Uncle); he then says Uncle Ned "was a darkey," without a name of his own, docile and cringing, and satisfied to be a darkey with his shovel, hoe, fiddle, and bow. Uncle Ned's son, however, must "*Hang up the fiddle and the bow.*" Uncle Ned was intensely religious, as the second poem, "De Baptis' Church," relates. That was good, Davis says, but today we want "*meat*" with the "gravy." The lecture continues. Uncle Ned loved his banjo and fiddle, illustrated by the poem, "Miss Liza's Banjer"; but one day he heard a different music, a "new note" from the grand piano in the great house. Uncle Ned's son "resolves to get a piano of his own and learn that music," which is "American civilization with all of its rights and privileges."

Similarly, in Davis's lecture "Paying the Fiddler," the poems "Hog Meat" (often criticized as the nadir of "epicureanism") and "Hants" (on superstitions) illustrate the shiftless and the ignorant slave, respectively, while "Jus Gib Him One ub Mine" and "De Chana Cup" reveal admirable qualities of the black man: his "cheerful and sunny" outlook and his religiosity. In one instance the poem explicitly conveys the critical message of the prose. Rastus's puzzled complaint in "De Nigger's Got to Go" defends the black man's right to American citizenship and is introduced by the remark, "We must reach the Promised Land as Negroes or not at all. This is God's country and not the white man's. He has the upper hand. God holds the Title" ("Jim Crow's Search").[16] The ten-stanza, tightly constructed monologue is Davis's most trenchant social commentary in verse. Rastus reviews the slaves' work—"Dey made Virginny like de rose"—and their loyalty in war and politics. He wonders if it is because blacks are now rising, "An' sum un us is gittin' rich,/ Wid do'-bells on de do'," that they are told "we all got to go":

> De Lord he made dis lubly lan'
> Fur white and black folks too,
> An' gin each man his roe to ten'—
> Den what we gwine to do?

16. Davis frequently insisted that America was his race's Promised Land. Not only was deportation (or voluntary emigration) logistically unsound, but it was also futile, for "the white man is everywhere on earth, in heaven and certainly in hell."

> We 'habes ourselbes an' 'specks de laws,
>   But dey's peckin mo' an' mo'.
> We ain't don nuffin 't all to dem,
>   Den huccum we mus' go?
>
> Fur ebry nashun on de glob'
>   Dis seems to be a hom';
> Dey welkums dem wid open arms,
>   No matter whar dey frum;
> But we, who here wuz bred an' borhn,
>   Don't seem to hab no show;
> We ho'ped to mek it what it is,
>   But still we'z got to go.

Rastus concludes that they "got a right to stay," and his Liza has the last word: "An' 'cepin' de Lord sez—'Forward march!'/ We'z not a-gwine to go."

It is inevitable that the dialect poetry of Davis and Dunbar be compared for aesthetic merit. Although the dialect medium confined both poets to humorous, pathetic, or ironic observations, Dunbar's topical range is broader and his emotions more varied than Davis's. Moreover, Davis sometimes breaks the mood or melody of his verses by lapsing into moralistic comment and metrical irregularity. His imagery is limited, less concrete and particularized than Dunbar's, and his dialogues are less forthright and picturesque. Davis's narratives often founder, while his settings, characters, and their sentiments may fade into stereotypes. Stanzas from Davis's "When de Sun Shines Hot" and Dunbar's "Song of Summer" may be compared as evocations of summertime:

"When de Sun Shines Hot"   (Davis)

(1)

> Yo' may talk erbout de snowflakes,
>   An' de pleasen' winter breeze;
> Ub de pledjurs foun' in skeetin',
>   When de ice begins to freeze;
> Ub de 'joyments ub de winter,
>   Dat yo' think a happy lot—
> But gib to me de summer,
>   When de sun shines hot.

(3)

> But 'long wid frogs an' lizzuds,
>   When de sun kums out,
> My bones begin er thawin',
>   An' I'm ready fur to shout.

Fur de happy thoughts ub summer
  Makes me feel all right
Fur de wadermillun's kumin'
  When de sun shines bright.

"Song of Summer"   (Dunbar)

(1)

Dis is gospel weathah sho'—
  Hills is sawt o' hazy.
Meddahs level ez a flo'
  Callin' to de lazy.
Sky all white wif streaks o' blue,
  Sunshine softly gleamin',
D' ain't no wuk hit's right to do,
  Nothin' 's right but dreamin'.

(3)

Squir'l a-tippin' on his toes,
  So 's to hid an' view you;
Whole flocks o' camp-meetin' crows
  Shoutin' hallelujah.
Peckahwood erpon de tree
  Tappin' lak a hammah;
Jaybird chattin' wif a bee,
  Tryin' to teach him grammah.

For this reader, the diction, pace, and simple, personalized observations of Davis's poem give it an authentic charm that Dunbar's more artistic song misses. Granting a lesser "white" talent to Davis does not deny aesthetic value to his dialect poems. Moreover, as has been shown, in the context of Davis's life and prose writings, his verse was designed to instruct while it pleased, and it retains historical and racial significance which Dunbar's entertaining melodies lack.

Davis, said Sterling Brown, is "merely a Negro Thomas Nelson Page," whose poems are "oddly free of difficulties, and therefore unbelievable." His humor, Brown continues, "is of the jokebook sort," his philosophizing "empty," and his writing "crude." [17] The effectiveness of Davis's humor and the depth of his insights into human nature need no further defense; the poet's abuse of the folk speech —with misspellings, inversions, and incongruous words—is common to many writers, white and black. To Davis's credit, he wrote from firsthand experience of Southern blacks (unlike the Ohioan, Dunbar), and he was a scholar of dialect. Noting variations of pronun-

17. *Negro Poetry and Drama* (Washington, D.C., 1937), p. 37.

ciation throughout the South, Davis worked with his publisher to achieve the "perfect line." [18] In *'Wey Down Souf*, he offers a two-page glossary of dialect words and their equivalents in standard English, such as these examples taken at random:

Fhar	fair
Ho'ped	helped
Huccum	how comes
Inchin'	coming slowly
Medjur	measure
Peckin'	impose upon
Reggin'	reckon
Shorz	sure as
Tak' hur	get out of the way

The introduction to both his poetry volumes discusses Afro-American dialect, and in his *Industrial History* Davis points to the similarities between black and white Southern speech as well as the differences in dialect among various Southern states and even in parts of the same state. In short, Davis worked seriously at his dialect poetry, and although it exhibits all the flaws of the genre, it numbers quite a few engaging, tuneful lyrics, which may be enjoyed as evocations of a bygone life "'weh down souf."

SELECTED SOURCES

Culp, 39.
*Harrison, Lottie D. "Daniel Webster Davis." 7 pp. Condensed in *NHB*, 18 (December, 1954), 55–57.
Hartshorn, William N., ed. *An Era of Progress and Promise, 1863–1910.* Boston: Priscilla, 1910. P. 454.
Redding, 53–56.
Wright, John L. "Three Negro Poets." *CAm*, 2 (April, 1901), 404–13.

18. Byron E. Helman, letter to John E. Bruce, MS 1281, Bruce Collection, NNSch. Other letters here by or about Davis are MSS 1395 and 1262.

JAMES EDWIN CAMPBELL
1867–95

The earliest and best collection of dialect poems of the nineteenth century was the work of James Edwin Campbell, a native of Pomeroy, Ohio. Born on September 28, 1867, Campbell attended public school in Pomeroy and graduated from its academy in June, 1884.[1] For two years he taught school in Buck Ridge, near Gallipolis, Ohio, and then moved to Charleston, West Virginia. Here, according to his friend and biographer, Carter G. Woodson, Campbell edited Christopher Payne's newspaper, *Pioneer*.[2] Subsequently he became principal of the Langston School in Point Pleasant, West Virginia. Campbell was writing poetry during these years; his ninety-six-page collection, *Driftings and Gleanings,* was published in Charleston in 1887, and a long poem, "The Pariah's Love," appeared in 1889.

In 1891, in conformance with the Morrill Act which funded land-grant colleges, the West Virginia legislature established an agricultural and mechanical arts school for black youths in Charleston. When this West Virginia Colored Institute opened with twenty students on May 3, 1892, Campbell was its young principal and professor of mathematical science. On the staff of the school were M. L. C. Campbell, secretary and librarian, and Mrs. Mary Camp-

1. Campbell's attendance at Miami University, reported by Harlan, could not be confirmed. I am indebted to Robert T. Howard, Director of Public Information, Miami University, Oxford, Ohio, for his extensive efforts at verification; also to Joyce C. Agnew, University of Cincinnati, and Marian H. Winters, University of Cincinnati College of Medicine (formerly Miami Medical College). Woodson says Campbell was not a college graduate.

2. Materials supplied by Carolyn J. Zinn, Director, West Virginia Department of Archives and History, and Rowell's *American Newspaper Directory* (New York, 1886) suggest that the newspaper Campbell edited was J. R. Clifford's *Pioneer Press* (Martinsburg and Moorefield, W.Va.), the only paper in the state devoted to black readers.

bell, instructor in music, but their relations to the principal, if any, are unknown.[3]

In the early 1890's a mining boom in West Virginia attracted many Afro-American workers from neighboring states. Woodson, who was one of these miners, recalls that their sudden affluence precipitated constant "drinking, gambling, rioting." Campbell, a forceful orator, spoke at meetings in the mines and persuaded several miners to reform and seek an education at the institute. Woodson describes Campbell at this time as a "fine-looking man, always neatly dressed, looking spick-and-span, and manifesting the qualities of a gentleman whom one had to respect." An oil painting of Campbell, hanging in the West Virginia State College library, shows a very light-complexioned man with a full oval face, high cheekbones, and prominent ears, sporting a pince-nez and dandyish handlebar moustache.

Enrollment at the Institute had doubled by May 29, 1894, when Campbell resigned and moved to Chicago. He joined the staff of the *Times-Herald* and in 1895 published his second volume of poetry, *Echoes from the Cabin and Elsewhere*. Campbell's poetry was appreciated during and after his lifetime. Richard B. Harrison, the actor, often gave it public readings; Harry T. Burleigh set some poems to music; two selections appeared in the *A.M.E. Church Review* as late as 1918. Campbell's promising career as a poet, educator, and journalist was cut short by his death at age twenty-eight. He had returned to his home in Pomeroy, Ohio, for the Christmas holidays in 1895 and died there after a brief illness.

Campbell's Poetry

The Ohioans Campbell and Dunbar were close friends and may have influenced one another. However, Campbell's *Driftings and Gleanings* appeared in 1887, six years before Dunbar's first slim book, *Oak and Ivy*, and Campbell's *Echoes from the Cabin* (1895) preceded Dunbar's celebrated *Lyrics of Lowly Life* by one year. Modern black critics have praised Campbell's dialect poetry. Sterling Brown admired his originality, his "hard realism missing in Dunbar," and the aptness of his phrasing, rhymes, and rhythms. "Campbell's dialect," said J. Saunders Redding, "is more nearly a

3. The Colored Institute is now West Virginia State College. Harlan and *West Virginia Bulletin*, copies courtesy of the Reference Department, West Virginia State College Library.

reproduction of plantation Negro speech sounds than that of any
other writer in American literature." James Weldon Johnson also
commended Campbell's dialect but found it "idiomatically and pho-
netically . . . nearer to Gullah [of South Carolina] or to the West
Indian dialect" of Claude McKay.[4]

Campbell's materials, purpose, and achievement are succinctly
defined by Richard Linthicum, editor of the *Chicago Sunday Times-
Herald*, in his introduction to *Echoes*:

> In his anti-bellum state the Negro was close to nature. He gave a
> language to the birds and beasts, and his simplicity and superstition
> formed the basis for a charming fiction. . . . American literature has
> preserved few of these types. . . . The author of this volume has
> caught the true spirit of the ante-bellum Negro, and in characteris-
> tic verse has portrayed the simplicity, the philosophy, and the humor
> of the race. In no instance has he descended to caricature, which has
> made valueless so many efforts in this fertile field of literary effort.

Campbell dedicated his dialect poems to "the Negro of the old
regime" and captured "the joy and pathos of his song" in over a
dozen lively lyrics. In the tradition of folk fables, the poet employs
animal antagonists. In "The Courting of Miss Lady-Bug," a flea, a
roach, and a gnat compete for her love; in "Ol' Doc' Hyar" wily Doc-
tor Hare loses a patient but not his fee:

> Ur ol' Hyar lib in ur house on de hill,
> He hunner yurs ol' an' nebber wuz ill;
>
> . . . . .
>
> He doctah fur all de beas'ses an' bu'ds—
> He put on he specs an' he use beeg wu'ds,
> He feel dee pu's' den he look mighty wise,
> He pull out he watch an' he shet bofe eyes;
> He grab up he hat an' grab up he cane,
> Den—"blam!" go de do'—he gone lak de train,
>   Dis Ol' Doc' Hyar,
>   Whar lib up dar
> Een ur mighty fine house on ur mighty high hill.

Doc' Hyar, summoned to the sickbed of Mr. B'ar, pierces his pa-
tient with a "sha'p li'l lawnce";

4. Brown, *Negro Poetry and Drama* (Washington, D.C., 1937), pp. 36–37;
Redding, 51–53; Johnson, *The Book of American Negro Poetry* (1922; rev. and
enl., New York, 1958), p. 64. Jean Wagner, in a sensitive analysis of Campbell's
poetry, stresses his independence from the minstrel and plantation themes, his
careful, sympathetic observation of people and folk values, and Campbell's
"racial consciousness," "satirical spirit," and religious skepticism, which fore-
shadow the poetry of the Harlem Renaissance. *Black Poets of the United States*
(Urbana: University of Illinois Press, 1973), pp. 129–38.

But de vay naix day Mistah B'ar he daid;
Wen dee tell Doc' Hyar, he des scratch he haid:
"Ef pashons git well ur pashons git wu's,
Money got ter come een de Ol' Hyar's pu's;
Not wut folkses does, but fur wut dee know
Does de folkses git paid"—an' Hyar larfed low,
        Dis sma't Ol' Hyar,
        Whar lib up dar
Een de mighty fine house on de mighty high hill!

In Campbell's vivid monologues and dialogues, "sound effect" description combines with a wealth of realistic detail and consistently supple rhythms. He adapts verse forms to suit the subject, as in the working "Song of the Corn." Here slightly varied internal and stanzaic repetitions take us through all stages of "plantin'," "hoein'," "cuttin'," "huskin'," "ginin'," and "eatin'" of the corn.

O, hits time fur de cuttin' ur de co'n,
    De blades am dry, de milk am ha'd—
    (Hack, hack, de co'n knives say,)
    De hawgs am killed an' ren'nered la'd—.
    (Hack, hack, de co'n knives say,)
O, hits time fur de cuttin' ur de co'n.

In a different mood are the tender "Negro Lullaby" and a plaintive "Negro Serenade":

O, de light-bugs glimmer down de lane,
    Merlindy! Merlindy!
O, de whip'-will callin' notes ur pain—
    Merlindy, O, Merlindy!
O, honey lub, my turkle dub,
    Doan' you hyuh my bawnjer ringin',
While de night-dew falls an' de ho'n owl calls
    By de ol' ba'n gate Ise singin'.

Common subjects of dialect verse like horse-trading, good eating, backsliding from church, and superstitions take on fresh vigor from Campbell's treatment of the cabin folk as individuals. Their idiosyncratic behavior and the poems' sensuous detail—sounds, odors, sights—arise directly from a particularized situation. Uncle Eph in "Uncle Eph—Epicure" does not merely catalogue traditional foods; he graphically hunts down, trees, and captures a possum with his pack of hounds, gives instructions on fattening, killing, freezing, and cooking the delicacy, and concludes: "I wouldn't stop my eatin' ef ol' Gab'ul blowed his horn!" Campbell's ability to convey a whole subculture through dialogue appears in "'Sciplinin' Sister Brown,"

an ironic commentary on stiff-necked clergy done in by banjo music.
The poem begins as visitors are sighted:

> Shet up dat noise, you chillen! Dar's some one at de do'.
> Dribe out dem dogs' you 'Rastus, tek Linkum off de flo'!
>
> Des ma'ch yo'se'f right in sah! (Jane, tek dem ashes out!
> Dis house look lak ur hog-pen; you M'randy, jump erbout!)

The guest, Ef'um, tells how the parson and board of deacons had
tried to pray for the "'po bac'slidah" Susan Brown, who was caught
dancing at a party. But as Ef'um strummed his banjo, the clergy-
men's hymns grew ever livelier, until:

> De pa'son an' de deacons jined han's right on dis flo',
> Su'cled right and su'cled lef'—it sutny wiz er show.
>
> Dey 'naded up an' down de flo' an' w'en hit come ter swing,
> De pa'son gin hisse'f a flirt an' cut de pidgin-wing!

The pious committee then declared Susan not guilty because "SHE
NEBBER CROSSED HER FEET."

Campbell's poetry in standard English toasts wine, women, song,
and the beauties of nature in verse that is serious, correct, and, com-
pared to his cabin lyrics, dull. He easily handles a generous variety
of metrical patterns, but language and rhyme are usually trite. How-
ever, his imagery of autumnal flora and fauna brightens "Through
October Fields," and he evokes an original scene in "When the Fruit
Trees Bloom," where "Falstaffian bumblebees/ Drain the blossoms
to the lees" as a poet carouses in the orchard, getting drunk on nec-
tar from the blossoms. Campbell seldom moralizes, and except for a
few laments over lost love, his vision is cheerfully optimistic. "Com-
pensation" claims that the best things in life are free, as an impover-
ished poet who loses his girl to a rich lord tells the victor:

> The boundless sky to me belongs,
> The paltry acre thine;
> The painted beauty sings thy songs,
> The lavrock lilts me mine;
> The hot-housed orchid blooms for thee
> The gorse and heather bloom for me,
>   Ride on young lord, ride on!

Also free, or at least inexpensive, is a writer's life in "Bohemia"
which Campbell praises in two poems. "My Friends in Bohemia"
begins:

> Friends have I in Bohemia three—
> My pipe, my dog, myself, you see

We make a jolly trinity—
We three are careless Bohemians.

When editors reject his work or the larder is bare, his pipe and faithful dog give succor. However, in "Amici Tres," Bohemia's secure isolation fails to shield the poet from faithless friends; now his "all sufficing trinity" become "wife, mother, CHRIST, the stronger three."

Campbell wrote no race protest poems, but an interracial love affair is the subject of "The Pariah's Love" (1888), a tale of about 300 lines.[5] The narrator-lover, sprung "of a mongrel race," dotes on a childhood sweetheart "of haughty lineage." Their stations in life—she the brahmin and "lily sought by all men," and he the pariah and "thistle shunned by all"—are effectively contrasted by parallel imagery. The mulatto lover keenly feels his frustration:

> Who was I, that I should love her?
> I, a hybrid, born of shame;
> I, a crawling, groveling object,
> Of a race without a name!
> Fair was I as her complexion,
> Honest came my fairness too!
> For my father and my mother
> Were in wedlock banded true.
> Yes, this mixing of the races
> Had been long, long years ago,
> That I could not trace the mingling
> Nor the fountain whence the flow.

Although the lover raised himself high through education, "caste's arrow, venom laden" struck him down, turned him bitter and cynical but unable to hate his blonde maiden. After many trials, the lovers achieve a tender reunion and agree on the moral of the tale:

> What care I for your lineage
> Or the harsh world's frown or smile?
> Men are noble from *their* actions,
> From *their* deeds and *theirs* alone;
> Father's deeds are not their children's
> Reap not that by others sown.
>
> . . . .
>
> Arm in arm we left the river
> And the lily-covered shore,
> Where the stream is constant landing
> Lily-kisses wafted o'er.

5. *AMECR*, 5 (April, 1889), 370–74. A shorter version, minus the happy ending, appears as "The Pariah" in *Echoes*.

Although Campbell's nondialect poetry is aesthetically superior to much of the black poets' work of this period, the cabin lyrics remain his most notable contribution. Unlike Dunbar, who seemed reluctant to win applause as a dialect poet, Campbell was proud of his songs, for he recognized their importance both as folk poetry and as an enduring historical record, however fragmentary, of the "Negro of the old regime." After nearly a century Campbell's gentle satires retain a vitality unique in the vast canon of dialect poetry.

SELECTED SOURCES

Harlan, John Clifford. *History of West Virginia State College, 1890–1965.* Dubuque, Iowa: William C. Brown, 1968? Pp. 8–11.

Robinson, Wilhelmina S. *Historical Negro Biographies.* New York: Publishers Co., 1967. Pp. 59–60 (data from Woodson).

The West Virginia Collegiate Institute Bulletin. Ser. 3, no. 2. Cat. no. 24, 1915–16. Pp. 10–11.

°Woodson, Carter G. "James Edwin Campbell, a Forgotten Man of Letters." *NHB,* 2 (November, 1938), 11.

JAMES EPHRIAM McGIRT
1874–1930

Why was I born if this ends all,
All that I'll ever be;
To feel a spirit that's divine,
No chance to let it free.

James McGirt craved the favor of a seductive Muse, Erato, all his
life, but she eluded him. Nevertheless, he felt compelled by nature
to sing and wrote nearly 100 poems before he realized that the
skill and fame of "masters of poetry" would never be his. Frustrated
in love as in art, McGirt lost the one love of his life to another
man, lived with his domineering mother, and, when past thirty,
composed fanciful love poems to schoolmates he had courted at
age twelve. At times McGirt also suffered the bitterness of poverty,
racial discrimination, and business failure; always he was tortured
by warring commands from Satan and Conscience.

This "poet of 'hope deferred,' " as John W. Parker called him,
was born in 1874 in Robeson County near Lumberton, North
Carolina.[1] He was one of four children—none of whom ever mar-
ried—of Madison "Mack" McGirt, whose family had been North
Carolinians for several generations, and Ellen Townsend McGirt,
a Bible-preaching matriarch whose sense of familial superiority iso-
lated the McGirts even from their closest neighbors. James farmed
the land with his family, but briefly he attended David Allen's
private school in Lumberton, where the Edith, Alice, and Anna of
his later poems captured his affections. The McGirts moved to

---

1. Parker's article in the *Historical Review* is the primary source of McGirt's
biography. McGirt's birthplace is variously given as Robeson, Robinson, and
Robertson County, North Carolina. I am indebted to C. F. W. Coker, Depart-
ment of Archives and History, State of North Carolina, for his extensive efforts
to locate materials on McGirt, and to Harriet C. Meloy, Librarian, Montana
Historical Society, for a photocopy of the *Plaindealer* article.

Greensboro about 1890; there Mack McGirt worked as a drayman, his wife as a laundress, and James held odd jobs and went to public school. In 1891 young McGirt enrolled in the English course at Bennett College in Greensboro, where he enjoyed the most tranquil and rewarding years of his life. In 1892 he joined the first-year normal class, and for the next three years he studied diverse subjects, from psychology and Virgil to chemistry and political economy, earning grades of "satisfactory" or better in all courses. His highest marks were in literature and music, and he maintained a perfect 100 in deportment. McGirt graduated from Bennett in 1895 but stayed on to take another course in the history of civilization.[2] Although he did well in college, McGirt seemed unable to capitalize on the knowledge and the B.A. degree he had earned.

His most productive years as a poet followed graduation. Living in Greensboro and working as a manual laborer, he published *Avenging the Maine* in 1899 (enlarged, then revised in 1900 and 1901), followed by *Some Simple Songs* in 1901. Disillusioned by mixed reviews and under pressure to support his invalid father and mother, McGirt fell into despair. In May, 1903, he wrote to Thomas Nelson Page, introducing himself as "the would-be-poet (colored) that called to see you last winter." McGirt asked Page for work as a houseman or handyman: "Give me a trial. I think I can please you."

> If you can give me anything to do, I hope you will consider me; and if God will give me the strength, I will add a line to American poetry for which you shall have the praise—for I must say that he who comes to my rescue at this time shall be the saving of my literary proclivities, if I have any, for it seems as though fate will conquer me at last.[3]

McGirt, it seems, rescued himself, for in August, 1903, he was in Philadelphia as editor and publisher of *McGirt's Magazine,* an illustrated monthly of "Art, Science, Literature and of General Interest." [4] Its purpose, McGirt wrote in the first issue of September,

2. Mary Mayfield Eady, Registrar, Bennett College, kindly supplied McGirt's complete record at the school in a letter to me.

3. Entire letter quoted by Parker, p. 329.

4. *McGirt's Magazine* appeared monthly from September, 1903, to August, 1908, and quarterly in 1909. Sixteen extant issues have been located in scattered lots at DHU, NNSch, and Atlanta University. See Penelope L. Bullock, *The Negro Periodical Press in the United States, 1838–1909,* dissertation, University of Michigan, 1971 (facsimile rpt. Ann Arbor, Mich.: University Microfilms, 1972), pp. 186–91, 374.

1903, was to acquaint readers of both races with "the many great men and women of the colored race and what they are saying and doing." *McGirt's Magazine* actually had three functions: to provide a showcase for creative writing by Afro-Americans, to aggrandize the personal fortunes of its editor, and to promote race advancement through the "Constitutional Brotherhood of America."

McGirt's own poetry and fiction regularly appeared with contributions from Dunbar, Harper, Kelly Miller, John E. Bruce, and Lucian B. Watkins; essayists like W. E. B. Du Bois, Mary Church Terrell, and Benjamin Tanner frequently joined them. To increase his income, the editor included in every issue large, prominently placed ads offering a get-rich-quick investment plan in the McGirt Publishing Company—"Safe as a Savings Bank"—which he formed late in 1905 to publish the *Magazine*; subscription "package deals" for the *Magazine* and McGirt's books; inducements to sales agents; and lavish testimonials to McGirt's work from "The Best Writers in America" and "The Leading Papers of the World."

In the last few years of publication, McGirt's articles and editorials urged political independence and activism, economic growth, and education for the race. He established an organization called the Constitutional Brotherhood of America, whose goal was "to organize the Negro-American voters throughout the country," to ascertain the racial attitudes of every candidate for public office, to exact a written statement from each declaring what he would do, if elected, to secure equal rights for blacks, and to publish this information in *McGirt's Magazine,* the Brotherhood's "official organ, in order that we may pass upon the worth and fitness of the candidate to represent the Negroes' interest."

McGirt's Publishing Company flourished for several years (it employed thirty-seven black workers in 1907), but his standing offer of "11% interest on every dollar" failed to attract investors, and when the Company failed in 1909, *McGirt's Magazine* disappeared with it. During these years in Philadelphia, McGirt published more poetry in *For Your Sweet Sake* (1906, 1909) and a book of eight stories, *The Triumphs of Ephriam* (1907), neither of which brought him the literary recognition he sought. In 1910 McGirt returned to Greensboro and bought a ten-room house in which he lived with his family.[5] With a sister, Mary Magdalene, he reorganized the

5. Although Parker says McGirt left for Greensboro in 1910, the Bennett College *Catalogue* for 1912–13 lists McGirt as an editor living in Philadelphia.

Star Hair Grower Manufacturing Company and prospered over the
next eight years selling hair grower and toilet articles in the United
States, Canada, and abroad. In 1918, now a financially secure prop-
erty owner, McGirt became a realtor in Greensboro, but within a
few years he had to relinquish this position because of "continuing
ill health, business incompetence, and dissipation" (Parker, 334).
McGirt's death certificate reveals that he was an alcoholic for the
last five years of his life, and he died of nephritis on June 12, 1930,
in Richardson Memorial Hospital.[6] It had been a journey of fifty-
six years from farm boy to college graduate, eager young poet, pub-
lisher, businessman, alcoholic. James McGirt, who yearned only for
a glance from the Muse and the love of a woman, now lies at rest
in Maplewood Cemetery, Greensboro, in an unmarked grave.

McGirt's Poetry

McGirt's verse in *Avenging the Maine* (1899, 1900, 1901) is uni-
formly weak in all poetic skills and remains of interest only for its
autobiographical and historical insights. Each volume offers about
an equal number of martial-patriotic, racial, sentimental, and di-
dactic verses. The title poem, "Avenging the Maine" (1899), is
typical of many narratives of the Spanish-American War which
stress the heroism of Afro-Americans and Cubans in the midst of
battle scenes. The poem begins:

> Sing, O Muse! the avenging of the Maine,
> The direful woes, the fate of Spain.
> A heinous deed to our ship they wrought,
> Untimely death to our crew they brought.
> Our soldiers' valor forever tell,
> Who for revenge both fought and fell;

McGirt's race poems include appeals from Africa for the gospel,
denunciations of color and class prejudice among blacks, and ob-
servations on superstitions, evils of slavery, and rights of freedmen.
McGirt writes in *Avenging the Maine* that most illiterate persons
living among the cultured "speak correctly one half of their words.
So I have written just as the masses impressed me." Consequently,
his half-dozen dialect verses here are almost unintelligible.

6. Data on death certificate (North Carolina) supplied by McGirt's mother
erroneously gives his age at death as 46. According to Parker, McGirt's mother
was killed at age 82 when she "rushed out of church into the path of a moving
vehicle" (p. 322).

A large number of sentimental verses like "The Girl and the Birds," "The End of Day," "Memory of Old Times," "My Lonely Homestead," and "The Stars" gush over nature, children, mothers, boyhood, and love. In his "Ode to Love" (1901), however, McGirt finds more heartache than joy in the experience:

> Love! O passion! O woman!
> Return what thou hast stole:
> Ambition, heart and treasure,
> O free the weary soul.
> Loose thy suffering victim;
> Unbar the prison door;
> Call them back that weary,
> Let them live once more.

McGirt's didactic verses are pathos-filled confessions of personal conflicts. Life's temptations in "Satan" ("He's always on duty/ Seeking a soul"), "Envy," and "Ambition" vie with an "Ode to Conscience," "The Boy's Opportunity" (for thrift and study), and "Virtue Alone Can Make Men Great." He campaigns for temperance in such verses as "The Memory of Frances Willard," "I'll Enter the Saloon No More," and "A Drunken A. B." In the latter narrative an intoxicated young man wears a medal which reveals that he has a college degree and was "the poet of his class—/ A valedictorian." The narrator contemplates this "genius" whom he rescued from the gutter, wondering "what caused him first to drink?" The resemblance to McGirt, A.B. and poet, in this early poem suggests that his problems with alcohol spanned several decades.

McGirt felt that his second collection, *Some Simple Songs* (1901), was "a great improvement" over the first, but these twenty-one selections are equally faulty in meter, language, and sentiment. Almost half are love poems, more hopeful in tone—perhaps because love finally came, "a cooing little dove." A tribute to Edith in the earlier volume is followed here by two for Alice, of the "rosebud lips and teeth of pearl" in "If Loving Were Wooing" and "A Test of Love." There is a long plea for world peace, "The Century Prayer"; an encomium in heroic couplets from the black race, "Victoria, the Queen"; and good advice in verses like "Weep Not" which counsels labor, prayer, and striving to climb the ladder of life.

The two editions of *For Your Sweet Sake* (1906, 1909) contain about twenty-nine new poems. Among the love poems "A Mystery" is metrically even and pleasing in tone as the poet confesses that

all nature reminds him of his beloved; and, for McGirt's third
childhood sweetheart, there is "Anna, Won't You Marry Me?" The
title poem was inspired by his frustrated love for Irene Gallaway,
who married another man when McGirt balked at the altar—he
was "forever confused by his mother's intervention" (Parker, 331):

> For you! For you! For your sweet sake alone,
> I live! I toil! And oh, with blistered feet,
> I rove! I rove! I seek thee in the dark.
> I pray that God may grant us some day soon to meet.

Perhaps his best effort is "Born Like the Pines," three stanzas of
musical, melancholy reflection on the poet's need to sing:

> Born like the pines to sing,
>   The harp and song in m' breast,
> Though far and near,
> There's none to hear,
> I'll sing at th' winds request.

Similar in mood is "A Magic Change," in which the poet laments
that his youthful desire to transcend earth through art was hindered
by his attachments to earthly things; but he still yearns for the
"beacon light" of inspiration. Brief testimonials to McGirt's art
appear in both editions of *For Your Sweet Sake* from Rebecca
Harding Davis, Ella Wheeler Wilcox, Julian Hawthorne, Thomas
Nelson Page, and, in 1909, Booker T. Washington. Their praise for
McGirt's poetic talent is difficult to justify. Despite some improve-
ment in technique and language over the years and his evident love
for poetry, McGirt's beacon light of inspiration flickered out before
he could grasp it.

SELECTED SOURCES

"Literary Laurels for Negro Poet." [Helena] *Montana Plaindealer*, April
    13, 1906, p. 1. Rpt. from Philadelphia *North American*.
Parker, John W. "James Ephriam McGirt." *North Carolina Authors: A
    Selective Handbook*. Chapel Hill: University of North Carolina Library
    Extension Publication, 18 (October, 1952), 79–80.
*——. "James Ephriam McGirt: Poet of 'Hope Deferred'." *North Caro-
    lina Historical Review*, 31 (July, 1954), 321–35.

CHARLES DOUGLAS CLEM
1876–1934

A versatile writer and peripatetic lecturer, Charles Clem was born in Johnson City, Tennessee, on July 10, 1876.[1] His parents, Henry C. and Melvina (Robinson) Clem, were former slaves, and Clem claimed direct descent from the white Kentucky orator and essayist Cassius M. Clay. In his *Upas Tree of Kansas* (1917) Clem describes Clay, "—that bosom friend of Lincoln,—that great duelist and Abolitionist,—" as a "beastly" slaveholder who raped his "helpless slave," Clem's maternal grandmother. Accounts of Clem's early life vary somewhat, but it seems he worked and attended school in Tennessee, Oklahoma, and Kentucky. When Clem was eleven his parents moved to Kentucky, where he labored in the coal mines for four years. About 1891, in Oklahoma, Clem completed a "common school course" and taught school for two years. Then he returned to Tennessee and supposedly graduated from Greeneville College (now Tusculum) in 1898, but no record of his attendance can be found.[2]

Charles Clem's first book, *Oklahoma, Her People and Professions*, appeared in 1892, and a volume of thirty-four poems, *Rhymes of a Rhymster*, may have been published as early as 1896, but the only edition located suggests a later date, 1900–1901.[3] The poems in *Rhymes*, Clem states, were written during the eight years prior to their publication by popular demand. In 1899 Clem moved to Okla-

1. Unless otherwise noted, biography is from a letter to me from Irene Clem, from *WWCR*, 68, and from a brief biographical sketch in *Rhymes*.
2. Jack C. Haaksma, Registrar, Tusculum College, in a letter to me. Mr. Haaksma suggests Clem may have graduated from Greeneville College High School.
3. Clem is listed under "Edmond" in M. H. Marable and E. Boylan, *A Handbook of Oklahoma Writers* (Norman, Okla.: University of Oklahoma Press, 1939), p. 221, reprint courtesy of Alene Simpson, Head Librarian, Oklahoma Historical Society. The DHU copy of *Rhymes* is annotated, "Edmond, Okla., 1901," but the 1896 date is given in *WWCR*.

homa, and in 1901–2 he edited the *Western World* in Oklahoma
City. Clem married Kitty Smothers, a schoolteacher, in Guthrie,
Oklahoma, on April 13, 1903, and they settled permanently in
Chanute, Kansas. The Clems had six children, two of whom died in
infancy. According to his daughter Irene Clem, now a teacher in
Kansas City, Missouri, her siblings Helen, Joseph, and Lawrence
were, like herself, college-educated, and all are living today.[4]

In 1905 Clem was assistant steward of the Elks Club in Chanute,
and in 1906 his name appears on the masthead of the *Coffeyville*
(Kansas) *Vindicator* as its editor.[5] He worked for a short time with
the Santa Fe Railroad, and from about 1909 until 1926 he was head
of the linoleum and rug department of the Rosenthal Department
Store of Chanute. Clem continued to write and publish: a slim
pamphlet of verse, *A Little Souvenir* (1908); a prose work, *Four-
teen Years in Metaphysics* (1913); and articles on economic and
philosophical subjects in newspapers and periodicals such as the
Kansas City Post and the *African Times and Orient Review.* He
traveled through Kansas, Oklahoma, and Colorado lecturing on
"metaphysical science, including psychic phenomena, hypnotism,
suggestive and psycho therapeutics, and telepathy." [6] Clem was an
active member of the NAACP, and as president of the Chanute
chapter he lectured widely on race problems, in particular urging
establishment of black schools, and he gave poetry recitals. He is
listed in *Who's Who of the Colored Race* as a spiritualist, socialist,
and Mason, and his daughter corroborates Clem's Masonic activities
as an officer of the Prince Hall Lodge for many years.

Clem's last-known publication is *The Upas Tree of Kansas* (1917),
a twenty-four-page essay, including two strong poems, which vigor-
ously denounces the Kansas Negro as deficient in race pride, race
consciousness, and support for race enterprises: he is "the only spe-
cies of the race . . . who can swallow a Caucasian camel, but choke
on an African gnat." It is "Negro Jim-Crowism" which is crippling
the race, Clem writes, and he blames the Kansas blacks' indifference
for the failure of a "million dollar movement" he had originated to
improve their economic development. At the root of all racial prob-

4. Children's names from Chanute, Kansas, *Directory* (1929), courtesy of
Mrs. George T. Hawley, Librarian, Kansas State Historical Society; and from
Roberta D. Thuston of Chanute, Kansas, in a letter to me.
5. Chanute *Directory* (1905); file of the *Vindicator* (December 17, 1904–
1907) is held by the Kansas Historical Society.
6. *WWCR.*

lems is Kansas's policy of white teachers only; this is the poisonous Upas Tree which must be uprooted, for only black teachers can instill race pride in their charges, keep them in school, and eradicate the adult blacks' sense of inferiority.

After 1926 Clem's health failed. In 1929 he was still living in Chanute and working as a janitor for the Rosenthal Mercantile Company, but shortly thereafter the family moved to Pittsburg, Kansas. Here in 1934 Charles Clem died and was given a Masonic funeral.

Clem's Poetry

> Let me not sing to entertain
>   Alone and cause an hour's mirth,
> Though millions join the glad refrain
>   And herald it throughout the earth;
> But let my song arouse in you
>   Just one moment of sober thought,
> Though it be heard by very few,
>   Millions will see the changes wrought.   (LS)[7]

This brief poem, "My Song," expresses Charles Clem's poetic principle, illustrated by the forty-four poems in *Rhymes of a Rhymster* (1900?), *A Little Souvenir* (1908), *The Upas Tree of Kansas* (1917), and a broadside, "Booker T. Washington" (n.d.). All, except a few verses in dialect, are sober thoughts: there are sentimental, nostalgic pieces like "The Old Homestead," "Childhood's Happy Dream," "Charity Rewarded," and "Power of Woman's Tears"; exhortations to racial justice and race pride; and moral-didactic lessons such as "God Knows Our Heart," "Was It Duty or Love?" and "A Good Name." Clem's versification, thought, and sentiment lack distinction, but his poetry is significant evidence of Booker T. Washington's influence on the black poets of the century's final decade. Clem's message in "Paddle Your Own Canoe" (R) is self-help and self-reliance, and in "My Voyage" (LS) his advice is to float carefully, "calm and merry," through life "in midstream." The thirty-two-line broadside, "Booker T. Washington," written sometime after Washington's death in 1915, exalts the man and his work:

> He lived a strenuous life; full-measured to the brim;
> He tested it at all its points, from center to outmost rim;

7. Volume in which a poem first appears: (R) *Rhymes of a Rhymster*, (LS) *A Little Souvenir*, (UT) *The Upas Tree*.

He fathomed the Saxon mind, weathered the calms and storms,
Found Deities, and demons, too, involved in human forms.

.   .   .   .

Let none of sable face, thick lip or crispy hair,
Enshroud himself with grief or stand in mute despair;
For though his mortal parts deep in the grave may lie,
His name, his fame, his life, his work, can never, never die.

At the same time that many Afro-Americans were inspired by
Washington's onward and upward teachings, white Americans were
treated to a similar philosophy of self-improvement in the luck and
pluck books of Horatio Alger (from 1867). Clem seems to have
adopted Alger's motto in his poem "Luck and Pluck" (R), where a
conversation between the two reveals that the secret of honor and
wealth is pluck:

Luck picked up his hat and departed from him
Whose mottoes were truthfulness, work, push, and vim;
Whose teachings were right—not in part, but in whole,
Being health to the body and life to the soul.

The black man will rise in society with "pluck," using his God-given
"energies of mind." "The Power of Mind" (UT) in six stanzas of
fairly smooth verse insists God's "kingdom is within you":

Think not, O millions of a mighty race,
    That it has been decreed by cruel fate,
That you, with crispy hair and sable face,
    Shall not attain success in man's estate;
Lift up your heads and with all men aspire
    To reach the highest goal, fear not, nor sin;
But with the strength of your intense desire,
    Look not without, but use the power within.

Clem's race pride is strong in several poems, notably "Herod's Sac-
rifice" (LS), a twenty-four-stanza indictment of Army officers who
in 1906 framed 167 black soldiers as rioters in Brownsville, Texas;[8]
in "How Long" (R), which anticipates the day "When every mem-
ber of my race/ Hails foreign emigration" to escape "Judge Lynch";

8. On September 28, 1972, the U.S. Department of Defense cleared the
Brownsville "rioters" of all guilt. This official exoneration was prompted by
Representative Augustus Hawkins's speech to Congress on March 18, 1971.
Hawkins, a black Democrat from California, had raised the issue after reading
John D. Weaver, *The Brownsville Raid: The Story of America's Black Dreyfus
Affair* (New York: W. W. Norton, 1971). On August 4, 1973, the Senate
passed a bill, introduced by Senator Hubert H. Humphrey, to compensate
Dorsie Willis, the sole survivor of the all-black 25th Infantry Regiment dishonor-
ably discharged at Brownsville.

and in "Afric's Reply to Saxon" (R), which insists that blacks are not "emigrants,/ Vile murderers, or slaves," but American heroes and builders. "The Jim Crow Negro" (UT), a later poem vehemently censuring accommodationists, is a tightly constructed and forthright appeal for independence and race consciousness:

> What is a Jim Crow Negro?
> It is one who never demands
> What is his by right, for fear that a fight
> Will be upon his hands;
> Who cringes and fawns at insults;
> Who submits to a coward's blow;
> Who kisses the foot that kicks him,—
> This cur is the real Jim Crow.
>
> . . . .
>
> Away with the Jim Crow Negro;
> The race needs stalwart men;
> Men who will fight for what is right
> With hand and tongue and pen. . . .

Clem shows skill and a sense of humor in a handful of rhythmic dialect verses. "Mr. Scroggins' Courtship" (R) is a lively tale of rivalry for Lucinda Snow's hand between "Cake-Walk Jim" and the speaker, Mr. Scroggins, which culminates in a cake-walk contest: "But Longleg Jim took off de cake,/ An I took off a wife." Clem's dialect is neither authentic nor consistent, but "When Gabel Blows de Ho'n" (R) is an engaging comparison of old and new style preachers:

> Dey goes off to de cadamies
>   An fixes up dey min',
> Till dey kin read ole David's sams
>   Er comin' an' er gwine.
> Dey doan sing ole time melodies
>   But hiferlutin songs;
> But bless de Lawd, dats gwine ter drap
>   When Gabel blows de ho'n.

Clem also wrote tributes to Crispus Attucks, Frederick Douglass, and Lincoln; a love poem to someone's "lips of rosebud tint with nectar tipped"; and a humorous impression of Oklahoma in which Farmer Squeers is convinced by monstrous centipedes and man-eating tarantulas to stay in "Nebrasky." Clem's verse varies in literary quality from very weak to mediocre, but it is a valuable mirror of Afro-American thought at the turn of the century.

ELOISE BIBB THOMPSON
1878–1927

Eloise Alberta Veronica Bibb was born in New Orleans on June 29, 1878, the daughter of Charles H. and Catherine Adele Bibb. Her childhood and early schooling were passed in New Orleans, where her father was a customs inspector. It was a Boston firm, however, that published her volume of verse, *Poems*, when she was seventeen years old. Miss Bibb attended the Oberlin Academy preparatory department from 1899 until 1901, after which she taught in the public schools of New Orleans for two years. She matriculated at Howard University in 1903 and graduated from its Teachers' College in January, 1908. In April of that year Miss Bibb became head resident of the Colored Social Settlement in Washington, D.C., a post she held until 1911.[1]

In Chicago on August 4, 1911, Eloise Bibb married Noah D. Thompson, a thirty-three-year-old widower.[2] Both Thompsons were devout Catholics, and when they moved to Los Angeles in 1911 they became active in church work. Mrs. Thompson was a special feature writer for the *Los Angeles Sunday Tribune* and the *Morning Sun*. She contributed articles and poetry to popular magazines, among them *Out West* and *Tidings*, official organ of the diocese of Monterey and Los Angeles. An address she made to the Catholic Women's Clubs of Los Angeles was highly praised, according to a biographer, Delilah Beasley, who also quotes Mrs. Thompson's re-

1. W. E. Bigglestone, Archivist, Oberlin College, in a letter to me. Information was taken from a form filled out by Miss Bibb in 1908; W. A. Sojourner, Registrar, Howard University, in a letter to me, gives Miss Bibb's graduation date from Howard as 1907. A statement in *WWCR* that she graduated from New Orleans University (now Dillard) could not be verified by C. L. Reynolds, Registrar.

2. Marriage license, Illinois. Miss Bibb was thirty-three in 1911 but gave her age as thirty.

iterated belief in Catholic training, a "quickening of the spirit," as the panacea for seven million of her race who had no religion.[3] As far as is known, the Thompsons lived in Los Angeles through the 1920's. They had one child, Noah Murphy Thompson. Mrs. Thompson died in 1927.

Miss Bibb's Poetry

Over half the poems in her one slim volume are romantic narratives of star-crossed lovers and agonized heroes. The narratives generally commence with descriptions of time and weather conditions: "The morn has risen clear and bright"; "Twas eve in sunny Italy"; "The sun has sunk neath yonder distant hill." They proceed to a story line that may be complicated and illogical, as in "Imogene," or, more often, single and smoothly developed with sustained suspense as in "Destiny," "Gerarda," and "The Hermit." Although her lovers' catastrophes differ, the characters vary in little more than their names from tale to tale, and inevitably the poetic sentiments are those of a teenage girl in love with love, the more tempestuous the better.

"Gerarda" is a typical young maiden who loves Nelville, the organist who played at her wedding. For years she suffers and laments their separation, until one day Nelville reappears:

> Forgetful then of hour and place
> He stoops to kiss the beauteous face,
> And at the touch the fire of love,
> So pure as to come from above,
> Consumes his heart and racks his brain,
> With longing fear and infinite pain.

The lady, equally moved, sends him away, for she is "alas! a wedded wife." But a fortunate fire soon destroys her home, husband, and family; Nelville rescues Gerarda from the flames, and they live happily ever after. Other lovers, including those in "Captain Smith and Pocahontas," are similarly rewarded, but disaster plagues many. Lucius is torn "limb from limb" when he violates the sacred cloister of Florinia in "The Vestal Virgin," and his beloved dies in a dungeon. The lovers—both poets—of "A Tale of Italy" die of broken hearts to meet in the "boundless sphere of eternity," and the hero of

3. I am indebted to Miriam Matthews of Los Angeles for calling my attention to the Beasley book and suggesting other black poets of California for further study.

"The Hermit" emerges from his sanctuary after twenty years to claim the princess Fahredeen, but when he renounces Christianity for her he is sent back to his cave, because "The man who to his god is false,/ To thee can ne'er be true."

Miss Bibb's biblical and historical subjects, such as "The Wandering Jew," "Eliza in Uncle Tom's Cabin," "Ann Boleyn," and "The Expulsion of Hagar," are often treated with pleasing simplicity. Their narratives are metrically even, consistent in tone and story line, and free from excessive sentimental embroidery. The tale of "Judith" is a good example of this type:

> Then from its scabbard soon his sword she draws,
> And lifts aloft—and then, one awful pause
>   Before it falls. She quickly grasps the head,
>   For Holofernes, Juda's foe is dead.
> Rejoice Bethulia, God has pitied thee,
> And noble Judith set thy people free.

Miss Bibb's short lyrics, including tributes to nature and to luminaries like Frederick Douglass and Alice Ruth Moore (later Mrs. Paul L. Dunbar), are trite, weak verses. It is in the longer narratives that she demonstrates a breadth of interest and talent for versification unusual in so young a poet.

SELECTED SOURCES

Beasley, Delilah L. *The Negro Trail Blazers of California.* Los Angeles, 1919.
WWCR, I, 262.

AARON BELFORD THOMPSON
1883–1929

A trio of poets was born in Rossmoyne, Ohio, to John Henry and Clara Jane Thompson, formerly of Virginia. Aaron Thompson and his sisters published seven volumes of poetry between 1899 and 1926. The girls, who did not marry, remained in Rossmoyne with an elder brother, Garland Yancey Thompson. Here their poetry was privately printed: Priscilla Jane's *Ethiope Lays* (1900) and *Gleanings of Quiet Hours* (1907), and Clara Ann's *Songs from the Wayside* (1908) and *A Garland of Poems* (Boston, 1926). Aaron Belford Thompson dedicated his first volume of poetry, *Morning Songs* (1899), to his sisters, and his second volume, *Echoes of Spring* (1901), to his brother Garland.[1]

Thompson was born on April 5, 1883. After attending public school in Rossmoyne, he purchased a small printing outfit and became his own publisher. In 1902 Thompson married and moved to Indianapolis, where at 2109 Howard Street he bought a cottage and installed a well-equipped print shop in the rear. Here he lived and worked for twenty-seven years until his death. In 1907 Thompson brought out a second edition of *Echoes of Spring* with a complimentary introduction by James Whitcomb Riley. This facsimile of Riley's handwritten endorsement was also prefixed to Thompson's final volume of poems, *Harvest of Thoughts* (1907). Thompson had

---

1. Dates of birth for the three poets are uncertain. For Aaron Thompson, Coyle gives 1873; Dabney and Thompson's death certificate, Indiana State Board of Health (copy in my possession, information supplied by his widow, Hallie) give 1883. From portraits in their four volumes, Priscilla's and Clara's birthdates may be about 1882 and 1887, respectively. Garland was probably the eldest child, and a poem by Clara Ann mourns another brother who died in childhood. Some family problem seems to have alienated Aaron from his siblings as early as 1900 (see the sisters' dedications—to Garland—in their volumes).

suffered from chronic heart disease and rheumatism for many years, and a heart attack took his life at age forty-five on January 26, 1929. He died at home, and following his funeral on January 29 at Mt. Zion Baptist Church, Thompson's body was sent to Cincinnati for burial. He was survived by his widow, Hallie, his two sisters, and a brother.[2]

Thompson's Poetry

In three volumes, among 100 verses, Aaron Belford Thompson offers very modest evidence of poetic talent. His subjects are conventional: religion, love, nature, race, childhood, and morality. His versification is trite, and even the simplest iambics prove troublesome. More than a dozen love poems like "To Helen," "Love's Passion," and "My Lady Love" share identical sentiments and diction:

> A song to the damsels, our Ethiope maids!
>   Her crisp curly locks, in beauty arrayed.
> Her voice is so gentle, so tender, so true;
>   Her smiles glow like sun-beams;
>   Her eyes spark like dew.
>   ("Our Girls")
>
> Love is divine; with love I adore thee;
>   Fair sable damsel, to thee I'll be true;
> As thy companion for e'er I'll be happy;
>   Thou gem of my casket that sparkles like dew.
>   ("My Queen")

Thompson's nature verse in praise of summer nights, an oak tree, wind, morning, a song bird, and autumn lacks intellectual or emotional content. "Farewell to Summer" is typical:

> Farewell to the summer,
>   For autumn is here,
> The skies they are cloudy,
>   The days dark and drear;
> Wild winds like a deluge,
>   Through fields shall descend,
> The trees of their beauty,
>   Must yield to the wind.

2. Funeral announcements in the *Indianapolis News*, January 28, 1929, p. 5, and *World*, February 1, 1929, p. 8. I am indebted to Caroline Dunn, Librarian, William Henry Smith Memorial Library, Indiana Historical Society, for photocopies of the newspapers and for her extensive efforts to locate information on Thompson; also to Jay W. Beswick, Cleveland Public Library; Ruth E. Ballenger, Rutherford B. Hayes Library, Fremont, Ohio; and Mary M. Fisher, Central State University, Wilberforce, Ohio, for their assistance.

Nostalgic verses like "Bygone Days" and "My Country Home," as well as Thompson's musings on time, life's journey, sin, friendship, and death never rise above triviality and a uniformly flat tone. "A Eulogy on the Farm" or "Fleeting Time" receive equal emphasis and care:

> For 'tis the farm with boys and girls,
>   And fruitful crops a growing,
> That constitutes our living world,
>   With health and plenty flowing.
>
>   . . . .
>
> Let us estimate its value,
>   While we through life's journey go,
> Let us gather in our harvest,
>   Ere the winter comes with snow.

Among his race poems "Emancipation," "The Chain of Bondage," and "The Foresight" celebrate liberty and Ethiopia's triumph, but without the poet's involvement, as in this stanza from "A Song to Ethiopia":

> So long we've been rejected!
>   For since Queen Sheba's reign,
> We've fell from wealth to servants;
>   Have worn the bondage chain.
> Unfurl your hidden banners,
>   In freedom's name for right!
> And show to foes our colors,
>   And sing with all your might.

Thompson's volumes contain a handful of weak dialect poems; a patriotic tribute, "Our National Flag"; a story of David and Goliath in nineteen nine-line stanzas: "I'm not afraid this man to fight,/ My God hath gave me grace"; and pieces on Ireland, Christmas, dancing parties, and a haunted dell. The work of another poet of Thompson's stature (Mrs. Josephine Heard) was kindly dismissed by a critic who said, "The special merit of this group of poems is, they all have a SUBJECT." For Aaron Thompson we can only add, "and they are nicely printed."

SELECTED SOURCES

Coyle, William. *Ohio Authors and Their Books.* Cleveland, Ohio: World, 1962. P. 629.
Dabney, Wendell P. *Cincinnati's Colored Citizens.* Cincinnati, Ohio: Dabney Publishing Co., 1926. P. 318.

BIBLIOGRAPHIES OF THE POETS' WORKS

JAMES MADISON BELL

POETRY

Bell's long poems were published separately and later included in *The Poetical Works*.

A Poem [delivered August 1, 1862]. San Francisco: S. F. Sterett, 1862. Copy: CU.

A Poem Entitled The Day and The War. San Francisco: Agnew & Deffebach, 1864. 27 pp. Dedicated to John Brown. Copy: DHU, DLC.

An Anniversary Poem Entitled The Progress of Liberty. San Francisco: Agnew & Deffebach, 1866. 28 pp. Dedicated to Rt. Rev. Jabez Pitt Campbell.

A Poem, Entitled The Triumph of Liberty. Detroit: Tunis Steam Printing Co., 1870. 32 pp. Dedicated to Henry P. Baldwin, Governor of Michigan. Copy: DHU.

The Poetical Works. Lansing, Mich.: Wynkoop Hallenbeck Crawford Co., n.d. [copyright 1901, Wilmot Johnson, Publisher]. 223 pp. 32 poems. Portrait.

Same: 2nd ed., copyright 1901.

Same: Reprint, 1904.

Copies: 1st ed.: DHU, DLC. 2nd ed.: DHU, NN, NNSch. 1904 ed.: NN, NNSch.

PROSE

A Discourse Commemorative of John Frye Bell, Member of Hopkins High School, Hadley [*Mass.*]. Northampton, Mass.: Gazette Printing Co., 1874. 30 pp. Copy: DLC#.

This memorial pamphlet, "A father's tribute to the memory of his eldest son (1859–1874)," is attributed to Bell in the Library of Congress *Catalogue*. Although Bell's dates are incorrectly given here as 1833–1901, the work is probably his.

ALFRED GIBBS CAMPBELL

POETRY

Poems. Newark, N.J.: Advertiser Printing House, 1883. 120 pp. 54 poems. Copies: DHU, DLC, NJR, NNSch.

Uncollected
"Hallowed Ground" (96 lines). MS A.D. C.2, 2260.
"The Last Man" (80 lines). MS A.D. C.3, 2261.
Copies of both: NNSch.

PROSE

The Alarm Bell. Paterson, N.J., July, 1851–October, 1852 (newspaper).
   Copy: NJP. Bound volume inscribed by Campbell to William Nelson,
   April 22, 1872.

JAMES EDWIN CAMPBELL

POETRY

Driftings and Gleanings. Charleston, W.Va., 1887. 96 pp.
   This volume could not be located; all selections were reputedly re-
   printed in *Echoes.*
Echoes from the Cabin and Elsewhere. Chicago: Donohue & Henneberry,
   1895. 86 pp. 44 poems. Portrait. Copy: DHU.

Uncollected
"The Pariah's Love." *AMECR,* 5 (April, 1889), 370–74.
"Home Sick." *AMECR,* 35 (July, 1918), 24.
"When Jeanie Danced the Hielan Fling." *AMECR,* 35 (July, 1918), 25.

NOAH CALWELL W. CANNON

POETRY AND PROSE

*The Rock of Wisdom; An Explanation of the Sacred Scriptures, . . . To
   Which Are Added Several Interesting Hymns.* N.p., 1833. 144 pp. 17
   poems. Copies: DHU, NNSch.

PROSE

Truth. Instruction to Youth. Seek Ye After Knowledge. Rochester: C. S.
   McConnell & Co., 1842; rpt. Rochester: James Nelson, 1843. 24 pp.
   4 hymns. Copy: DHU (pp. 19–22 missing).

CHARLES DOUGLAS CLEM

POETRY

Rhymes of a Rhymster. No title page [Edmond, Okla., 1896/1901]. 52
   pp. 34 poems. Portrait. Copy: DHU, bound with *Little Souvenir* and
   broadside, below.
A Little Souvenir. N.p.: Author, 1908. 8 pp. 6 poems. Portrait. Copies:
   DHU, KHi, NNSch.
"Booker T. Washington" (broadside). N.p., n.d. Copies: DHU, KHi.

PROSE AND POETRY

The Upas Tree of Kansas. Chanute, Kans.: Tribune Publishing Co., 1917.
   24 pp. Essay and 2 poems. Copy: KHi.

The following books by Clem are cited in *WWCR:*
Oklahoma, Her People and Professions. 1892#.
Fourteen Years in Metaphysics. 1913#.

JOSEPH SEAMON COTTER, SR.

POETRY

A Rhyming. Louisville, Ky.: New South Publishing Co., 1895#. 32 pp. Copy: DLC.

Links of Friendship. Louisville, Ky.: Bradley & Gilbert Co., 1898. 64 pp. 54 poems. Portrait. Copies: DHU, DLC, NN, NNSch.

A White Song and a Black One. Louisville, Ky.: Bradley & Gilbert Co., 1909. 64 pp. 48 poems. Copies: DHU, DLC, NN, NNSch copy inscribed: "With compliments of Joseph S. Cotter."

Collected Poems. New York: Henry Harrison, 1938. 78 pp. 73 poems. Portrait. Copies: DHU, DLC, NN, NNSch.

Sequel to the "Pied Piper of Hamelin" and Other Poems. New York: Henry Harrison, 1939. 93 pp. 69 poems. Copies: DHU, DLC, NN, NNSch.

POETRY AND PROSE

Negroes and Others at Work and Play. New York: Paebar Co., 1947. 63 pp. 7 poems, aphorisms, tales, sketches, plays, songs. Copies: DHU, DLC, NN, NNSch.

DRAMA

Caleb, The Degenerate. Louisville, Ky.: Bradley & Gilbert Co., 1903. 57 pp. Portrait. Copies: DHU, DLC, NNSch copy inscribed by Cotter to the Rev. Edward Everett Hale.

PROSE

Negro Tales. New York: Cosmopolitan Press, 1912. 148 pp. 17 tales. Copies: DHU, NNSch.

Twenty-fifth Anniversary of the Founding of Colored Parkland or "Little Africa," Louisville, Ky., 1891–1916. Louisville, Ky.: I. Willis Cole Publishing Co., 1934. Copy: DHU.

MANUSCRIPT

Papers, 1920–34 (unpublished poems, essays, songs, stories, plays, lesson plans). Louisville Free Public Library, Western Branch, 602 South Tenth Street, Louisville, Ky.

DANIEL WEBSTER DAVIS

POETRY

Idle Moments. Baltimore, Md.: Educator of Morgan College, 1895. 81 pp. 38 poems. Portrait. Dedicated to his mother. Copies: DHU, ViHi.

'Weh Down Souf. Cleveland, Ohio: Helman-Taylor Co., 1897. 136 pp.
42 poems (21 new). Illus. William L. Sheppard. Dedicated to his wife.
Copies: DHU, DLC, NNSch.

Uncollected

"Echoes from a Plantation Party," *Southern Workman*, February, 1899,
pp. 54–59; "The Black Woman's Burden," *VN*, 1 (July, 1904), 308;
"Green Apples," *VN*, 2 (November, 1905), 770; "Jes Gib Him One Ub
Mine," *CAm*, 2 (March, 1901), 353; "I Once Knew a Darkey," "The
Old Ring Plays," "Only a Nigger," TS, ViHi.

PROSE

The Life and Public Services of Rev. Wm. Washington Browne. Philadel-
phia: A.M.E. Book Concern, 1910. 192 pp. Portrait. Illus. Copies:
DHU, DLC, NNSch, ViHi.
With Giles B. Jackson. *The Industrial History of the Negro Race in the
United States.* Richmond, Va.: Virginia Press, 1908. 400 pp. Portrait.
Illus. Copies: DLC, ViHi.
Same: Rev. ed. Richmond, Va.: Negro Educational Assoc., 1911. 369
pp. Portrait. Illus. Copies: DHU, NNSch.

MANUSCRIPT (PROSE)

Notebook A: "Paying the Fiddler," "Jim Crow's Search for the Promised
Land," "Uncle Ned and His Son," "Some Fools I've Known" ("Gumps").
Notebook B: "Negro Ideals, A series of lectures for the Hampton Summer
Normal Institute, held at Hampton Normal School, July 1–26, 1902." All
in Davis's hand. Notebooks and other memorabilia at ViHi.

TIMOTHY THOMAS FORTUNE

POETRY

Dreams of Life: Miscellaneous Poems. New York: Fortune and Peterson,
1905. 192 pp. 50 poems. Portrait. Dedicated to "Jessie and Frederick
White, My Beloved Children." Copies: DHU, NJR, NNSch.

Uncollected

"Bartow Black," *AMECR*, 3 (October, 1886), 158–59.

SELECTED PROSE

Black and White: Land, Labor and Politics in the South. New York: Ford,
Howard & Hulbert, 1884. 310 pp.
"Civil Rights and Social Privileges," *AMECR*, 2 (1886), 119–31.
The Negro in Politics. New York: Oglivie & Rowntree, 1885. 61 pp.
"The Negro's Place in American Life at the Present Day." In *The Negro
Problem.* New York: James Pott & Co., 1903. Pp. 213–34.
The New York Negro in Journalism. Publication 5 of New York State
Commission, National Negro Exposition, Richmond, Va. New York,
1915. 15 pp.
"Whose Problem Is This?" *AMECR*, 11 (October, 1894), 253–61.

Bruce Collection, NNSch; Robert Russa Moton Papers, Tuskegee Inst.; Booker T. Washington Papers, DLC.

CHARLOTTE FORTEN GRIMKÉ

POETRY, UNCOLLECTED

A single source is given for each poem; however, most of them are additionally found in Cooper, II, and several are hand copied in Scrapbook 3, NNSch. Dates and places of composition, when known, follow each entry.

"The Angel's Visit." Brown, *BM*, 196–99.
"At Newport." *AMECR*, 4 (1888), 258.
"Charles Sumner. On Seeing Some Pictures of the Interior of His House." Cooper, II, 24 (June, 1874; Columbia, S.C.).
"Charlotte Corday: Suggested by Two Pictures in the Corcoran Art Gallery." Cooper, II, 22–23 (Washington, D.C.).
"The Grand Army of the Republic" (also titled "The Gathering of the Grand Army"). Cooper, II, 25–26 (August 12, 1890; Boston).
"In Florida." Cooper, II, 21–22 (March, 1893).
"In the Country." *National Anti-Slavery Standard,* September 1, 1860 (July, 1860).
"A June Song." *The Dunbar Speaker and Entertainer.* Ed. A. R. Dunbar-Nelson. Naperville, Ill.: J. L. Nichols, 1920. Pp. 26–27 (June 15, 1885; Washington, D.C.).
"A Parting Hymn." Brown, *BM*, 191 (July, 1856?).
"Poem" (graduation). *Liberator,* August 24, 1856 (July, 1856?).
"The Slave Girl's Prayer." *Liberator,* February 3, 1860 (1859; Salem).
"To W[illiam] L[loyd] G[arrison] on Reading His 'Chosen Queen'." *Liberator,* March 16, 1855.
"The Two Voices." *National Anti-Slavery Standard,* January 15, 1859 (December 14, 1858; Philadelphia).
"The Wind among the Poplars." *Liberator,* May 27, 1859 (March, 1859; Philadelphia).
"Wordsworth." Cooper, II, 23.

SELECTED PROSE

Essays and Letters

"At the Home of Frederick Douglass." Cooper, II, 56–61.
"The Centennial Exposition: Philadelphia, 1876." Cooper, II, 62–77.
"Glimpses of New England." *National Anti-Slavery Standard,* June 19, 1858.
"Letters from St. Helena's Island." *Liberator,* December 12 and 19, 1862, pp. 119, 203.
"Life on the Sea Islands." *Atlantic Monthly,* 13 (May and June, 1864), 587–96, 666–76.

"Personal Recollections of Whittier." *New England Magazine*, NS 8 (June, 1893), 468–76.

Journal

The Journal of Charlotte L. Forten. Ed. Ray A. Billington. New York: Dryden, 1953; rpt. Collier, 1961.

Translation

Erckmann, Emile, and Chatrian, Alexandre. *Màdame Thérèse; or, The Volunteers of '92.* New York: Charles Scribner, 1869. 289 pp. Copy: NNSch.

MANUSCRIPT

Original diaries and miscellaneous items, Francis J. Grimké Papers, Negro Collection, DHU.

FRANCES ELLEN WATKINS HARPER

POETRY

Poems on Miscellaneous Subjects. 2nd ed. Boston: J. B. Yerrington & Son, 1854. [No first edition known.] 40 pp. 19 poems, 3 essays. Copy: NNSch.
  Same: 1856#.
  Same: Tenth Thousand. Philadelphia: Merrihew & Thompson, 1857. 48 pp. 23 poems, 2 essays, 1 letter (19 poems and essays same as 1854). Copy: NNSch.
  Same: 1858, 1864, 1866#.
  Same: 20th ed. Philadelphia: Merrihew & Son, 1871. 56 pp. 26 poems (3 new), same prose. Copy: NNSch.
  Same: 1874. Copy: DHU.
Moses: A Story of the Nile. 2nd ed. Philadelphia: Merrihew & Son, 1869. [No first edition known.] 47 pp. 1 poem, 1 essay. Portrait. Copy: NNSch.
  Same: A "third edition," 1870#.
  Same: 2nd ed. Philadelphia: 1006 Bainbridge Street [Author], 1889. 52 pp. 3 poems (2 new), same essay. Copy: NNSch.
  Same: *Idylls of the Bible.* Philadelphia: 1006 Bainbridge Street, 1901. 64 pp. 8 poems (five new). Copy: NNSch, inscribed by author.
  (Same as 1901 ed.: editions dated 1893 and 1895#).
Poems. Philadelphia: Merrihew & Son, 1871. Preceding t.p., added t.p.: *Poems.* Providence, R.I.: A. Crawford Greene & Sons, 1880. 48 pp. 31 poems. Copy: DHU. (See *Poems*, 1896.)
Sketches of Southern Life. Philadelphia: Merrihew & Son, 1872. 24 pp. 10 poems. Copy: NNSch.
  Same: 1873#.
  Same: Philadelphia: Ferguson Bros. & Co., 1888. 58 pp. 16 poems (7 new), 1 tale. Copy: NNSch.
  Same: 1891. 58 pp. 15 poems and tale, same. Copy: DHU.
  Same: 1896. 48 pp. 10 poems and tale from 1888 ed. Copy: NNSch.

The Sparrow's Fall and Other Poems. N.p., n.d. [1890?]. 22 pp. 10 poems. Portrait. Copy: NNSch.

The Martyr of Alabama and Other Poems. N.p., n.d. [1894?]#. 12 poems. (See *Atlanta Offering.*)

Atlanta Offering. Philadelphia: 1006 Bainbridge Street, 1895. 70 pp. 34 poems (4 from *Poems,* 1871; 2 from *Sketches,* 1888; 10 from *Sparrow's Fall,* 1890?; 9 from *Martyr of Alabama,* 1894?; 9 new). Portraits of author and daughter. Copy: NNSch.

Poems. Philadelphia: 1006 Bainbridge Street, 1896 [copyright 1895, George S. Ferguson Co.]. 74 pp. 36 poems. Portrait. Copy: DHU. Same: 1898 [copyright 1895]. Copy: DHU. Same: 1900 [copyright 1895]. 90 pp. 36 poems. Copy: NNSch, with MS poem, "Saved at Last," in Harper's hand.

(N.B.: Selections in *Poems* (1895–1900) appear in previous volumes.)

Light Beyond the Darkness. Chicago: Donohue & Henneberry, n.d.#. 8 pp.

SELECTED PROSE

Novel

Iola Leroy, or Shadows Uplifted. Intro. William Still. 2nd ed. Philadelphia: Garrigues Brothers, 1893. Same: Boston: James H. Earle, n.d. Both copyright 1892. Copies: NNSch.

Short Story

"The Two Offers." *Anglo-African Magazine,* 1 (September and October, 1859), 288–91, 311–13.

Essays

"The Democratic Return to Power." *AMECR,* 1 (1884), 222–25.

"The National Women's Christian Temperance Union." *AMECR,* 5 (1889), 242–45.

"True and False Politeness." *AMECR,* 14 (1898), 339–45.

Letters

To John Brown, November 25, 1859. In *The Mind of the Negro as Reflected in Letters.* . . . Washington: Association for the Study of Negro Life and History, 1926. Pp. 508–9.

To William Still, 1854–72. In Still, 755–80 *passim.*

GEORGE MOSES HORTON

POETRY

The Hope of Liberty. Containing a Number of Poetical Pieces. Raleigh: J. Gales & Son, 1829. 22 pp. 21 poems. Copies: DLC; NcU (microfilm) #.

Same: *Poems by a Slave.* 2nd ed. Philadelphia: Lewis Gunn, 1837. 23 pp. 21 poems. Copies: DHU, NcU, NN, NNSch.

Same: *Memoir and Poems of Phillis Wheatley, a Native African and a*

Slave. Also, Poems by a Slave. 3rd ed. Boston: Isaac Knapp, 1838.
155 pp. 21 poems by Horton. Copies: DHU, NNSch.
The Poetical Works. Hillsborough, N.C.: D. Heartt, 1845. 99 pp. 44
poems. Copies: MH, NcU.
Naked Genius. Raleigh, N.C.: Wm. B. Smith & Co.: Southern Field and
Fireside Book Publishing House, 1865. 160 pp. 132 poems (90 new).
Copies: MBAt; NcU (microfilm).

Manuscript

"The Emigrant Girl" (1836?); "On Ghosts"; "An Acrostic, Mr. Daven-
port's Address to His Lady"; "An Acrostic, His Lady's Reply"; "An Acrostic,
to Their Little Daughter." Pettigrew Family Papers, Southern Historical
Collection, NcU.

PROSE MANUSCRIPTS

"The Stream of Liberty and Science: An Address to the Collegiates of
the University of North Carolina." 1859. 29 pp. (Includes poetry.)
North Carolina Collection, NcU.
Letters: to Garrison (September 3, 1844); to Greeley (September 11,
1853); first letter to Swain (n.d.). David Lowry Swain Papers, South-
ern Historical Collection, NcU.
Second letter to Swain (n.d.). Miscellaneous Papers, Department of
Archives and History, Raleigh, N.C.

GEORGE MARION McCLELLAN

POETRY

Poems. Nashville, Tenn.: A.M.E. Church Sunday School Union, 1895.
145 pp. 57 poems, essay, and 5 sketches. Copies: DHU, DLC.
Songs of a Southerner. Boston: Press of Rockwell and Churchill, 1896.
16 pp. 12 poems (same as *Poems*). Portrait. Copy: DHU.
The Path of Dreams. Louisville, Ky.: John P. Morton & Co., 1916. 76 pp.
43 poems (10 new). Copies: DHU, DLC, NNSch copy inscribed, gift
of Joseph S. Cotter to A. A. Schomburg(1925).
Same: Nashville, Tenn.: A.M.E. Sunday School Union, 1916. 206 pp.
43 poems (same), 4 stories and novella (from 1906). Copies: DHU,
NNSch copy inscribed by author (1934).

PROSE

Old Greenbottom Inn and Other Stories [Louisville, Ky.: Author, 1906].
N.p., n.d. 210 pp. Novella and 4 stories.
"The Negro as Writer." In Culp, 275–86.

POETRY AND PROSE

"Especial Book Announcements." N.p., 1929. Copy: Case Memorial Li-
brary, Hartford Seminary Foundation.

MANUSCRIPT

Letters to Hartford Seminary, 1906–33. Case Memorial Library, Hartford
Seminary Foundation.

JAMES EPHRIAM McGIRT

POETRY

Avenging the Maine. Raleigh, N.C.: Edwards & Broughton, 1899. 86 pp. 42 poems. Portrait. Copies: DHU, DLC, NcU.
  Same: 2nd ed., enl., 1900. 109 pp. 59 poems. Portrait. Copies: NcU, NNSch.
  Same: 3rd ed., rev. and enl. Philadelphia: George F. Lasher, 1901. 119 pp. 61 poems. Copies: DHU, NcU, NNSch.
Some Simple Songs and A Few More Ambitious Attempts. Philadelphia: George F. Lasher, 1901. 72 pp. 21 poems. Portrait. Copies: DHU, NcU, NNSch.
For Your Sweet Sake. Philadelphia: John C. Winston Co., 1906. 79 pp. 44 poems. Portrait. Copies: DHU, DLC, NNSch.
  Same: 1909. 77 pp. 51 poems. Copy: DHU.

SHORT STORIES

The Triumphs of Ephriam. Philadelphia: McGirt Publishing Co., 1907. 131 pp. Copies: DHU, NNSch.

ESSAYS, FICTION, AND POETRY

McGirt's Magazine (Philadelphia), September, 1903–1909.

JOHN WILLIS MENARD

POETRY

Lays in Summer Lands. Washington: Enterprise Publishing Co., 1879. 84 pp. 63 poems. Portrait. Copies: NNSch, DHU copy inscribed by author to Col. John Hay, December 6, 1879.

Uncollected

"The First of January, 1863." *Liberator,* February 13, 1863, p. 28.
"The Heart's Harvest." *AMECR,* 2 (1886), 211–12.

PROSE

"A Reply to Frederick Douglass, by a Colored Man." *Douglass' Monthly,* April, 1863, pp. 820–21.

ANN PLATO

POETRY AND PROSE

Essays; Including Biographies and Miscellaneous Pieces, in Prose and Poetry. Hartford, Conn.: Author, 1841. 122 pp. 20 poems. Copies: DLC, NNSch.

HENRIETTA CORDELIA RAY

POETRY

Lincoln. New York: J. J. Little & Co., 1893. 11 pp. Copy: DLC.
Sonnets. New York: J. J. Little & Co., 1893. 29 pp. 12 poems. Copies: DHU, DLC.

Poems. New York: Grafton Press, 1910. 169 pp. 146 poems (12 from 1893). Copies: DHU, DLC, NNSch copy inscribed: "To Mariteha from Cordelia. Jan. 1–1911."

PROSE

"Charles Lamb." *AMECR*, 8 (July, 1891), 1–9.

With Florence T. Ray. *Sketch of the Life of Rev. Charles B. Ray.* New York: J. J. Little & Co., 1887. 79 pp. Copy: NNSch, inscribed: "With the esteem of the family."

CHARLES LEWIS REASON

POETRY

"Freedom." In *The Man: The Hero: The Christian: . . . Thomas Clarkson: Delivered in the City of New-York; December, 1846. By the Rev. Alexander Crummel . . . Together with Freedom: A Poem, Read on the Same Occasion by Mr. Charles L. Reason.* New York: Egbert, Hovey & King, 1847. Pp. 39–44. Copy: NNSch.

"Hope and Confidence." In *Autographs for Freedom.* Ed. Julia Griffiths. Auburn, N.Y.: Alden, Beardsley & Co.; Rochester, N.Y.: Wanzer, Beardsley & Co., 1854. Pp. 226–29.

"Silent Thoughts." In Simmons, 1111–12.

"The Spirit Voice; or Liberty Call to the Disfranchised. (State of New York)." In Simmons, 1108–11.

PROSE

"Caste Schools." *Liberator,* January 4, 1850.

"The Colored People's Industrial College." *Autographs for Freedom.* Pp. 11–15.

"Letter to the Editor of the *Daily Register.*" Rpt. in *Frederick Douglass' Paper,* February 10, 1854.

ELYMAS PAYSON ROGERS

POETRY

A Poem on the Fugitive Slave Law. Newark, N.J.: A. Stephen Holbrook, 1855. 11 pp. Copy: DHU.

The Repeal of the Missouri Compromise Considered. Newark, N.J.: A. Stephen Holbrook, 1856. 24 pp. Copies: DHU, DLC, NNSch.

MANUSCRIPT

Letters to the Reverend George Whipple, December, 1860, and January, 1861. American Missionary Association Archives, Amistad Research Center.

GEORGE CLINTON ROWE

POETRY

Thoughts in Verse. Charleston, S.C.: Kahrs, Stolze & Welch, 1887. 113 pp. 71 poems. Portrait. Copies: DHU, DLC, NNSch, ScU.

Our Heroes. Patriotic Poems on Men, Women and Sayings of the Negro Race. Charleston, S.C.: Walker, Evans & Cogswell Co., 1890. 68 pp. 15 poems. Copies: DHU, DLC, ScU.

A Memorial Souvenir of Rev. T. Wofford White. Charleston, S.C., January 11, 1890#. 9 pp. 1 poem.

Decoration: A Poem for Decoration Day Celebration at Beaufort, S.C., May, 1891. Charleston, S.C., 1891#. 3 pp. 1 poem.

A Noble Life, Memorial Souvenir of Rev. Jos. C. Price. Charleston, S.C., 1894. 7 pp. 1 poem. Copies: DHU, NNSch.

Rev. Salem Mitchell. A Memorial Souvenir. Charleston, S.C., 1903. 7 pp. 1 poem. Copy: DHU.

PROSE

The Aim of Life: Live, Learn, Labor, Love. Charleston, S.C., 1892. 27 pp. Address delivered at Claflin University, Orangeburg, S.C., April 26, 1892#.

Items not examined are listed in *Congregational Year-Book,* p. 41, and mentioned by Rowe in 1897 letter to Furman.

MANUSCRIPT

Letters to Professor Furman, 1895–1901. Charles James McDonald Furman Papers, South Caroliniana Library, ScU.

JOSHUA McCARTER SIMPSON

POETRY AND PROSE

The Emancipation Car. Zanesville, Ohio: Sullivan and Brown, 1874. 154 pp. 53 poems and essays. Copies: DHU, NNSch.

AARON BELFORD THOMPSON

POETRY

Morning Songs. Rossmoyne, Ohio: Author, 1899. 84 pp. 40 poems. Portrait. Copy: DHU.

Echoes of Spring. Rossmoyne, Ohio: Author, 1907 [1901?]. 78 pp. 37 poems. Portrait. Copy: DHU.

Harvest of Thoughts. Indianapolis: Author, 1907. 106 pp. 45 poems (23 new). Portrait. Copies: DHU, In.

ELOISE BIBB THOMPSON

POETRY

Poems. Boston: Monthly Review Press, 1895. 107 pp. 26 poems. Copies: DLC, NNSch copy inscribed: "Presented by Noah D. Thompson, Esq. . . . June 23rd 1902."

GEORGE BOYER VASHON

POETRY

"Vincent Ogé." In *Autographs for Freedom*. Ed. Julia Griffiths. Auburn, N.Y.: Alden, Beardsley & Co.; Rochester, N.Y.: Wanzer, Beardsley & Co., 1854. Pp. 44–60. 391 lines.

"A Life-Day." In Daniel A. Payne, *The Semi-Centenary and the Retrospection of the African Methodist Episcopal Church*. Baltimore: Sherwood, 1866. Pp. 172–75. 126 lines.

"Ode on the Proclamation of the Fifteenth Amendment." *New Era*, I:13 (erroneously numbered 12) (April 7, 1870). 108 lines.

Translation

"The Diver." From the German of Schiller. *New Era*, I:6 (February 17, 1870). 162 lines.

PROSE

"Africa as a Field for Missions." *New Era*, I:15 (April 21, 1870).

"The Citizenship of Colored Men." *New Era*, 1:7 (February 24, 1870).

"The Lasting Benefits of Poetry." *New Era*, I:10 (March 17, 1870).

"Letter from Geo. B. Vashon" ("To His Excellency Abraham Lincoln"). *Douglass' Monthly*, 5 (October, 1862), 727–28.

"The Nile." *New Era*, I:14 (April 14, 1870).

"The Proclamation and Its Promise." In Benjamin T. Tanner, *An Apology for African Methodism*. Baltimore, 1867. Pp. 299–304.

"The Successive Advances of Astronomy." *Anglo-African Magazine*, 1 (July, 1859), 204–8.

MANUSCRIPT

Correspondence, Howard University Papers, DHU.

ISLAY WALDEN

POETRY

Miscellaneous Poems. 2nd ed. Washington: Author, 1873. 99 pp. 55 poems. First edition of 50 pages with same title was published in 1872 (Washington: Reed and Woodward) and is included in the 1873 edition. Copies: 1872: DLC. 1873: DHU, DLC, NNSch.

Sacred Poems. New Brunswick, N.J.: Terhune & Van Anglen's Press, 1877. 23 pp. 13 poems. Copies: DLC, NJR, New Brunswick Theological Seminary.

MANUSCRIPT

Letter to Dr. Demarest, September 21, 1878. Gardner A. Sage Library, New Brunswick Theological Seminary, New Brunswick, N.J.

JAMES MONROE WHITFIELD

POETRY

America and Other Poems. Buffalo, N.Y.: James S. Leavitt, 1853. 85 pp. 23 poems. Copies: DHU, DLC, NNSch.

"A Poem Written for the Celebration of the Fourth Anniversary of President Lincoln's Emancipation Proclamation." In Ezra Rothschild Johnson, *Emancipation Oration . . . and Poem. . . .* San Francisco: *Elevator* Office, 1867. Pp. 23–32. Copy: Bancroft Library, CU.
"Poem by J. M. Whitfield." *San Francisco Elevator,* April 22, 1870, p. 3.

In Periodicals

The North Star: August 10, December 14 and 21, 1849; March 5 and 22, April 12, 1850; *Frederick Douglass' Paper:* January 22, November 12, December 17, 1852; July 8, 1853; February 29, 1856; *Liberator:* November 18, 1853; *Elevator:* January 11, December 6, 1867; April 10, August 14, 1868; May 6, 1870; *Pacific Appeal:* May 23, 1863.

PROSE

Letters to *The North Star.* Rpt. in Frederick Douglass, W. J. Watkins, and J. M. Whitfield, *Arguments, Pro and Con, on the Call for a National Emigration Convention. . . .* Detroit: M. T. Newsome, 1854. Copy: DHU.

ALBERY ALLSON WHITMAN

POETRY

Essays on the Ten Plagues and Miscellaneous Poems. 1871? [Mentioned by Whitman in *Leelah Misled;* copy not located.]
Leelah Misled; A Poem. Elizabethtown, Ky.: Richard LaRue, 1873. 33 pp. 1 poem (1,180 lines). Dedicated to the Hon. Charles G. Wintersmith. Copy: DHU.
Not a Man, and Yet a Man. Springfield, Ohio: Republic Printing Co., 1877. 254 pp. 19 poems. Portrait. Dedicated to "The Abolition Fathers." Copies: DHU, DLC, NNSch.
The Rape of Florida. St. Louis: Nixon-Jones Printing Co., 1884. 95 pp. 1 poem. Portrait. Dedicated to the Rt. Rev. H. M. Turner. Copies: DHU, DLC, NNSch.
  Same: *Twasinta's Seminoles; or, Rape of Florida.* Rev. ed. St. Louis: Nixon-Jones Printing Co., 1885. 97 pp. 1 poem. Portrait and dedication, same.
  Same: 3rd ed., rev. 3 vols. in 1. St. Louis: Nixon-Jones Printing Co., 1890. 96 pp. Portrait, same.
    Volume I: *Twasinta's Seminoles.* Dedicated to the Hon. Charles Robinson, ex-governor of Kansas.
    Volume II: *Not a Man, and Yet a Man.* 2nd ed., rev. Dedicated to Bishop Benjamin W. Arnett.
    Volume III: *Drifted Leaves, A Collection of Poems.* 23 poems. Dedicated to the Rt. Rev. T. M. D. Ward.
  (*N.B.:* Revisions in above editions consist of occasional changes in a word or phrase.)
  Copies: DHU, NNSch copy inscribed: "What woman loves is manliness in man With Resp't Caddie Whitman April 20 '91."

World's Fair Poem. Atlanta, Ga.: Holsey Job Print, n.d. ["Read in Memorial Art Palace, Chicago, Sept. 22, 1893."] 9 pp. 2 poems. Portraits of Whitman and wife. Copies: DHU, NNSch.

An Idyl of the South: An Epic Poem in Two Parts. New York: Metaphysical Publishing Company, 1901. 126 pp. 2 poems. Copies: DHU, DLC, NNSch.

BIBLIOGRAPHICAL ESSAY

The bibliographies and finding aids, books of biography and criticism, periodicals, anthologies, and manuscript collections discussed below were consulted for this study in addition to materials listed under sources and notes for each poet and generally not repeated here. All of the primary works—ninety volumes of poetry and the poets' prose—are out of print and were examined principally in the Schomburg Collection of Negro Literature and History of the New York Public Library (103 West 135 Street) and in the Moorland and Spingarn Collections of Howard University (Washington, D.C.). Although publishers have announced some reprints of poetry in recent years, few volumes have appeared. Similarly, many secondary works are available only in special collections of Afro-Americana. This essay concentrates on materials for research in nineteenth-century black literature, with emphasis on poetry, but it includes sources of value to twentieth-century studies.

Bibliographies and Finding Aids

The earliest bibliography of black literature is "Works by Negro Authors," comp. Benjamin Arnett et al. for the U.S. Bureau of Education Report for 1893–94 (Government Printing Office, 1896), pp. 1056–61. Daniel Murray, Preliminary List of Books and Pamphlets by Negro Authors, for Paris Exposition (Washington, D.C., 1900), lists 500 of the 1,100 titles Murray had found; in "Bibliographia-Africana," VN, 1 (May, 1904), 186–91, Murray claims to have identified 2,200 works by black authors but does not record them. W. E. B. Du Bois, A Select Bibliography of the Negro American, 3rd ed., Atlanta University Publication no. 10 (Atlanta, 1905) includes books by seven nineteenth-century poets but makes no reference to them in his twenty-two-page index to periodical literature. Du Bois's bibliographical essays in Atlanta University Publication no. 14 (1909) and (with Guy B. Johnson, eds.) Encyclopedia of the Negro: Preparatory Volume (New York, 1946) are very weak on literature. The pioneer Arthur A. Schomburg, Bibliographical Checklist of American Negro Poetry (New York, 1916), although incomplete and inaccurate, offers twenty-two pages of volumes and single poems and is the basis for most later compilations. Appended to Schomburg's Checklist is Charles F. Heartman, "Bibliography of the Poetical Works of Phillis Wheatley."

An earlier "Heartman Series" bibliography is Oscar Wegelin, *Jupiter Hammon* (1915).

The Negro Yearbook, ed. Monroe Work (Tuskegee, Ala., 1912–38), lists works by and about black authors. A comprehensive summary of bibliographies, books, pamphlets, and articles in black literature (and many other areas) to 1928 is Work's *Bibliography of the Negro in Africa and America* (New York, 1928). Several bibliographies compiled by Arthur Schomburg for *The New Negro,* ed. Alain Locke (New York, 1925) are still valuable, particularly for post-1900 studies. The extensive bibliographies of Lorenzo D. Turner, *Anti-Slavery Sentiment in American Literature to 1865* (Washington, D.C., 1929) include a few black authors but do not identify them by race. Vernon Loggins appends a detailed bibliography of black writings to his study, *The Negro Author: His Development in America to 1900* (New York, 1931). Loggins emphasizes prose writings, but his volume remains the best literary history of the early period yet published. Dorothy B. Porter, *North American Negro Poets . . . 1760–1944* (Hattiesburg, Miss., 1945) furnishes exhaustive data on volumes, broadsides, and pamphlets, accurately notated with locations given. Her "Early American Negro Writing," *Bibliographical Society of America Papers,* 39 (1945), 192–268, is the most scholarly account of prose and poetry to 1835, and her introduction here is essential reading for researchers in early black literature. An outstanding contribution is Janheinz Jahn, *A Bibliography of Neo-African Literature from Africa, America, and the Caribbean* (New York, 1965), listing *volumes* only *by* black authors from the 1700's to date. Locations are not given, but Jahn's is the most thorough bibliography of its kind.

Other useful literary bibliographies are John Lash, "The American Negro and American Literature," *Bulletin of Bibliography,* 19 (1946), 12–15; (1947), 33–36, excellent annotated guides to 572 items, anthologies, articles, and books by and about black writers; also Maxwell Whiteman, *A Century of Fiction by American Negroes, 1853–1952* (Philadelphia, 1955). Louis D. Rubin, *A Bibliographical Guide to Southern Literature* (Baton Rouge, 1969) and bibliographies in *Images of the Negro,* ed. S. Gross and J. E. Hardy (Chicago, 1966), both list books and articles by and about black authors and on the image of blacks in American literature. Although the "representative works" of only six nineteenth-century poets (and Dunbar) are in Darwin Turner, *Afro-American Writers* (New York, 1970), this is the best attempt at a comprehensive guide to periodical articles and books in all areas of black literature and to bibliographies for modern black writers.

Among black studies bibliographies, few contribute significantly to literature. Edgar and A. M. Thompson, *Race and Region* (Chapel Hill, 1949), describes materials in North Carolina libraries, and all but two items in the brief literature section are for twentieth-century studies. Elizabeth Miller, *The Negro in America* (Cambridge, Mass., 1966), allows 5 pages out of 190 to literature, all twentieth century; the 2nd ed., rev. and enl., comp. Mary L. Fisher (1970) has extensive references to folklore, black authors, and literary criticism, but no nineteenth-century poets are included. Other modern bibliographies by Earl Spangler (1963),

Irving Sloan (1965), Erwin Welsch (1965), Abraham Chapman (1966), Erwin Salk (1966), and Donald Dickinson (1969) are sketchy and/or inaccurate in the literature areas.

Dwight Dumond, *Bibliography of Anti-Slavery in America* (Ann Arbor, 1961) locates reports, minutes, newspapers, magazines, sermons, speeches, and literary works of the antebellum period but mentions only one black poet, Joshua McCarter Simpson. Dorothy B. Porter, *The Negro in the United States* (Government Printing Office, 1970) is a fine 313-page guide to secondary (biographical-critical) sources but very weak in early literature. Under "Poetry," only Dunbar represents the nineteenth century. However, Porter's earlier *Working Bibliography on the Negro in the United States* (Ann Arbor, 1969) does include eight early poets.

Major nineteenth- and twentieth-century American literature bibliographies fail to mention any of the black poets of this study. Among these guides, however, two by Clarence Gohdes are valuable for locating secondary materials like histories, papers, and state literary studies: *Bibliographical Guide to the Study of the Literature of the U.S.A.* (Durham, N.C., 1963), and *Literature and Theater of the States and Regions of the U.S.A.* (Durham, N.C., 1967).

Finding Aids to Periodicals and Periodical Literature

Bibliographies of Afro-American newspapers of the last century are found in George W. Williams, *History of the Negro Race* (New York, 1885); W. E. B. Du Bois, Atlanta University Publication no. 14 (Atlanta, 1909), which lists 261 newspapers founded between 1852 and 1909; and Monroe Work's *Bibliography* (1928). Also valuable are two fine studies of black journalism: I. Garland Penn, *The Afro-American Press and Its Editors* (Springfield, Mass., 1891), and Frederick Detweiler, *The Negro Press in the United States* (Chicago, 1922). Data on many black newspapers are offered by two directories: *N. W. Ayer & Son's Directory of Newspapers and Periodicals* (Philadelphia, 1880–); and *Rowell's American Newspaper Directory* (New York, 1869–80, 1885, 1890, 1900).

Among more recent newspaper bibliographies are Warren Brown, *Checklist of Negro Newspapers in the United States* (Jefferson City, Mo., 1946), listing 467 papers published between 1827 and 1946 with their locations, if known. Armistead L. Pride, "A Register and History of Negro Newspapers in the United States" (dissertation, Northwestern University, 1950), covers publications from 1827 to 1950 and notes library locations and microfilm copies available. (See also Pride's *Negro Newspapers on Microfilm* [Washington, D.C., 1953], and the recent *Guide to Microforms in Print* [Washington, D.C., 1971].

No similar finding aids to early black magazines were available until 1972, with Penelope L. Bullock, *The Negro Periodical Press in the United States, 1838–1909* (dissertation, University of Michigan, 1971; facsimile rpt., Ann Arbor: University Microfilms, 1972). Bullock offers annotated bibliographies of eighty-four magazines published from 1838 to 1909 and describes their publishing histories, general contents, and availability of original copies and microreproductions. Several excellent appendices and a bibliography of sources additionally make this work a unique and valuable finding aid.

Indexes to the contents of early magazines and newspapers are not available. Some literary bibliographies (e.g., Work, Lash, D. Turner) list articles in magazines of the early 1900's; W. E. B. Du Bois's magazine, *Horizon* (1907–10), offers monthly bibliographies of articles in selected black periodicals. For articles of the 1940's there is "A Guide to Negro Periodical Literature," comp. Albert P. Marshall (Winston-Salem, N.C.), an index to about twelve publications issued in mimeographed quarterlies that are not generally obtainable. Since 1950 articles in all areas of black studies are listed in *The Index to Selected [Negro] Periodicals,* compiled by the staffs of the Hallie Q. Brown Memorial Library and the Schomburg Collection. About twenty-six periodicals are currently indexed quarterly; a decennial cumulation, 1950–59, and annual indexes from 1960 are available (although the *Index* now appears to be published some two years after the articles it lists). Another ongoing guide is the bimonthly *Bibliographic Survey: The Negro in Print,* of the Negro Bibliographic and Research Center (Washington, D.C., 1965–), which annotates new books, reprints, and some periodical literature. Among black journals, bibliographies of periodical literature are a regular feature of the *Journal of Negro Education* from 1931 to the present; reviews of new publications and occasional bibliographical essays are found in *Black Books Bulletin, Black World (Negro Digest), Phylon, College Language Association Journal, Journal of Negro History, Black Scholar,* and others. Of exceptional value are the penetrating critiques and literary surveys of Ernest Kaiser in *Freedomways,* from 1961 to date.

Guides to unpublished theses in black studies are Earle H. West, *Bibliography of Doctoral Research on the Negro, 1933–66* (Ann Arbor, 1969), and typescript or printed lists of master's theses from such Universities as Atlanta, Howard, Fisk, Hampton, and Tuskegee.

Comprehensive bibliographies of works by and about Afro-American writers and indexes of early periodicals are yet to be compiled. In their absence, most useful to this study for identifying black poets and their works and for locating primary and secondary books and articles were the bibliographies of Work, Loggins, Schomburg (1916), Porter (1945), Lash, and Jahn; the *Dictionary Catalog of the Schomburg Collection* in nine volumes and two-volume *Supplement* (1962, 1967); card catalogue of the Moorland and Spingarn Collections, since published as *Dictionary Catalogs* (1970); and the Library of Congress *National Union Catalogue: Pre-1965 Imprints,* all of which identify American Negro authors. Published catalogues of the Heartman Collection (Texas Southern University), Bancroft Library (University of California), and the Boston Athenaeum, among others, were of more limited value.

Books: Biography and Criticism

There is virtually no reliable published biography or criticism on nineteenth-century black poets. Existing accounts are secondhand, inaccurate, and heavily biased by racial attitudes. The early black poets are not included in white biographical dictionaries, collective biographies, or state literary histories. Exception is sometimes made for Bishops Daniel Payne and Benjamin T. Tanner, unrepresentative poets, and occasionally for Dunbar, Mrs. Harper, and T. Thomas Fortune (primarily a journalist). *American Authors, 1600–1900*, eds. S. J. Kunitz and H. Haycraft (New York, 1938) lists none of the poets; the six-volume *Appleton's Cyclopedia of American Biography*, eds. J. G. Wilson and J. Fiske (New York, 1887–89), includes the bishops; the twenty-three-volume *National Cyclopedia of American Biography* (New York, 1892–1947) has the bishops and Dunbar; *Who Was Who in America: Historical Volume, 1607–1896* (1967) includes Payne and James Madison Bell; and only Dunbar appears in *Who's Who in America* (1901–2). Two author dictionaries offer very brief notations on a handful of black poets: *American Authors and Their Books, 1640–1940*, eds. W. J. Burke and W. D. Howe (New York, 1943), and *Dictionary of North American Authors Deceased before 1950*, comp. W. Stewart Wallace (Detroit, 1968). The *Dictionary of American Biography*, ed. D. Malone (New York, 1928–37) lists Payne, Bell, Albery Whitman, and Dunbar.

The black poets fare even worse in collective biographies. For example, Frances E. Willard and M. A. Livermore, *American Women* (New York, 1897) contains 1,500 biographies of nineteenth-century women, none of whom are black. Among sketches of 1,000 women, Phebe Hanaford, *Women of the Century* (Boston, 1877), includes a paragraph on Mrs. Harper. No black poets appear in the dozens of multivolume state histories and "Who's Who" registers consulted. State literary histories such as William Coyle, *Ohio Authors and Their Books* (Cleveland, 1962) and *North Carolina Authors* (Chapel Hill, 1952) include two black poets each.

Biographies, dictionaries, and literary histories by and about Afro-Americans are more helpful. There are three autobiographies by early black poets: James D. Corrothers, *In Spite of the Handicap* (New York, 1916); Charlotte Forten, *Journal* (New York, 1953); and Daniel Payne, *Recollections of Seventy Years* (Nashville, 1888). Four poets have received individual study: Charlotte Forten by Anna J. Cooper, *Life and Writings of the Grimké Family* (N.p., 1951); Fortune by A. Terry Slocum, "Timothy Thomas Fortune: A Negro in American Society" (thesis, Princeton, 1967), and by Emma L. Thornbrough, *T. Thomas Fortune: Militant Journalist* (Chicago, 1972); Mrs. Harper by Theodora Daniel, "The Poems of Frances E. W. Harper" (dissertation, Howard University, 1937); and George Horton by Richard Walser, *The Black Poet* (New York, 1966). Of these studies, only the Thornbrough and Walser books are easily obtainable, as are the many biographies of Dunbar listed in my preface.

Afro-American collective biographies reinforce the myth that there were no black poets between Wheatley and Dunbar, as in Russell L. Adams, *Great Negroes Past and Present* (Chicago, 1964). Not even these two poets are mentioned in Joel A. Rogers, *Africa's Gift to America* (New York, 1959, 1961), and only Dunbar appears in his two-volume *World's Great Men of Color, 3000 B.C. to 1946 A.D.* (New York, 1946). Among hundreds of biographies in seven volumes of Arthur B. Caldwell, *History of the American Negro and His Institutions* (Atlanta, 1917–23), none is of a nineteenth-century black poet.

From two to five poets appear in each of the following volumes, but the biography is almost invariably derivative. In chronological order, they are: Benjamin T. Tanner, *An Apology for African Methodism* (Baltimore, 1867); Lawson A. Scruggs, *Women of Distinction* (Raleigh, 1893); Monroe Majors, *Noted Negro Women* (Chicago, 1893); Mrs. N. F. Mossell, *The Work of Afro-American Women* (Philadelphila, 1894, 1898, 1908); *Afro-American Encyclopaedia*, comp. James T. Haley (Nashville, 1896); G. F. Richings, *Evidences of Progress among Colored People* (Philadelphia, 1896, 1900); Charles Alexander, *One Hundred Distinguished Leaders* (Atlanta, 1889); H. F. Kletzing and W. H. Crogman, *Progress of a Race or the Remarkable Advancement of the Afro-American* (Naperville, Ill., 1901) (10 poets); J. W. Gibson and W. H. Crogman, *Progress of a Race: The Remarkable Achievement of the Afro-American* (Atlanta, 1902, 1920); *Twentieth Century Negro Literature,* ed. W. D. Culp (Naperville, Ill., 1902); Monroe Work, *Negro Year Book* (Tuskegee, Ala., 1912–38); Leila A. Pendleton, *A Narrative of the Negro* (Washington, 1912); [Centennial] *Encyclopedia of the AME Church,* ed. R. R. Wright (Philadelphia, 1916, 1947); Delilah Beasley, *Negro Trail Blazers of California* (Los Angeles, 1919); *National Cyclopedia of the Colored Race,* ed. Clement Richardson (Montgomery, Ala., 1919); Hallie Q. Brown, *Homespun Heroines* (Xenia, Ohio, 1926); Richard Bardolph, *The Negro Vanguard* (New York, 1961).

Literary histories of some biographical and/or critical value were Benjamin Brawley, *The Negro in Literature and Art* (New York, 1930) and *The Negro Genius* (New York, 1937); Benjamin E. Mays, *The Negro's God as Reflected in His Literature* (Boston, 1938); M. J. Butcher, *The Negro in American Culture* (New York, 1956); Janheinz Jahn, *Neo-African Literature* (New York, 1968). Also, two articles—I. Garland Penn, "Rise and Progress of Afro-American Literature," in *The College of Life,* ed. Henry Northrup et al. (Chicago, 1895), pp. 86–102; and Arna Bontemps, "The Negro Contribution to American Letters," *The American Negro Reference Book,* ed. J. Davis (Englewood Cliffs, 1966), pp. 850–78. Jean Wagner, *Black Poets of the United States* (Urbana Ill., 1973), concentrates on Dunbar and poets of the Renaissance but offers original and sensible criticism of many earlier poets and analyses of folk poetry and the minstrel and plantation traditions in nineteenth-century literature. Basic Afro-American histories which mention a few black poets are George W. Williams, *History of the Negro Race* (New York, 1885); John W. Cromwell, *The Negro in American History* (Washington, 1914); W. E. B. Du Bois, *The Gift of Black Folk* (Boston, 1924); and L. Hughes and M. Meltzer, *Pictorial History of the Negro in America* (New York, 1968).

Only eight books can be considered major sources of biography and criticism for early black poets, and even these are not free from inaccuracy and bias. William J. Simmons, *Men of Mark: Eminent, Progressive, and Rising* (Cleveland, 1887) includes material on Fortune, Payne,

Charles Reason, and Whitman; William Wells Brown, *The Black Man: His Antecedents, His Genius, and His Achievements* (Boston, 1863) and, largely repetitive, *The Rising Son* (Boston, 1874) are valuable for Brown's first-hand descriptions of several poets and for some criticism. Sterling Brown, *Negro Poetry and Drama* (Washington, 1937), offers detailed criticism of some ten poets with additional general remarks on nineteenth-century poetry. J. Saunders Redding, *To Make a Poet Black* (Chapel Hill, 1938) (and, to a much lesser extent, *The Lonesome Road* [New York, 1958]), contributes criticism. Vernon Loggins, *The Negro Author: His Development in America to 1900* (New York, 1931) remains the best all-around introduction to nineteenth-century black literature. Two dictionaries—*Who's Who of the Colored Race*, ed. Frank Mather (Chicago, 1915), and *Who's Who in Colored America*, ed. Joseph J. Boris (New York, 1927, 1929), ed. Thomas Yenser (Brooklyn, 1933)—offer nine and eight biographies, respectively. Additional biography in anthologies (see below) is usually brief, wholly derivative, and incorrect. Only Benjamin Brawley, *Early Negro American Writers* (Chapel Hill, 1935), includes biographies of a page or more with some evidence of original source material.

A recent annotated guide to collective biographies and reference tools for biographical research (1860–) is Barbara Bell, *Black Biographical Sources* (New Haven: Yale University Library, 1970). Although not available at the time of this study, *Sources* appears to be a good starting point for locating biographical data. However, for black writers of the last century the scanty and unreliable facts in published works—including the writers' own prefaces, speeches, essays, letters, and poems—must be verified and supplemented, as they were for this study, by correspondence with historical societies, boards of health and education, Chambers of Commerce, Probate Courts, colleges, and church-affiliated and racial societies throughout the United States. Slavery records and birth certificates for the early writers were not available, but marriage and death certificates, academic records, city directory listings, copies of correspondence, and, in a few cases, surviving friends and relatives of the poets were found and provided accurate biographical details. Two inexpensive directories which greatly facilitated such research by correspondence were *College and University Archives in the United States and Canada*, comp. Society of American Archivists (Ann Arbor, 1966); and *Directory: Historical Societies and Agencies in the United States and Canada, 1969–1970*, comp. M. M. LaGodna for the American Association for State and Local History (Washington, D.C., 1969).

Periodicals: Articles in Periodicals and Collections

The best sources of poetry and prose by Afro-Americans (outside of their individually published volumes) and important sources of biography and criticism were periodicals, those directed to black readers and others supporting abolitionism. Among newspapers, the most valuable were: *Freedom's Journal* (1827–30), *Liberator* (1831–65), *National Anti-Slavery Standard* (1840–70), and *North Star* and *Frederick Douglass' Paper* (December, 1847–1860). The most valuable early magazines were

Douglass' Monthly (1858–August, 1863), *Anglo-African Magazine* (January, 1859–March, 1860), *African Methodist Episcopal Church Review* (1883–1927), *Voice of the Negro* (1904–7), and *Alexander's Magazine* (1905–9).

Research in nineteenth-century black literature should concentrate on these periodicals, on the publications of various anti-slavery societies (1834–61), and on other magazines like *National Baptist Magazine* (1894–1908) and *Colored American* (1900–1909). Also recommended are newspapers such as *National Era* and *New Era* (Washington, D.C.), the *San Francisco Elevator* and *Pacific Appeal,* and church publications like the *A.M.E. Christian Recorder.* Many magazines and anti-slavery society organs are now available in facsimile reprints from Negro University-sities Press, while the major newspapers are found on microfilm in libraries. Dozens of other Afro-American periodicals which published for a year or two exist in scattered issues, if at all, and must be examined in local libraries or repositories of Afro-Americana (see "Finding Aids" and "Manuscripts").

The white press of the century is virtually barren in the area of black literature. Julian D. Mason, Jr., "The Critical Reception of American Negro Authors in American Magazines, 1800–1885" (dissertation, University of North Carolina, 1962), finds, for example, that *"The North American Review* never reviewed any works by American Negroes during the eighty-six years of its existence in the nineteenth century" (33). The record for all but a few of fifty-six magazines Mason examines is little better, and the score for poetry is dismal. From 1800 to 1885, not one magazine reviewed an Afro-American's poetry (259). During these years only two poems appeared in white journals, both by Horton in the *Southern Literary Messenger* (April, 1843).

In the present study, most periodical articles concerning the black poets are found in the sources or notes for each section. A few, however, are general surveys mentioning several poets, like Alice E. Dunnigan, "Early History of Negro Women in Journalism," *NHB,* 28 (Summer, 1965), 178–79, 193, 197; and "Negro Poets, Singers in the Dawn," *NHB,* 2 (November, 1938), 9–10, 14–15. *The African Methodist Episcopal Church Review,* a major source of poetry, biography, and criticism for this entire study, carries five general articles between 1885 and 1898: Mrs. N. F. Mossell, "The Colored Woman in Verse," 2 (1885), 60–67, discusses eight poets; Joseph T. Wilson, "Some Negro Poets," 4 (1888), 236–45, ten poets; Fannie C. L. Bentley, "The Women of Our Race Worthy of Imitation," 6 (1890), 473–77, three poets; Katherine D. Tillman, "Afro-American Women and Their Work," 11 (1895), 477–99, seven poets; and the same author's "Afro-American Poets and Their Verse," 14 (1898), 421–28, thirteen poets.

These sympathetic accounts of the early literature contrast with W. H. A. Moore, "The New Negro Literary Movement," *AMECR,* 21 (1904), 49–54, which dismisses all nineteenth-century Afro-American poets as imitative and unconvincing, and Newman Ivy White, "American Negro Poetry," *South Atlantic Quarterly,* 20 (October, 1921), 304–22, which concludes that American literature would not be greatly affected by the total loss of all black poetry to 1920. Also of this opinion are Robert E. Park, "Negro Race Consciousness as Reflected in Race Literature," *American Review*, 1 (1923), 505–17, who calls the period before Dunbar "the dark ages of Negro poetry"; and John Chamberlin, "The Negro as Writer," *Bookman*, 70 (1930), 603–11, who finds all poetry before Dunbar "dismal," offering "nothing that might form the material of a usable past." M. J. C. Echeruo, "American Negro Poetry," *Phylon*, 24 (September, 1963), 62–68, is essentially in agreement with Park but makes exception for a few poems which appeal to "basic norms of decency." The nadir of criticism comes with Wallace Thurman, "Negro Poets and Their Poetry," *Bookman*, 67 (1928), 555–61. Thurman viciously ridicules the poets' intelligence, sincerity, and talent, and he vituperates their poetry as totally worthless "religious cant and doggerel jeremiads."

Dozens of other articles with "Negro Poetry" in their titles were found to deal with either white poets' work on Negro subjects or with only twentieth-century black poets. Three exceptions are Phoebe Ann Heath, "Negro Poetry as an Historical Record," *Vassar Journal of Undergraduate Studies*, 3 (May, 1928), 34–52, which summarizes material from the Kerlin and Johnson anthologies; Newman Ivy White, "Racial Feelings in Negro Poetry," *South Atlantic Quarterly*, 21 (January, 1922), 14–29, which reviews the prevalence of race consciousness in the work of some fifteen pre-1900 poets; and M. W. Bennett, "Negro Poetry," *NHB*, 9 (May, 1946), 171–72, 191, which names eight early poets. Another article of interest is Charles H. Good, "The First American Negro Literary Movement," *Opportunity*, 10 (March, 1932), 76–79, a discussion of the New Orleans Creole poets and their anthology, *Les Cenelles* (1845). (See Appendix F.) A significant essay which includes the early poets is Richard Wright, "The Literature of the Negro in the United States," in his *White Man, Listen!* (New York, 1957).

Several general articles on black literature and history or on problems of the black author, in addition to those mentioned in my Introduction, proved useful, although they did not mention nineteenth-century poets. Among those are two whole issues of *Annals of the American Academy of Political and Social Science*, 49 (September, 1913) and 140 (November, 1928); the Harlem issue of *Survey Graphic* (March, 1925); an issue of *Phylon*, 11 (December, 1950); the Emancipation Centennial issue of *Ebony* (September, 1963); and *Midcontinent American Studies*, 11 (Fall, 1970). Also useful were Edward Bland, "Racial Bias and Negro Poetry," *Poetry*, 63 (March, 1944), 328–33, and J. Saunders Redding, "American Negro Literature," *American Scholar*, 18 (Spring, 1949), 137–48. Essays and symposia papers of significance are in collections such as *The New Negro*, ed. Alain Locke (New York, 1925); *Anthology of American Negro Literature*, ed. S. Watkins (New York, 1944); John O. Killens *et al.*, *The American Negro Writer and His Roots*, American Society of African Culture Conference, March, 1959 (New York, 1960); *Black and White in American Culture*, ed. J. Chametzky and S. Kaplan (anthology from *The Massachusetts Review*, 1959); and *The Black American Writer*, ed. C. W. E. Bigsby, two volumes of critical essays on fiction (I), poetry and drama (II) (Baltimore, 1971).

Anthologies

Without exception, black poets are excluded from nineteenth-century American poetry anthologies. Since poems are anonymous in many early anthologies, it is possible, but very unlikely, that a black poet is represented. In one of Wilson Armistead's several volumes, for example, the 400-page *Garland of Freedom* (London, 1853), James Whitfield's "How Long?" appears without attribution. *Freedom's Lyre: Or, Psalms, Hymns, and Sacred Songs* (New York, 1840), comp. Edwin Hatfield, contains two poems signed "James Horton" which are the work of his slave, George Moses Horton. All other contributors are leading white abolitionists. It is likely that some black poets contributed to William Wells Brown, *Anti-Slavery Harp* (Boston, 1848), but none of the song-poems is signed. *Autographs for Freedom,* ed. Julia Griffiths (Rochester, N.Y., 1853, 1854), an abolitionist gift-book, is significant as the only source of George Vashon's "Vincent Ogé" and two poems by Charles Reason. Lydia Maria Child's potpourri, *The Freedman's Book* (Boston, 1865), includes five poems by Frances Harper, four by Horton, and one each by "Mingo," Bell, and Whitfield.

Many periodicals of the century were essentially anthologies of poetry, stories, and brief essays in support of abolitionism or civil rights. One, *The Liberty Bell* by Friends of Freedom, was published in Boston for the National Anti-Slavery Bazaar from 1839 to 1858. Examination of the entire series yielded hundreds of poems by more than sixty white poets, two poems in Spanish by "Placido," but none by Afro-Americans.

Among anthologies of "Negro Writing," the only nineteenth-century contribution is the "Thoughts, Doings and Sayings of the Race" section of the *Afro-American Encyclopedia,* comp. James T. Haley (Nashville, 1896), with over two dozen poems, most by minor poets. Twentieth-century black literature anthologies which include a few to none of the early poets are: *The Dunbar Speaker and Entertainer,* ed. Alice Dunbar-Nelson (Naperville, Ill., 1920), with seven poets; *The Anthology of American Negro Literature,* ed. V. F. Calverton (New York, 1929), with one poem for each of four poets; *Negro Anthology,* comp. Nancy Cunard (London, 1934), with none. Only Dunbar appears in *Singers in the Dawn,* ed. Robert Eleazer (Atlanta, 1935); *American Literature by Negro Authors,* ed. Herman Dreer (New York, 1950); *Dark Symphony,* ed. J. Emanuel and T. Gross (New York, 1969); and *Black Literature in America,* ed. Houston A. Baker, Jr. (New York, 1971). In addition to Dunbar, *Kaleidoscope,* ed. Robert Hayden (New York, 1967), includes Horton and Harper; *Black American Literature: Poetry,* ed. Darwin Turner (Columbus, Ohio, 1969), includes Horton; *3000 Years of Black Poetry,* ed. A. Lomax and R. Abdul (New York, 1970), includes Harper.

A greater selection of early black poetry appears in several major anthologies. In order of publication, *The Book of American Negro Poetry,* ed. James Weldon Johnson (New York, 1922, 1931, 1958), concentrates on twentieth-century poets, but offers thirty-one selections by seven earlier writers. This collection remains valuable for Johnson's two introductory histories of black poetry (both reprinted in the 1958 edition). Sterling Brown, *Outline for the Study of the Poetry of American Negroes*

(New York, 1931) is a study guide to the Johnson anthology with useful questions and commentary. Robert Kerlin's history-biography-criticism anthology, *Negro Poets and Their Poems* (Washington, D.C., 1923, 1927), includes poems and excerpts by ten poets of this study (and of four dozen others from 1900 to 1920), all highly overpraised. *An Anthology of Verse by American Negroes,* ed. Newman Ivy White and Walter C. Jackson (Durham, N.C., 1924), is remarkable for inclusiveness: thirty poems by twelve early poets and thirty-one by Dunbar. Each poet receives a biographical sketch (inaccurate) and strongly negative criticism, not untinged with ridicule. Several additional early poets receive biographical-critical notice, although their poems are not included. The best coverage by far for seven major antebellum poets is *Early Negro American Writers,* ed. Benjamin Brawley (Chapel Hill, 1935), with twenty-six poems by Horton, Payne, Whitfield, Reason, Vashon, Bell, and Harper. Brawley's criticism, largely from Loggins, is more objective than that of his predecessors. *Negro Caravan,* ed. Sterling Brown *et al.* (New York, 1941), an anthology of prose and poetry, includes twelve poems by six nineteenth-century poets and fourteen by Dunbar. Its chronology of parallel white and black literary-historical events, although incomplete, is useful. *The Poetry of the Negro: 1746–1949,* ed. Langston Hughes and Arna Bontemps (Garden City, 1949), offers only nine poems by six poets and nine by Dunbar. A recent effort, *Early Black American Poets,* ed. William H. Robinson (Dubuque, Iowa, 1969), is outstanding for quantity, with about ninety poems or excerpts from long poems by nineteen poets in this study. Unfortunately, the work is marred throughout by gross factual errors in bibliography, biography, transcription of the poetry, and by careless writing and editing. A major new anthology is *Cavalcade: Negro American Writing from 1760 to the Present,* ed. A. P. Davis and J. Saunders Redding (Boston, 1971). Selection and format are excellent, but *Cavalcade* offers only the work of Horton, Harper, Corrothers, and Dunbar (23 poems in all), and an excerpt from Forten's *Journal.*

Among other anthologies of interest, "Scrapbook 3" (MS 2200, Bruce Collection, NNSch), contains hand-written, typed, or newsprint copies of seventy-three poems, many nineteenth-century. "Anthology of Negro Poetry by Negroes and Others," eds. B. F. Wormley and C. W. Carter (WPA, Newark, N.J., 1937) is a mimeographed anthology with brief comments relying heavily on Kerlin. William Moore, "The Literature of the American Negro prior to 1864: An Anthology and a History" (dissertation, New York University, 1942), a four-volume typescript available on microfilm, includes newspaper and periodical verse, selections from several early black poets, brief biographies (with sources), and related historical essays. Of much less value, but interesting for its origin, is Hermine Barz, "The Development of the Poetry of the Negro in North America" (dissertation, Johannes Gutenberg University, Mainz, Germany, 1952), available in German and English on microfilm.

Manuscripts

Identification of archives for black literary studies and publication of their holdings has become an urgent and continuing task. An early contribution was Arthur A. Schomburg, "The Negro Digs up His Past," *The Survey*, 53 (March, 1925), 670–72. Later articles include Arnett G. Lindsay, "Manuscript Materials Bearing on the Negro in America," *JNH*, 27 (January, 1942), 94–101; and Arna Bontemps, "Special Collections of Negroana," *Library Quarterly*, 14 (July, 1944), 187–206, a fine historical survey of the origins and contents of major Afro-American collections. Some contemporary efforts are *Materials by and about Negroes*, ed. Annette Phinazee (Atlanta, 1967); two articles by Lorenzo Greene, *NHB*, 30 (March and October, 1967), 20, 14–15; and Dorothy B. Porter, "Documentation on the Afro-American: Familiar and Less Familiar Sources," *African Studies Bulletin*, 12 (December, 1969), 293–303. An accessible, concise summary of the field is Ernest Kaiser, "Public, University and Private American Library Holdings on the Negro," *In Black America*, ed. Patricia Romero (Washington, D.C., 1969), pp. 333–53.

For this study, several general manuscript guides were used: *National Union Catalog of Manuscript Collections* (1959–68); *A Guide to Archives and Manuscripts in the United States*, ed. Philip Hamer (New Haven, 1961); *Subject Collections*, 3rd ed., eds. Lee Ash and D. Lorenz (New York, 1967); and *American Literary Manuscripts*, comps. Joseph Jones et al. (Austin, Texas, 1960). Two specialized finding aids of value were *A Guide to Documents in the National Archives: For Negro Studies*, comp. Paul Lewinson (Washington, D.C., 1947), and the early *Library Resources for Negro Studies in the U.S. and Abroad*, comp. Lawrence D. Reddick (New York, 1944). Highly useful were finding aids by Robert B. Downs, his particularized guides to resources of state and college libraries, and his general *American Library Resources* (Chicago, 1951, 1962). The latter lists published guides, catalogues, periodicals, bibliographies, and annual reports which describe existing collections and accessions in regional, state, public, and college libraries and societies (books as well as manuscripts).

Although some archives of Afro-American materials have compiled their own catalogues, such as the *Calendar of Manuscripts in the Schomburg Collection* (1942), these are not readily available except at the source. A major boon to scholars, therefore, is the *Directory of Afro-American Resources*, ed. Walter Schatz, Race Relations Information Center (New York, 1970). Detailed descriptions of 5,365 collections at 2,108 institutions, geographically arranged, and a bibliography of some 275 publications on Afro-American source materials make this *Directory* the most comprehensive in the field, and excellent indexes facilitate its use. The *Directory* was not available at the time this study was written, but all references it gives to the nineteenth-century poets have been included in their bibliographies or Appendix A. Despite the thoroughness of the *Directory*'s listings, it is far from complete: for example, some of the manuscript items found for this study but omitted from the *Directory* are the letters of George McClellan, Islay Walden, Albery Whitman, George Rowe, and Elymas Rogers, and the manuscript poems of George Horton and Frances Harper. Still needed is the publication and distribution of manuscript resources by individual repositories of Afro-Americana.

Key to References in Appendices

BOOKS AND PERIODICALS

Alexander	Charles Alexander, *One Hundred Distinguished Leaders* (Atlanta, 1899).
AMECR	*African Methodist Episcopal Church Review.*
Barton	Rebecca Barton, *Witnesses for Freedom: Negro Americans in Autobiography* (New York, 1948).
Brown, *BM*	William Wells Brown, *The Black Man* (Boston, 1863).
Brown, *RS*	———, *The Rising Son* (Boston, 1874).
Caldwell	Arthur B. Caldwell, ed., *History of the American Negro and His Institutions* (Atlanta, 1922), VI.
CAm	*Colored American Magazine.*
Coan	Josephus Coan, *Daniel Alexander Payne* (Philadelphia, 1935).
Culp	D. W. Culp, ed., *Twentieth Century Negro Literature* (Naperville, Ill., 1902).
DAB	*Dictionary of American Biography,* ed. A. Johnson and D. Malone (New York, 1928–37).
Davis	D. W. Davis and Giles B. Jackson, *The Industrial History of the Negro Race of the United States* (Richmond, 1908).
JNH	*Journal of Negro History.*
Kerlin, *NP*	Robert Kerlin, *Negro Poets and Their Poems* (Washington, D.C., 1923).
Kletzing	H. F. Kletzing and W. H. Crogman, *Progress of a Race* (Naperville, Ill., 1901).
Loggins	Vernon Loggins, *The Negro Author* (New York, 1931).
McGinnis	Frederick McGinnis, *A History and an Interpretation of Wilberforce University* (Wilberforce, Ohio, 1941).
Mossell	Mrs. N. F. Mossell, *The Work of the Afro-American Woman,* 2nd ed. (Philadelphia, 1908).
Murray	Daniel Murray, *Preliminary List of Books and Pamphlets . . . Paris Exposition* (Washington, D.C., 1900).
NCAB	*National Cyclopaedia of American Biography* (New York, 1892–1947).
NHB	*Negro History Bulletin.*
Nichols	J. L. Nichols, *New Progress of a Race* (1929).
NUC	*National Union Catalogue,* Library of Congress.

Penn   I. Garland Penn, *The Afro-American Press and Its Editors*
                (Springfield, Mass., 1891).
Pipkin   J. J. Pipkin, *The Negro in Revelation, in History, and in
                Citizenship* (St. Louis, 1902).
Redding   J. Saunders Redding, *The Lonesome Road* (New York,
                1958).
Richings   G. F. Richings, *Evidences of Progress Among Colored Peo-
                ple*, 6th ed. (Philadelphia, 1900).
Rogers   Joel A. Rogers, *World's Great Men of Color* (New York,
                1946).
Simmons   William Simmons, *Men of Mark* (Cleveland, 1887).
VN   *Voice of the Negro*.
W&F   J. G. Wilson and J. Fiske, eds., *Appleton's Cyclopedia of
                American Biography* (New York, 1887–89).
WWA   *Who's Who in America*, ed. A. N. Marquis.
WWCAm   *Who's Who in Colored America*, ed. Joseph J. Boris (New
                York, 1929); ed. Thomas Yenser (Brooklyn, 1933).
WWCR   *Who's Who of the Colored Race*, ed. Frank L. Mather
                (Chicago, 1915).
Wright   Richard R. Wright, ed., *Centennial Encyclopedia of the
                AME Church* (Philadelphia, 1916).

LIBRARIES

DHU   Howard University, Moorland and Spingarn Collections
DLC   Library of Congress
NJP   Princeton University
NNSch   Schomburg Collection of the New York Public Library

SYMBOLS

+   Additional material available
++   Large quantity of additional material available
*   Most valuable source
#   Volume not examined

APPENDIX A: Poets for Further Research

The thirty-five individuals in Appendix A are Afro-Americans known to have published many poems or volumes of poetry (and prose). All were writing poetry during the nineteenth century and, with few exceptions, their work appeared in print before 1900.[1]

BENJAMIN, ROBERT C. O.

    b. 1855. Attorney, journalist, lecturer, teacher.

    Poetry: *Poetic Gems* (Charlottesville, Va.: Peck & Allan, 1883), 14 pp., 18 poems (DLC, NNSch).+

    Prose: 10 vols., 1891– (DHU, DLC, NNSch).

    Reference: Alexander; Murray; *AMECR*, 5 (1888), 173–74, 11 (1895), 439; Kletzing; Simmons.

BLACKSON, LORENZO DOW

    b. 1817, Delaware. Methodist preacher.

    Poetry and Prose: *The Rise and Progress of the Kingdoms of Light and Darkness; or, The Reigns of Kings Alpha and Abadon* (Philadelphia: J. Nicholas, 1867), 288 pp. (DHU, NNSch).

    Reference: Loggins; *AMECR*, 10 (1894), 561.

BOYD, FRANCIS A.

    b. 1844, Kentucky. Evangelist.

    Poetry: *Columbiana; or, The North Star, Complete in One Volume* (Chicago: Steam Job & Book Printing House of B. Hand, 1870), 69 pp. (DLC)#. "Gamos" (Ercildown, Pa., 1895), about 300 ll., MS 1186 (Bruce Coll., NNSch).

    Prose: Memorial pamphlet, 1872. 8 pp. (DLC).

    Reference: *NUC*

BROOKS, WALTER HENDERSON

    1851–1945, Richmond, Va. Baptist minister, chaplain of Anti-Saloon League.

1. For their efforts to supply data, I am obliged to Edmund Berkeley, Jr., University of Virginia Library; E. P. Caruthers, Meharry Medical College; Sylvester Dunn, Fisk University; John L. Ferguson, Arkansas History Commission; A. K. Johnson, Jr., Society of American Archivists; Clifford H. Johnson, Amistad Research Center; Annette L. Phinazee, North Carolina Central University; Elizabeth Promer, American Newspaper Publishers Association Foundation; W. A. Waters, Rust College; and B. K. Williams, Barber-Scotia College.

Poetry: Broadsides (DHU); "Scrapbook 3" (NNSch); *AMECR*, 4 (1888), 420–21, 9 (1892), 20–26; *Original Poems* (Washington, D.C., 1932), 40 pp.; *The Pastor's Voice* (Washington, D.C., 1945) (both DHU, NNSch). *National Baptist Magazine* (1894–1908).

Prose: 2 vols. (NNSch).+

Reference: *WWCAm* (1929); *WWCR;* Culp; Caldwell; *Crisis* (April, 1921; May, 1922).+

BRUCE, JOHN EDWARD ("Bruce-Grit")

1856–1924, Piscataway, Md. Journalist.

Poetry: 18 MSS poems (NNSch).+

Prose: *Selected Writings*, ed. Peter Gilbert (New York: Arno, 1971); plays, stories, articles, monographs (MSS and published) (DHU, NNSch).

Manuscript: Bruce Collection and Arthur A. Schomburg Papers, NNSch; Carter G. Woodson Coll., DLC.

Reference: Penn.

CLARK, BENJAMIN CUTLER

b. 1825?, slave.

Poetry: "John Brown Avenged," *Liberator*, June 27, 1862.

Poetry and Prose: *The Past, Present and Future, in Prose and Poetry* (Toronto, 1867), 168 pp. (DHU, DLC).

Prose: 3 vols., 1850–. (DHU, DLC, NNSch).+

Reference: Loggins.

COFFIN, FRANK BARBOUR

1870?–1951, Holly Springs, Miss. Pharmacist.

Poetry: *Coffin's Poems with Ajax' Ordeals* (Little Rock, Ark.: Colored Advocate, 1897), 248 pp., 90 poems (DLC, NNSch); *Factum Factorum* (New York: New Haven Press, 1947), 190 pp., 50 poems and prose (DHU, NNSch).

Reference: Kletzing; Richings; *WWCR*.

CORROTHERS, JAMES DAVID

(James R. Corruthers) 1869–1917, Cass County, Mich. Minister, journalist.

Poetry: *Century Magazine*, NS 35–45 (1899–1904); *Howard's American Magazine* (1899–1900); *CAm*, 3 (1901); *VN*, 1 (1904); 2 (1905, 1906); *Crisis*, 7 (1913, 1914), 9 (1915).+

Prose: *VN*, 3 (August, 1906).+

Autobiography: *In Spite of the Handicap* (New York: George H. Doran, 1916), 238 pp.

Reference: Bruce MSS 1350, 1354, 1365 (NNSch); Pipkin; Barton; *WWCR; Crisis*, 9 (January, 1915).+

DELANEY, ALEXANDER DUMAS

Teacher.

Poetry: *AMECR*, 2 (1885), 20 (1903), *passim*.

FORDHAM, MARY WESTON

b. 1862?

Poetry: *Magnolia Leaves* (Charleston, S.C.: Walker, Evans & Cogswell Co., 1897), 104 pp., 66 poems (DHU, NNSch).

Reference: Poems in *Magnolia Leaves;* review, W. S. Braithwaite, *CAm,* 3 (November, 1901), 73–74.

FRANKLIN, JAMES THOMAS

Poetry: *Jessamine Poems* (Memphis, Tenn., 1900) (not located).

Poetry and Prose: *Mid-day Gleanings. A Book for Home and Holiday Reading* (Memphis, Tenn.: Tracy Printing & Stationery, 1893), 144 pp., 46 poems (DHU, DLC).

Reference: *NUC; Mid-day Gleanings.*

HEARD, JOSEPHINE DELPHINE (HENDERSON)

1861–19(?), Salisbury, N.C.

Poetry: *Morning Glories* (Philadelphia, Pa.: Author, 1890), 108 pp., 78 poems (DHU, NNSch); 2nd ed. (Atlanta, Ga.: Franklin Printing and Publishing Co., 1901), 142 pp., 144 poems (66 new) (DHU).

Reference: "Historical Sketch," *Morning Glories;* Heard, William Henry, *From Slavery to the Bishopric in the A.M.E. Church: An Autobiography* (Philadelphia: A.M.E. Book Concern, 1924).

HOLLY, JOSEPH CEPHAS

1824–54.

Poetry: *Freedom's Offering, A Collection of Poems* (Rochester: Chas. H. McDonnell, 1853), 39 pp. (DHU).+

Reference: Flyleaf and preface, *Freedom's Offering.*

JACKSON, A. J.

Poetry: *A Vision of Life, and Other Poems* (Hillsborough, Ohio: Highland News Office, 1869), 52 pp. (DHU).

Reference: Preface, *Vision.*

LAINE, HENRY ALLEN

b. 1870?, Kentucky.

Poetry: *Footprints* (Richmond, Ky., 1924), 80 pp. (NNSch); 2nd ed. (New York, 1947), 144 pp. (DHU).+

Reference: P. Jones, "Two Kentucky Poets," *VN,* 3 (August, 1906), 583–86. Includes poetry.

LAMBERT, MARY ELIZA (PERINE) TUCKER

(*NUC:* Tucker; others: Mrs. J. H. or M. E. Lambert.)

b. 1838. Editor, *St. Matthew's Lyceum Journal.*

Poetry: *Loew's Bridge, A Broadway Idyl* (New York: M. Doolady, 1867), 78 pp. (DLC, NJP)#; *Poems* (New York: M. Doolady, 1867), 216 pp. (DLC, NJP)#; *AMECR,* 1, 2 (1885), 284–85, 170–72.

Prose: *Life of Mark M. Pomeroy* (New York, 1868), 230 pp. (DLC).

Reference: *AMECR,* 1885–94 *passim;* Mossell.

LATIMER, LEWIS HOWARD

1848–1929. Inventor.

Poetry: "Scrapbook 3" (NNSch); *Poems of Love and Life* (N.p.: Private, 1925), 22 poems (DHU, NNSch).
Prose: *Incandescent Electric Lighting* (New York, 1890) (DHU, NNSch).+
Reference: Richings; Rogers; Nichols; *The Story of Lewis Latimer* (New York, 1964).

LIPSCOMBE, EDWARD HART

b. 1858, North Carolina. Educator, editor, Baptist minister.
Poetry: Bruce MS 1234 and "Scrapbook 3" (NNSch).
Reference: Simmons.

MAPPS, GRACE

Poetry: *Anglo-African Magazine*, 1 (1859), 345–46.+
Reference: Mossell.

MARTIN, JOHN SELLA

b. 1832, North Carolina. Baptist minister, lecturer, editor *New Era* (Washington, D.C.).
Poetry: *Anglo-African Magazine*, 1 (1859), 361–62.+
Prose: *New Era*, 1870–. (DHU).
Reference: Brown, *BM, RS; Douglass' Monthly*, January, June, 1861, and February, 1862; *Liberator*, March 6, 1863.

MOORE, WILLIAM H. A.

New York. Journalist.
Poetry: Kerlin, *NP* (includes reference); *AMECR*, 10 (1894), 543–48.
Prose: *AMECR*, 31 (1914), 145–55; *Opportunity* (November, 1928).+

MOSSELL, GERTRUDE S. (Mrs. Nathan F.)

b. 1855, Philadelphia
Poetry: Mossell, 149–76; *AMECR* (July, 1888, and 1889).
Prose: Mossell, editions 1894, 1898, 1908; *AMECR* (1885–1901), *passim; CAm*, 3 (August, 1901), 291–305.
Reference: *NHB*, 28 (Summer, 1965); *Crisis*, 13 (December, 1916); *VN*, 3 (February, 1906).

NELSON, ALICE RUTH (MOORE) DUNBAR

1875–1935, New Orleans. Teacher, social worker, editor, clubwoman.
Poetry: Kerlin, *NP; Dunbar Speaker and Entertainer* (Naperville, Ill., 1920); *AMECR*, 35 (1918), 22–23; *NHB*, 31 (April, 1968), cover.+
Prose: 2 vols. stories (1895, 1899); 2 vols. compiler (1914, 1920); essays: *JNH* (1916–17); *AMECR*, 30, 31 (1914).++
Manuscript: Letters, Dunbar Papers, NNSch.+
Reference: Culp; *WWCR; WWCAm* (1933); obituary, *JNH*, 21 (January, 1936).++

PAYNE, DANIEL ALEXANDER

1811–93, Charleston, S.C. AME Bishop, President of Wilberforce University, editor-in-chief, *Repository of Religion and Literature and of Science and Art* (1858–63).

Poetry: *The Pleasures and Other Miscellaneous Poems* (Baltimore: Sherwood & Co., 1850), 43 pp. (DHU); "An Original Poem," *Liberator,* May 28, 1841; "The Mournful Lute," *Recollections.*

Prose: 7 vols. sermons, histories, treatises (DHU, NNSch).++

Autobiography: *Recollections of Seventy Years* (Nashville: AME Sunday School Union, 1888), 335 pp.

Manuscript: Payne Collection, Wilberforce University (4,500 items).

Reference: *DAB;* Redding; Coan; McGinnis; Simmons; *NCAB; AMECR,* 1894–1926 *passim.*++

RHODES, JACOB

b. 1835? Gardener.

Poetry: *The Nation's Loss: A Poem on the Life and Death of the Hon. Abraham Lincoln* (Newark, N.J.: F. Starbuck, 1866). 18 pp., includes essay (DLC).

Reference: *New Jersey and the Negro, A Bibliography, 1715–1966* (Trenton, 1967), p. 101.

SHOEMAN, CHARLES HENRY

Poetry: *A Dream and Other Poems,* 2nd ed. (Ann Arbor: George Wahr, 1899–1900), 202 pp. (46 poems of 1899 ed. plus 22) (DHU, NNSch).

SMITH, ELIJAH W.

b. 1825? Printer.

Poetry: Brown, *RS,* iii–iv, 552–55; *New Era,* April 28, 1870, and June 2, 1870; *Freedomways,* 2 (Fall, 1962), 400–401.

Reference: Brown, *RS.*

TANNER, BENJAMIN TUCKER

1835–1923, Pittsburgh. AME Bishop, editor *Christian Recorder* and *AMECR.*

Poetry: *In Memoriam . . . O. V. Catto* (N.p., 1871?), 4 pp. (NNSch); *Stray Thoughts* (N.p., n.d.), 20 pp. (DHU); *AMECR* (1880's–1912), *passim,* several dozen poems.+

Prose: *An Apology for African Methodism* (Baltimore, 1867); about 10 vols.: sermons, histories, church government (DHU, DLC, NNSch).

Reference: *WWA; NCAB;* W&F; Loggins; *NHB,* 10 (April, 1947), 147–52, 167.++

TEMPLE, GEORGE HANNIBAL

Reading, Pa. Musician.

Poetry: *The Epic of Columbus' Bell and Other Poems* (Reading, Pa.: Reading Eagle, 1900), 80 pp. (DHU, DLC, NNSch); "King Kobbena Eljen," *AMECR,* 16 (1899), 266–67.

Reference: *AMECR,* 17 (1900), 74–77 (includes poetry).

WALKER, JAMES ROBERT

Poetry: *Poetical Diets* (N.p., 18—), 146 pp. (NNSch).

WATKINS, JAMES ROBERT

Poetry: *Poems, Original and Selected, by James Watkins, a Fugitive Slave* (N.p., 1859?) (NNSch)#.

Prose: *Struggles for Freedom, or the Life of James Watkins,* 19th ed. (Manchester, England, 1860), 104 pp. (DHU). A slave narrative.

WHITFIELD, CUPID ALEYUS

b. 1868, Quincey, Fla. AME minister, teacher, editor.

Poetry: *Poems of [to] Today, or Some from the Everglades.* 1893? [not located].

Reference: Wright.

WILLIAMS, EDWARD W.

Poetry: *Views and Meditations of John Brown* (Washington, D.C., 1893), 16 pp. (NNSch).

WILSON, JOSEPH THOMAS

1836–91, Virginia. Historian.

Poetry: *Voice of a New Race* (Hampton, Va.: Normal School Steam Press, 1882), 43 pp. (DLC); "Scrapbook 3" (NNSch).

Prose: *Emancipation* (Hampton, Va., 1882); *The Black Phalanx* (Hartford, Conn., 1892).+

Manuscript: Letters, James M. McKaye Papers, DLC.

Reference: Davis.

WILSON, WILLIAM J. ("Ethiop")

Teacher, essayist.

Poetry: *Anglo-African Magazine,* 1 (February, May, 1859), 58, 150.

Prose: *Anglo-African Magazine,* 1 (1859); *Frederick Douglass' Paper; AMECR; Autographs for Freedom* (Rochester, 1854).+

Reference: Brown, *BM, RS.*

APPENDIX B: Occasional Poets

The following Afro-Americans published one or more poems in magazines, newspapers, and anthologies of the last century, such as *AMECR, Anglo-African Magazine,* Mossell, *Liberator, National Anti-Slavery Standard,* "Scrapbook 3" (NNSch), or *Afro-American Encyclopaedia,* comp. James T. Haley (Nashville, 1896). Those marked with an asterisk wrote several poems and were best known among their contemporaries.

*Aldridge, Ira
Arneaux, J. A.
Barber, Nannie A.
Beard, Jessie E.
Bolivar, W. Carl
Brown, Lucy Hughes
*Brown, Solomon G.
*Brown, William Wells
Chancellor, Miss A. E.
*Chapman, Katie D.
Clarke, Edward A.
Clayton, Robert A.
Cottin, Thomas L.
*Crogman, W. H.
Diggs, J. Thomas (Rev.)
*Douglass, Frederick
Drake, Linnie H.
Ensley, N. H.
*Fisher, Leland M.
Ford, R. Edgar
Forten, Robert B.
Forten, Sarah
*Fox, Mamie Eloise
Garnet, Esta
Gordon, Charles B. W. (Rev.)
*Gordon, J. E.
*Greener, Richard T.
Hammond, Edward S. W. (Rev.)

Hardy, Charles
Hughes, James C.
Jackson, Josephine B. C.
Jones, J. A. M.
Jonson, Ida F.
Knight, O. W.
*Lewis, Randolph C.
Luckie, Ida Evans
Mathews, William D.
Mingo
Monroe, Henry A.
Morris, William H.
Nash, C. H.
Newsome, Jonathan T. C.
Nicholson, G. W. (Rev.)
Parker, Fannie A.
Peck, Thomas
Perry, William L.
Pyle, W. D. F. (Rev.)
Sampson, James G.
Sangster, Margaret E.
Sherly, R. H. (Rev.)
Sidney, R. Y.
*Simpson, Ida V.
Stickum, Alfred B.
Stites, Wilson Hunt
Strong, James
Taylor, D. F. (Rev.)

THOMAS, EDITH M.
THOMPSON, MISS C. M.
THOMPSON, LILLIAN V.
*TURNER, HENRY MCNEAL (BISHOP)
WADE, P. W.
WALKER, JAMES RICHARD

WARD, T. M. D. (BISHOP)
WASSOM, MRS. F. E. H.
*WHITSETT, VIRGIE
WILLIAMS, D. T., JR.
WILLIAMS, J. W. (REV.)
WILLIAMSON, DAVID THOMAS

APPENDIX C: Anonymous Poets and Ada

(Authors are identified in parentheses)

"The Black Beauty" (a son of Africa). *Freedom's Journal,* June 8, 1827.
"Black Heroes" (a black girl). *Liberator,* February 5, 1864, p. 24.
"Hymn of Freedom" (a leader of the intended slave insurrection in South
    Carolina, 1813). *JNH,* 50 (January, 1965), 52.
"Marching Song" (adjutant of the First Kansas Colored Volunteers). *Na-
    tional Anti-Slavery Standard,* January 24, 1863.
"The Negro's Prayer" (a black slave in Virginia, 1790). In Olaudah
    Equiano, *The Life of Olaudah Equiano, or Gustavus Vassa* (Boston,
    1837), p. 36.
"O, Give Us a Flag" (private in Co. A, 54th Reg., Massachusetts Volun-
    teers). *Liberator,* June 19, 1863, p. 100.
"The Sorrows of Angola." *Freedom's Journal,* June 8, 1827.
"Tears of a Slave" (Africus). *Liberator,* March 10, 1832, p. 40.
Untitled (an aged contraband in imitation of *The New England Primer*).
    Liberator, January 23, 1863, p. 16.

ADA

A "young and intelligent lady of color" from Philadelphia contributed
twelve poems to Garrison's *Liberator* in 1831–37. The poems are little
more than doggerel, but the pathos and urgency of their antislavery senti-
ments are characteristic of this early, vigorous period of abolitionism.
Ada's poems are listed in order of their appearance in *The Liberator*:

1831
"The Grave of the Slave," January 22, p. 14.
"The Slave Girl's Address to Her Mother," January 29, p. 18.
"Past Joys," March 19, p. 1.
"Prayer," March 26, p. 50.
"The Slave," April 16, p. 62.

1833
"To the Hibernia," May 25, p. 84.
"The Separation," December 21, p. 203.

1834

"My Country," January 4, p. 4.
"An Appeal to Woman," February 1, p. 20.

1835

"The Slave Girl's Farewell," June 27, p. 104.

1837

"The Slave," March 11, p. 44.
"Legislation—No. II," June 16, p. 100.

APPENDIX D: Turn-of-the-Century Poets

The following Afro-American poets, sometimes listed among nineteenth-century writers, did not publish before the twentieth century. Their earliest date of publication, as far as could be ascertained, follows their names:

JUNIUS MORDECAI ALLEN (1906)
EFFIE DEAN (THREAT) BATTLE (1914)
WILLIAM STANLEY BRAITHWAITE (1904)
BENJAMIN G. BRAWLEY (1902)
CARRIE W. CLIFFORD (1911)
CHARLES ROUNDTREE DINKINS (1904)
GERTRUDE A. FISHER (1910)
DAVID BRYANT FULTON (1909)
GILMORE F. GRANT (1908)
M. N. HAYSON (1906?)
ELLIOT BLAINE HENDERSON (1904)
ADOLPHUS JOHNSON (1915)
H. T. JOHNSON (1904)
JEFFERSON KING (1906)
J. W. PAISLEY (1907)
GEORGE WASHINGTON PORTER (1910)
OTIS M. SHACKELFORD (1907)
ARMOREL STERNE (1916)
CLARA ANN THOMPSON (1908)
PRISCILLA JANE THOMPSON (1900)
WALTER E. TODD (1905)
RICHARD E. S. TOOMEY (1901)
IRVINE W. UNDERHILL (1905?)
LUCIAN B. WATKINS (1903)
BENJAMIN FRANKLIN WHEELER (1907)
JULIUS C. WRIGHT (1906)

APPENDIX E: Poets Erroneously
Identified as Afro-Americans

The following individuals are listed in various bibliographies as nineteenth-century black American poets. However, they were either white, of doubtful racial origin, or foreign born. Brief data and reasons for their exclusion from this study follow each name.

JOHN BOYD. *The Vision and Other Poems, in Blank Verse* (London, 1834) (DHU, DLC). Bahamian black author.

HATTIE BROWN. *Cantoninetales* (London, 1891). Pseudonym of William James Linton, white author.

JOHN BURKE, pseud. SENNOIA RUBEK (d. 1873). 3 vols. poetry (DLC). White author.

WILLIAM HENRY BURLEIGH (1812–71). 5 vols. prose and poetry (DHU, DLC, NNSch). White author.

GEORGE WASHINGTON CLARK (b. 1812). Comp., *The Liberty Minstrel* (New York, 1844; Boston, 1845) (NNSch, DHU, respectively); comp., *The Free Soil Minstrel* (New York, 1848); comp., *The Harp of Freedom* (New York, 1856) (NNSch). White author.

JOHN A. COLLINS (1810–79). *The Anti-Slavery Picknick* (1842) (DLC) (Boston, 1843) (DHU); *The Slave-Mother* (Philadelphia, 1855) (NNSch). White author.

WILLIAM JOHN GRAYSON (1788–1863). *The Hireling and the Slave* (Charleston, S.C., 1856) (DHU, NNSch). White proslavery politician and poet of South Carolina.

JAIRUS LINCOLN. Comp., *Anti-Slavery Melodies* (Hingham, Mass., 1843) (DHU, NNSch). White author.

EGBERT MARTIN, pseud. "LEO" (1862–90). *Leo's Poetical Works* (London, 1883) (DHU, NNSch). British Guianan black author.

ADAH ISAACS MENKEN (1835–68). *Infelicia* (New York, 1868) (DLC, NNSch). Race in doubt. See John S. Kendall, "The World's Delight," *Louisiana Historical Quarterly*, 21 (July, 1938), 846–68; *DAB*.++

JAMES MONTGOMERY (1771–1854). 25 vols. poetry and prose (DHU, DLC, NNSch). White author, born in Scotland.

BERTRAND SHADWELL. *America and Other Poems* (Chicago, 1899) (DHU, DLC). Race in doubt.

ABEL CHARLES THOMAS (1807–80). *The Gospel of Slavery* (New York, 1864) (NNSch). White Universalist clergyman.

APPENDIX F: The Creole Poets of *Les Cenelles*

Armand Lanusse, Pierre Dalcour, Victor Séjour, Camille Thierry *et al.*, *Les Cenelles. Choix de Poésies Indigènes* (New Orleans: H. Lauve and Company, 1845).

The contributors to this anthology of poetry in French were seventeen free blacks, all born in New Orleans. Most of them were sons of white Frenchmen and their octoroon mistresses, and many were educated in France. The poetry and prose of several contributors first appeared in a small literary magazine, *L'Album Litteraire*, established in 1843 by J. L. Marciacq to carry the work (in French) of the Creole writers. Armand Lanusse (1812–67), a journalist, Confederate soldier, and principal of the Catholic School for Indigent Orphans of Color in New Orleans, compiled the eighty-five poems for *Les Cenelles* (*The Holly Berries*). This highly decorated, illustrated volume was the first anthology of black poetry published in America. Best known among the contributors were Camille Thierry (1814–75), who emigrated to France and published his own volume of poetry, *Les Vagabondes* (Bordeaux, 1874), and Victor Séjour (1817–74), a popular dramatist who produced twenty-one successful plays in Paris in 1844–74.

See Charles H. Good, "The First American Negro Literary Movement," *Opportunity*, 10 (March, 1932), 76–79; Edward L. Tinker, *Les Cenelles, Afro-French Poetry in Louisiana* (New York, 1930); Charles B. Roussève, *The Negro in Louisiana* (New Orleans, 1937); Rodolphe L. Desdunes, *Nos Hommes et Notre Histoire* (Montreal, 1911); and *Creole Voices*, ed. Edward M. Coleman (Washington, D.C., 1945), a reprint of the original volume which is held at NNSch.

APPENDIX G: Phillis Wheatley and Jupiter Hammon—Bibliographies

<hr />

PHILLIS WHEATLEY (afterward Phillis Peters)

1753?–1784

BIBLIOGRAPHY

Heartman, Charles F. "Bibliography of the Poetical Works of Phillis Wheatley." In A. A. Schomburg, *Bibliographical Checklist of American Negro Poetry*, pp. 47–57 (New York: Heartman, 1916).

*Porter, Dorothy B. "Early American Negro Writings: A Bibliographical Study." *Bibliographical Society of American Papers*, 39 (1945), 261–67. Full titles and locations given.

BROADSIDES

"An Elegiac Poem, on the Death of . . . The Reverend and Learned George Whitefield . . ." (Boston: Ezekiel Russell, 1770), 8 pp. Editions: Newport, R.I.; New York; Philadelphia, 1770, with variations in title.

"To Mrs. Leonard, on the Death of Her Husband" (Boston, 1771).

"To the Rev. Mr. Pitkin, on the Death of His Lady" (1772).

"To the Hon'ble Thomas Hubbard, Esq.; On the Death of Mrs. Thankfull Leonard" (Boston, January 2, 1773).

"An Elegy, To Miss Mary Moorhead, on the Death of her Father, The Rev. Mr. John Moorhead" (Boston: William M'Alpine, 1773).

"An Elegy, Sacred to the Memory of . . . Dr. Samuel Cooper . . ." (Boston: E. Russell, 1784), 8 pp.

"Liberty and Peace, a poem" (Boston: Warden and Russell, 1784), 4 pp.

"A Beautiful Poem on Providence" (Halifax: E. Gay, 1805), 8 pp.

COLLECTED POEMS

Poems on Various Subjects, Religious and Moral (London: A. Bell, 1773). 124 pp.

    Same: Philadelphia: Joseph Crukshank, 1786; 1789. 66 pp.

        Philadelphia: Joseph James, 1787. 55 pp.

        Albany, N.Y.: Barber & Southwick for Thos. Spencer, 1793. 89 pp.

Walpole, N.H.: David Newhall for Thomas & Thomas, 1802.
86 pp.
Hartford, Conn.: Oliver Steele, 1804. 92 pp.
New England, 1816. 120 pp.
With memoirs by W. H. Jackson. Cleveland: Rewell, 1886. 149
pp.
Memoir and Poems of Phillis Wheatley, A Native African and a Slave
(Boston: G. W. Light, 1834). 103 pp. Memoir by Margaretta M.
Odell. Added t. p.: *Poems on Various Subjects, Religious and Moral*
(London: A. Bell, 1773).
Same: 2nd ed. Boston: Light & Horton, 1835. 110 pp.
Same: *Also, Poems by a Slave* [George Moses Horton]. 3rd ed. Bos-
ton: Isaac Knapp, 1838. 155 pp.

LETTERS

Proceedings of the Massachusetts Historical Society, 7 (November, 1863),
267–79.
Letters of Phillis Wheatley. Boston: Private, 1864. 19 pp.
Deane, Charles. *Letters of Phillis Wheatley.* Boston, 1864.

COLLECTED WORKS, MODERN EDITIONS

Poems and Letters: First Collected Edition. Ed. Charles F. Heartman
(New York: Heartman, 1915). 111 pp.
Renfro, G. Herbert. *Life and Works of Phillis Wheatley, . . . Complete
Poetical Works. . . . Letters, and a Complete Biography* (Washing-
ton, D.C., 1916). 112 pp.
The Poems of Phillis Wheatley. Ed. Charlotte R. Wright (Philadelphia:
The Wrights, 1930). 104 pp.
*The Poems of Phillis Wheatley. Ed. with intro. by Julian D. Mason,
Jr. (Chapel Hill: University of North Carolina Press, 1966). 113 pp.

BIOGRAPHY AND CRITICISM (selected)

Brawley, Benjamin. *Early Negro American Writers.* 1935; rpt. (Freeport,
N.Y.: Books for Libraries, 1968), pp. 31–36.
Davis, Arthur. "Personal Elements in the Poetry of Phillis Wheatley,"
Phylon, 14 (1953), 191–98.
Heartman, Charles F. *Phillis Wheatley: A Critical Attempt and a Bibliog-
raphy of Her Writings.* New York: Author, 1915.
Loggins, Vernon. *The Negro Author.* 1931; rpt. (Port Washington, N.Y.:
Kennikat, 1964), pp. 16–29.
Renfro, G. Herbert. "A Discourse on the Life and Poetry of Phillis Wheat-
ley." *AMECR,* 7 (July, 1891), 76–109.
Slattery, J. R. "Phillis Wheatley, The Negro Poetess." *Catholic World,* 39
(1884), 484–98.
Yeocum, William H. "Phillis Wheatley—The First African Poetess."
AMECR, 6 (January, 1890), 329–33.
[See also Mason and Renfro, above.]

JUPITER HAMMON
1711–1800?

BIBLIOGRAPHY

*Porter, Dorothy B. "Early American Negro Writings: A Bibliographical Study." *Bibliographical Society of America Papers,* 39 (1945), 236–37. Full titles and locations given.

Wegelin, Oscar. *Early American Poetry.* 2nd ed., rev. and enl. New York: Peter Smith, 1930. I: 41–42.

BROADSIDES

"An Evening Thought. Salvation by Christ." December 25, 1760. 88 ll.

"An Address to Miss Phillis Wheatly [*sic*]." Hartford, Conn., August 4, 1778. 84 ll.

POETRY AND PROSE

An Evening's Improvement. . . . To Which Is Added . . . The Kind Master and Dutiful Servant (Hartford, Conn.: Author, n.d.). 28 pp.

A Winter Piece (Hartford, Conn.: Author, 1782). 24 pp. Includes "A Poem for Children with Thoughts on Death."

An Address to the Negroes in the State of New York (New York: Caroll & Paterson, 1787). 20 pp. Reprints: Philadelphia, 1787; New York, 1806.

COLLECTED WORKS

Jupiter Hammon, American Negro Poet; Selections . . . and a Bibliography. Ed. Oscar Wegelin (New York: C. F. Heartman, 1915). 51 pp.

America's First Negro Poet: The Complete Works. Ed. with intro. by Stanley A. Ransom, Jr. (Port Washington, N.Y.: Kennikat, 1970). 122 pp. Biography, O. Wegelin; Criticism, V. Loggins; Bibliography.

INDEX

Abolitionists: activities of, xviii–xix,
xxii, 23, 27–28, 53, 63–64, 75, 88–89,
129; and periodicals of, xxii–xxiii.
See also Race protest; Slavery as
literary subject

Accommodation, 146–47, 149, 174,
177–78; as subject of poetry, xxvii,
167, 203

Ada (anonymous poet), vii, 247–48

Afric-American Repository, 44–45

Africa, 3, 21, 23–24, 99; emigration
to, 7, 37, 148, 167; and mission-
aries, 23–24, 56; as subject of
poetry, 41, 67–68, 84, 148, 158–59,
167, 196, 209. *See also* Colonization

African Civilization Society, 23

African Colonization Society, xviii, 28

African Education Society of Pitts-
burgh, 53

African Free School (New York City),
xix, 27

African Historical Society, 145

African Methodist Episcopal Church.
See Churches

African Repository, 136

African Times and Orient Review, 200

Afro-American Council, 144

Afro-American League, 144, 175

Afro-American Press Association, 145

Agassiz, Louis, 90

Alarm Bell, The, 75–78

Alcoholism: and Horton, 7–8; and
Whitman, 116; and Fortune, 147;
and McGirt, 196, 197. *See also*
Intemperance; Temperance

Aldridge, Ira, 27, 245

Alexander's Magazine, 165

Alger, Horatio, 202

Alienation, 38–39, 49–52

Allegory, 60, 127

Allen, Junius Mordecai, xxix, 249

Alumni Journal, 136

American Association of Educators
of Colored Youth and Author's
Association, 65

American Colonization Society, xviii,
20, 28. *See also* Colonization

American history: related to Afro-
American poetry, xx, xxi–xxix

American literature: compared with
Afro-American literature, xv, xx–xxi,
xxvi, xxix

American Missionary, 136

American Missionary Association, 106.
See also Ministry

Amsterdam News, 147, 149

Anglo-American Magazine, xxiii

Animals: in poetry, 188–89

Antislavery. *See* Abolitionists

Antislavery Society: American, xxii,
75, 88; of Pittsburgh, 53; Juvenile,
of Pittsburgh, 53; of Maine, 63; of
Pennsylvania, 63; Salem Female, 89

Appeal, David Walker's, xxii, 7

Arnett, Bishop Benjamin, 80, 83, 87

Assimilation, xxi, xxv, xxvi, 37, 148.
See also Interracial love

Association for the Study of Negro
Life and History, 165

Atlanta Exposition (1895), 137, 178